WHERE THE TRAILS RUN OUT

JOHN BLASHFORD-SNELL

WHERE THE TRAILS RUN OUT

HUTCHINSON OF LONDON

HUTCHINSON & CO (*Publishers*) LTD
3 Fitzroy Square, London W1

London Melbourne Sydney Auckland
Wellington Johannesburg Cape Town
and agencies throughout the world

First published 1974
© John Blashford-Snell 1974
Maps © Hutchinson & Co (*Publishers*) Ltd 1974

Printed in Great Britain by
R and R Clark, Edinburgh, Scotland

ISBN 0 09 121360 6

To Sergeant Major Ian Donald,
Royal Engineers (1937–1973)
and men like him

CONTENTS

ILLUSTRATIONS

Mission accomplished
Kay Thompson and Johnnie Johnson
With His Imperial Majesty Haile Selassie I at the end of the Great
    Abbai Expedition
The old prison on 'Devil's Island', Nocra
A Dahlak sumbacca

Between pages 176 and 177

Sheikh Seraj's Balilla truck
Blind villagers of Sahelia, Norah Island
Before Darien: raft trials
Before Darien: pistol training with the girls
A struggle to save a Range-Rover
On the Tuira River
At our base in El Real
Bridging ladders got us out of many difficulties

Between pages 240 and 241

David Bromhead prepares a marker balloon
Rafting on the Bayano River
Fallen trees made our going very difficult
The bridge at the beginning of the southern part of the Pan
    American highway
Ulster, 1973
An incident in Armagh
The SES gives a dinner to announce the Zaire River Expedition
    (*Fox Photos*)

MAPS IN TEXT

ACKNOWLEDGEMENTS

I HAVE tried to write this book not as an autobiography, but more as a collection of experiences involving a great many people. I owe much to those named in these pages and a very great deal to those who are not mentioned. If any credit is due, it is to them. Indeed, I count myself fortunate to have such an understanding and helpful circle of relatives and friends and privileged to have led some of the finest people – explorers and servicemen – in the world. I am only sorry that space and circumstances do not allow me to tell all the tales – but perhaps there will be an opportunity at a future date.

I am most grateful to Mr. H. M. Stephen, managing director of *The Daily Telegraph*, for his help and support over the years and to Mr. Maurice Green, editor of *The Daily Telegraph* and Mr. John Anstey, editor of *The Daily Telegraph Magazine* for their kind permission to publish the photographs taken by Paul Armiger, Chris Bonington and Stuart Heydinger and also the piece by Anthony Haden-Guest.

I am grateful to Chatto and Windus Ltd. and my old friend, Richard Snailham, for allowing me to base maps on those originally published in *The Blue Nile Revealed*. I also thank Mrs. George Bambridge for permission to include the lines from Rudyard Kipling's *The Explorer*.

I can think of no other organization that would give an employee as much encouragement and opportunity to explore the world on full pay as the British Army and my biggest thank-you is to the services, all of which have played a leading part in many of our ventures.

I

FOOLISH YOUTH

THE needle on the pressure gauge was well inside the red danger zone. In a few more deep breaths the air supply would stop abruptly and the aqua-lung had no reserve. I cursed my stupid stubbornness for causing me to neglect one of the basic safety rules of diving that would now probably cost me my life.

Letting go the inscribed marble slab, I fought to control my breathing and watched the precious artefact twirling down into the tangled seaweed. For ten minutes I had struggled, using up far too much air, to bring the slab to the surface from its watery grave forty feet below. I had found it jammed between rocks a mile off shore and felt certain that the inscription would provide a valuable clue to the riddle of the origins of the great port of Paphos.

Above me the late afternoon sun glittered on the waves, and as I rose quickly to the surface, still the air held out, although the needle was now right against the stop and I hardly dared to glance at the gauge.

My fourteen-pound weight belt was on the sea-bed, so I tried to control the ascent with my breathing. 'Too fast, too fast,' I kept saying as I rose in the cloud of bubbles. I felt a twinge in my leg, but thankfully I had not been down long enough to risk the dreaded bends.

As I broke the surface the valve went clunk, signifying the end of my air supply. Tearing the mouth-piece out, I sucked in air and sea-water. The dipping sun was blinding and the strong wind was blowing the waves into my face. Looking under water, I noticed with interest that the sea-bed was sliding past. Two more mouthfuls of water left me feeling horribly sick and an awful rattling noise came from my chest. A red film was clouding my vision.

'In an emergency, don't panic, think,' I repeated the advice I had so often given my divers, but I felt terribly tired and even thought was an effort. To get a good mouthful of air, I turned over on my back and, at the same time, tried to release the useless aqua-lung. One shoulder strap came off at once, but the other was sticking. Now I was drifting with the running tide, straight towards the foaming outline of the Moulia reef. How ironical that the rocks, whose earlier victims I had been investigating, should claim me as well.

Suddenly the breathing set dropped away and I rolled over to notice that it had already reached the sea-bed, now only twelve feet below. I still had a chance, and in the far distance I saw the grey bridge of the expedition mother-ship $Z\,II$, rising and falling in the swell. My instinctive cry for help only wasted valuable energy. I tried to swim, but, despite the fins I wore, my leaden legs could not even hold me against the current. The waves breaking on the jagged rocks of the reef were clearly audible.

Two hundred yards, I thought. Five minutes if I'm lucky. What a damned silly thing to do, leave the other divers and go off alone after some antique tombstone.

Again I tried to swim, but my legs refused to answer the command.

'Conserve your energy for the reef. There's still a chance of clinging onto a rock, if you can get through the outer breakers,' said optimism.

'Some hope, you've seen the dragon's teeth, they even slice you open if you touch them in calm conditions,' replied pessimism and realism together.

'You're a bit off course,' said another voice and I turned my head to see one of the expedition's boats about thirty yards away. Kneeling in the bows was a young Army public relations officer, who had come out to cover the story.

Drowning men are supposed to relive their past in the last few seconds, but I must confess that I had been too busy trying to survive to consider my short life history. However, had I done so, I feel I could have looked back on twenty-two full and exciting years. It would be rather like being caught in the slips after hitting a couple of fours and a good six in one's first game for the school cricket XI.

My father, born in Jersey in 1903, was the son of a sea captain, who had died when he was a child. Father had a good brain and during his time at the island's public school, Victoria College, he had intended to try for a commission in the Indian Army. However, he had always been religious and, in his final year, decided to enter the Church and in due course attended a theological college in Essex.

Here he met the attractive daughters of the wealthy squire, George Sadler, and in July 1924 at a dawn ceremony in St. Helier Parish Church, Jersey, he married the elder, Gwendolen.

My mother, like all her family, was a great character. Full of fun, she loved life and adventure. She claimed a strange assortment of forebears, including Louis XV, Oliver Cromwell and Judge Jeffreys! My father's ancestors were largely seafaring people and their graves are to be found in the West Country as well as in the Channel Islands. I believe our name came about through there being a family of Snells at the village of Blashford in Hampshire.

After twelve years of travel, father became rector of a busy parish on the outskirts of Hereford and here it was that I was born in 1936. My parents were enormously energetic people, they had travelled widely, been pioneers in New Zealand and the rectory in which we lived was always full of people. In 1939 my father was becoming a leading figure in local affairs; the council, RSPCA, Territorial Army and, of course, the Church. Our friends and the parishioners were many and varied. Everyone who came to the rectory, be he duke or dustman, was given the same cheerful reception. Our home was the centre of parish activity, and to enjoy it one simply had to like people.

At first I was a shy child, but this rapidly disappeared and I learned to make friends easily. My babyhood had been marred by a shrivelled left arm, the result of a difficult birth. Indeed it was only the attention of our old family doctor and my mother's persistent strapping of the offending limb that eventually induced it to grow properly. Mother had a great love of animals, which we all shared, and seeing her bandage up a sparrow's broken wing in later years, I could imagine her treating me in exactly the same way. She certainly had plenty of opportunity to practice her healing because in spite of being well built, I suffered from a host of ailments.

Father's involvement with the Army had originated in the OTC in Jersey, and during his time in New Zealand he had been the padre of the Southland Regiment. As war clouds gathered over England, Pa or 'Bish' as his friends knew him, foretold the coming conflict and made himself unpopular in many quarters amongst people who refused to face facts. However, his reputation as a preacher was well known and his fiery, forthright sermons from the pulpit, coupled with his infectious good humour out of church, won him a wide circle of friends, especially amongst the more radical. As a boy, I met many dashing young officers and soldiers, who told me stories of hair-raising adventures and it is not surprising that from my earliest days I longed for a life of travel and excitement.

We were surrounded by animals; horses, donkeys, cows, dogs, cats, foxes, rabbits, guinea pigs, tortoises, pigeons, chickens, budgerigars, a parrot and even a monkey. Today we should probably have been classed as a private zoo and, to the local children, that is what my home was. The dogs usually included alsatians, which at least twice had saved my mother from serious injury when she had been attacked. The first occasion was one night in a narrow country lane in Jersey. Driving a drophead coupe, she had come upon another car blocking the road, with its headlights blazing. Hooting produced no sign of life, and mother was about to reverse when an arm came through the open nearside window and switched off the ignition. The black alsatian bitch sitting on the back seat had the hand in her mouth in a split second and it was only with some difficulty that mother managed to prise the teeth apart and release the screaming man, who fled into the night. A day or two later, a man was admitted to the hospital with a severely mauled hand. He said he had been attacked by a dog in a field. The police thought otherwise, but no charges were pressed. He eventually lost the hand through gangrene.

On another occasion mother was mistaken for the St. Helier Prison Governor's wife and attacked by a demented escaped prisoner. The faithful alsatian nearly killed the man and father arrived in the nick of time to stop the unequal struggle by breaking a priceless antique vase over the rogue's head. Father was the prison chaplain at the time and much liked by the inmates. On discovering his dreadful error, the would-be murderer wrote my mother a letter of apology and complimented her on her guard dog!

Without doubt mother had an extraordinary power over animals. As the years went by I saw her calm a mad, half-starved dog that had been locked in a caravan without food and with little water for a week, and mend the broken limbs of countless small creatures that people brought to her, in some cases, after a vet had pronounced them beyond help. Originally I accepted these cures as being perfectly normal and it was not until I reached manhood that I realized many of them were almost miraculous. Perhaps they were. Somehow she seemed to know the correct tone of voice to use to each particular animal, the right expressions, where to touch or hold them and how never to show fear, although at times she must have felt it.

'They can smell fear, you know,' mother once said. 'You watch how a dog will immediately sense someone who is frightened of him.'

My attempts to imitate the methods my mother used have been fairly successful, although my skill could never compare with hers.

It is to my deep regret that I did not know my maternal grand-mother. By all accounts she was a great personality with many attributes, including being an accomplished shot, and I particularly like one tale which illustrates her prowess. The ladies of the village had gathered for tea on the terrace, when my grandmother or Ferdie as she was known, spied a large carrion crow perched vulture-like above the pheasant pen, some seventy yards away. Ringing the tea-bell, she summoned her maid and, with accustomed nonchalance, said, 'Please ask Wootton to bring me the Rook Rifle.' The girl scurried away and a few minutes later the butler delivered the fire-arm. Hardly interrupting conversation, Ferdie raised the gun to her shoulder and despatched the offending predator!

My grandfather George Sadler was a large, jolly man and had reached twenty stone in his prime. His house was always full of wild men friends, who, by all accounts, were the scourge of the county. The stories of their escapades are legion; George killing an escaped circus python with a tractor or collecting a runaway bull on the bonnet of his new Armstrong Siddley, as the enraged beast fled down Braintree High Street. Or on one occasion, returning from an hilari-ous shopping spree in London with a trick truncheon (one side of which was sorbo rubber) he came upon the vicar, a nervous intro-vert, taking sherry with my grandmother, and raising the club, George bellowed, 'The Philistines are upon us,' and struck the cleric over the head. Unfortunately he had neglected to use the soft face and the poor man was downed on the spot!

The story I like best was that of the Zeppelin raid. My mother told me that one night during the Great War, the family had just retired to bed when the butler tapped on the door of my grand-parents' bedroom and announced that an enemy dirigible was hovering over the park. Immediately the household was woken up. Whilst the governess led the ladies to the summer house, George climbed on to the roof with Wootton and the keeper. There, for all to see, like a giant cigar, was a Zeppelin, poised one thousand feet above the hall. Possibly to aid its navigation, it was dropping flares which illuminated the surrounding countryside with an eerie green light. The opportunity to strike a blow for England and defend his heritage was too strong for even George, who had not seen a day's military service, to let pass. Rifles and ammunition were passed from the gun-room and, encouraged by the ladies, George engaged the enemy. History does not relate whether it was the squire's gunfire, the weather or some whim of the German airman that saved the village from destruction. However, George gave a great party on the strength of it.

My own memories of war started on the day it broke out in September 1939, with father coming home with a regular army colonel, whom, years later, I was to meet when he was a field-marshal. The rectory became a centre of activity and was designated the local ARP HQ. Sand-bag blast walls were built across the front of the house, an Anderson bomb-shelter was installed in the dining-room and the study became the control-room. Nearby an RAF Station had opened and a regiment of Indian Cavalry, complete with horses, was camping on Hereford racecourse. At night a band of portly gentlemen armed with shot-guns and pitchforks patrolled the parish on bicycles. The Home Guard, as it was named, was led by our church warden, the redoubtable Captain Faulkner. For a small boy it was all very exciting and I wished I could grow up quickly and rush off to fight the Germans, but if the posters that adorned the walls were anything to go by, it was likely that the Germans would come to fight me anyway. I cannot remember exactly the date that it happened, but I do recall it was a summer's afternoon when I was in my playroom at the rear of the rectory. Hereford housed an important ammunition factory and air-raid alarms were not uncommon. The sirens had been wailing on and off that day and the thump, thump of anti-aircraft guns were clearly audible to the east. A new sound caused me to stand on a bench and peer out of a high window. Low over the fields a green-and-grey, twin-engined aeroplane was gliding earthward. A trail of black smoke streamed from one engine and the other was emitting a spluttering roar. Above it, in close formation, two spitfires followed, red-and-blue roundels on their wings standing out against the green countryside. Through the smoke I could see emblazoned on the fuselage of the bomber a black cross.

I did not see the crash, but the ting-a-ling of the fire engines and the sight of the Home Guard speeding by on bicycles told me the bomber had come down nearby. In the study Bill Bailey, the duty warden was on the phone.

'Down by the Canny Brook,' he shouted, 'they've got one of the Jerrys alive.'

A short time elapsed before I confronted the Jerry. To one so young, he looked a tall, slim, blond-haired man, although, in retrospect, he was probably barely out of his teens. He was dressed from head to foot in a black flying-suit with a silver eagle and a swastika on his breast. His boots and gloves were also black, and in contrast, a mass of wavy straw-coloured hair fell untidily over his pale face. Captain Faulkner stood by the door clutching his twelve-bore, which occasionally he waved menacingly at the enemy. To my amazement, the pilot said in perfect English, 'Do you mind if I smoke?' The church warden nodded his assent and our visitor drew out an elegant silver cigarette case from a rather natty breast pocket. As he lit it, I noticed his hands were shaking very slightly. From my perch on the desk I enquired, 'Were you in that bomber?'

'Yes,' he said without emotion.

'Now you'll go to prison,' I pointed out unnecessarily.

'But not for long,' he smiled.

The significance of his remark was lost on me, but the men in the room stiffened. At that moment a khaki-coloured fifteen-hundred-weight utility full of burly military policemen swept up the drive. 'Aufwiedersehn,' said the German officer, as he was escorted away.

My grandmother and godmother were terribly cross that I should have even spoken to him. There was no love of the Boche in our house. Jersey was occupied, and, for all we knew, everything that father's side of the family had possessed was now German loot. My godmother, Aunt Jess, had served as a Red Cross nursing sister in France in 1914 and her aged father and brother were still in the Channel Islands. After the war we learned how father Le Brun had defied the enemy. When their military band passed beneath his window, the cantankerous and supposedly bedridden old Jerseyman had emptied his chamber pot over them, shouting as he did so, 'Sal Boche.' His arrest was only averted by his housekeeper's protest that he had TB, was insane and should not be approached!

My mother spent much of her time helping welfare organizations and ran the parish whilst father was abroad with the 53rd Welsh Division. Granny was left to run the house and attempt to keep me in order. She was a grand little lady, very Victorian with a stubborn Jersey personality. Married twice, she was again a widow and thought to be on the look out for a third husband. For her the war years were hard, but she managed to relieve the tension by a wee nip of whisky from a bottle kept concealed in a boot in her cupboard. I discovered that she kept her false teeth in a weak solution of brandy and I suppose this made them bearable when inserted in the morning.

Father's infrequent leaves were always the cause of much excitement. It was usually the middle of the night when he arrived, or the train got bombed or he had something unusual with him. Meeting him at Hereford station on one occasion, I perceived he was accompanied by a tall laundry basket. As he stepped from the train I went to help with this container and when about to lift it, a small black hand emerged and gripped my sleeve. It belonged to a very angry monkey. Jacko had a crooked tail, the unfortunate outcome of an accident with the NAAFI door, resulting in a permanent hatred of anyone in khaki, thus the ex-regimental mascot became my new pet. We had much in common; he was as mischievous as I was alleged to be, loved eggs, hated cats, pulled little girls' hair and screamed with rage when he couldn't get his own way. Together we went on safari through the 'jungle' of orchards, copses and rose-gardens. The long grass behind the church became a Serengeti in which lurked a fearsome lion, obligingly played by an over-fed ginger tom-cat. On siting our prey, Jacko would chatter excitedly and with Tarzan-like whoops, I would pursue the fleeing quarry with an ancient maori war spear, brought home by my parents from New Zealand. Sometimes the monkey got too near to the cat and was badly scratched for his pains and occasionally I suffered the same fate. It served us right, but also added greatly to the realism. Alas, Jacko developed a liking for birds, which he feathered and ate alive. But as he aged, long fangs protruded from his mouth and, one day when teasing him, I was bitten to within half an inch of my jugular vein. Wisely, mother decided he must live in a cage, from which he frequently escaped and terrorized the parish. His exploits are legendary and eventually he rather overdid it by climbing into the machine-gun post outside the ARP Headquarters and swivelled the ancient Maxim, resplendent with its belt of ammunition, to point at the curate, who did not approve of Jacko anyway, and liked him even less when he was forced to dive for cover into the freshly manured rose-garden. Ironically, my erstwhile chum was shortly despatched by a local farmer in, of all things, a monkey-puzzle tree.

However, I had other animal friends to console me. There was Brutus, the huge St. Bernard who adored being dressed up and always won the prize for the best attired dog at the church fete. There were cats, twenty-eight of them at one time! Unfortunately I was allergic to the cats; my eyes ran, I came up in spots and sneezed uncontrollably whenever they approached. An irritation that was to prove strangely useful in later years.

Meanwhile my faith in the Home Guard had diminished and, unable to play a more active part in the war, other than run messages for the ARP, I decided to raise a small private army that would be ready to defend the parish when the time came. Recruiting was easy. Before the war mother had laid in a plentiful stock of tinned pineapple and other mouth-watering delights. These, plus our fruit orchards and the abundance of cuddly pets, attracted hoards of children from all over the country. From this host I was able to select some thirty loyal followers of both sexes, to make up my gang. We had our headquarters in an old stable, shared with a pet fox and from here would sally forth against the enemy, who in the absence of German paratroopers, was provided by a rival organization of uncouth lads, whose sole occupation was to raid the apple orchards. Epic battles involving dozens of children raged back and forth across the Herefordshire countryside. Our weapons included catapults, spears, slings, bows and arrows and later, air-guns, home-made grenades and molotov cocktails.

By the time I was fourteen the need to defend the parish from Hitler had long receded and my schooling was making serious inroads into the conduct of the campaign. However, early scientific education gave a new impetus to our activities, and brought about the construction of a lethal cannon, mounted on an old invalid carriage and, worse still, a great mortar that could hurl a two-pound projectile over two hundred paces.

It was a bright summer's afternoon when my gallant little band, already suffering depletion as some, whose voices had broken, showed more interest in the choir girls than their military duties, made its last stand. After the first engagement the scrumpers, as the fruit-thieves were known, used all their low cunning to draw us to one side of the churchyard, whilst a nimble group scaled the eight-foot garden wall and wrought havoc amongst the Cox's Orange Pippins. These were similar tactics to those used by Prince Rupert at Marsden Moor to raid my ancestor's baggage train. We were not unprepared. Concealed in a yew hedge was the invalid carriage cannon and in a trench by the rhubarb bed sat the great mortar. The two possible escape routes through the allotments were liberally sown with mines, consisting of kilner jars filled with a fearful mixture of chemicals and acid. Leaving a handful of archers and air riflemen to deal with the enemy feint, I joined the artillery and catapulteers in the yew hedge. There were now some fifteen scrumpers busy looting the best tree in the orchard. 'Now, Hitchin,' I hissed in the ear of my master gunner, who obediently applied his illicit cigarette to the touchhole. The cannon roared, hurling half a pound of dried peas across the kitchen garden. Even as the carriage was careering backwards, I heard the screams of the enemy, but noted with some dismay that we had at least one innocent victim. Meredith, the gardener, rose phoenix-like from the spinach patch, clutching his posterior and mouthing a dreadful oath. But he who hesitates is lost, and having gained the advantage of surprise, we followed it up with a volley of catapult missiles and charged the enemy. As expected, they ran into the mine-field. At least half turned back and were seized. Now the mortar came into action to cut off the survivors. With a loud crump, it fired a bundle of fizzing fireworks inside a tin can high into space. Alas, the senior chorister's aim was bad and the bomb overshot, to fall and explode immediately behind an old lady, who, with her pekingese, was snuffling in the long grass. Scared out of their wits, dog and owner fled into the distance, clearing two stiles with extraordinary ease. The mortar's second shot landed on the rectory roof and brought down an avalanche of tiles. I accepted the senior chorister's resignation, apologized to Meredith, released all my prisoners unharmed and offered to pay for the roof as soon as I could negotiate a loan from my mother. It was to no avail. My father, now a JP, spent a week calming the populace and my private army disbanded. It is ironical that much of my military service has been spent at the receiving end of missiles very similar to those with which I had disturbed that peaceful shire. Father decided the Church was not my vocation and thereafter did all he could to encourage me to join the Army, where my destructive nature might be put to good use. At the age of nine a .45 revolver was thrust into my hand and, in spite of mother's protest, and to granny's terror, I was 'taught to shoot'. I was thirteen before I shot both myself and the village idiot and learned a useful lesson on safety with guns.

The Army was a natural choice, for throughout the war years I had watched the continuous stream of military men moving through our house. Travelling with my mother in a dilapidated van, we toured the county delivering school meals. The van broke down frequently. Several times we got stuck in slow-moving convoys of American tanks, and on two occasions I fell out when the string that secured the door gave way. Early one morning we came upon a messy road-accident in which a negro soldier was badly hurt. His cheek was slashed open and I was amazed to see that on the inside, his flesh was pink and his blood red, just like everyone else's. 'They are no different from us,' said mother, noting my surprise. I never forgot those words.

It was in Wales that my aunt and uncle lived, in a beautifully renovated miner's cottage near Devil's Bridge. The wild mountains, tumbling streams and the chance of meeting an infamous wall-eyed, black billy-goat fascinated me and I spent many happy holidays in the hills and learnt to appreciate the wonders of nature through the instruction of my uncle Laurie, himself a keen naturalist.

Another keen observer in our family was great-uncle Albert, whom I had met in his garden by the Solent. As I was brought forward to be introduced by a timorous aunt he sat, enormous in his deck-chair, a flowing grey beard cascading over his massive chest. Raised to his eye was a naval telescope. The old sea dog growled, 'So it's young John, is it?' and without looking down, 'What ship's that?' he said, swinging the lens to view a sleek destroyer sea-ward bound. 'Nice lines,' he muttered, 'that's what I like, nice lines.' His telescope had swung to some scantily-dressed girls, bathing on the far shore. 'Go out and see the world,' he roared, fixing me for a moment with a twinkling, blood-shot eye and then turned his attention back to the bathers.

Prep school years at a select choral college in Worcestershire were not terribly successful. In spite of my ecclesiastical upbringing, I had no singing voice and was pretty slow to learn anything. By the time I was ten I weighed almost nine stone and began a life-long battle of the bulge. But I soon discovered my weight was of no use unless I could put it to advantage, and after a fight with the school bully, which he won, I learnt to box.

In 1950 I arrived at Victoria College, Jersey. Built fortress-like of giant granite blocks, the school stood, defiantly, overlooking St. Helier. Father had made his mark at the same school and had risen to become its first Scout Master. After early days in his old troop, I found the attractions of the Combined Cadet Force irresistible. Transferring to join the brutal and licentious military, I was able to indulge my love of shooting and with the School VIII made the annual pilgrimage to Bisley.

Studies at Victoria were made more tolerable by the many un-official extra-mural activities available for the adventurous. Some of my contemporaries gained early experience with the French maids, but, for me, the great attraction was the maze of underground tunnels left behind by the German army of occupation. The island abounded with a liberal quantity of ammunition, mines and weapons. It was only years later during my training as a Sapper officer, that I discovered how lucky I had been to survive the experiments we carried out with assorted explosive devices.

Hans Hass and Jacques Cousteau were headline news in the new world of underwater adventure, and together with my friends, Adrian Troy and Tony Titterington, I manufactured my own diving equipment. Every week-end we weaved our way amongst the seaweed and rocks of Jersey's treacherous coastline to hunt the great grey conger eel, and the ugly wrasse. Our adventures were numerous, and when I regaled my mother with them she must have been horrified, but she simply smiled encouragingly and helped me to buy a powerful harpoon gun to continue the battle. Tony was the mechanical genius who could convert German submarine escape apparatus into underwater breathing equipment. We should have used soda lime to re-purify the air, but being short of funds, employed caustic soda for the task. The effects were almost fatal.

My great failure was with the opposite sex. Girls did not seem to appreciate bombs, guns, underwater fishing or my dancing. The ones that did were singularly unattractive.

During school holidays I became a part-time TA soldier in the Heavy Anti-Aircraft Regiment based at Abergavenny of which Father was the padre. The unit consisted mainly of ex war-time soldiers and very tough Welsh miners. In between bombarding airborne targets, we drank, danced, made eyes at the ATS girls and as Welshmen always will, sang lustily. Those fortnights at firing camp were the times when I really grew up. And it was from here I mounted my first expedition.

A schoolfriend and I set out from my uncle's Welsh mountain cottage at dawn one August morning. On our backs we carried enormous rucksacks filled with enough camping equipment for an army. The packs were badly balanced and it was almost impossible to stand upright. On our heads were Australian-style bush-hats and we each carried a four-foot ash-staff. I had a .22 revolver, with which to shoot rabbits when inevitably our rations were all gone and starvation threatened.

The first day was sheer hell and by early afternoon our feet were raw and our shoulders ached. A mountain mist dropped suddenly upon us and within minutes, we were utterly lost. It was with some relief that we decided to camp for the night. The next day was as bad as the first. It was late afternoon when we were following some sheep along a narrow track. Suddenly, to my astonishment, I saw my colleague sink waist-deep into a pool of bright green slime. The sheep scattered and ran back to dry ground, leaving us in the middle of a very treacherous bog. There was no point in looking around for help – we had seen no-one all day. Clifford, in spite of his considerable strength, was quite unable to move. Slipping off my cumbersome rucksack, I unwound the eight-foot toggle-rope we both carried.

'For God's sake, hurry,' was all he said, as I tossed the free end to him. The ground on which I stood shook like a jelly, so to spread my weight, I lay face down upon it. We both pulled hard, with the result that I began to slide towards my friend.

'It's no good,' he shouted, with a note of fear in his voice. 'I can feel the bloody stuff sucking me down.'

'Can't you get your own rope off?' I asked, but I knew immediately that if he took his arms and hands off the surface, he would probably sink right under. Overhead a lone buzzard circled and around us, oblivious to our plight, the sheep baahed contentedly.

'Wait,' I said, 'I've got an idea.'

'I hope it's a good one,' was Cliff's reply.

Crawling back to my pack, I undid the waist- and shoulder-straps and buckled them together. It gave me an extra six feet of line. Sliding back across the oozing surface, I joined it to the toggle-rope. It was just sufficient to enable me to get behind a hummock of long grass that stood like an island in the swamp. Now we had an anchorage and we began to pull. I'll swear nothing happened for ten minutes. The sweat was being forced out of our pores and neither of us said a thing, but went on pulling. Suddenly it was a little easier and to my great relief I realized that, inch by inch, Cliff was beginning to move towards me. Thirty minutes later we lay laughing together on the mountainside. For a further ten days we marched on, exploring ancient ruins, crossing fast-flowing streams, being chased by bulls and getting lost time and time again. When eventually we emerged, we were thinner, fitter and wiser for our experience.

I managed to pass my entrance exam to Sandhurst and, with a year to kill, took every opportunity to broaden my knowledge, whilst remaining at school to debate, shoot, swim underwater and take a few A-levels. By the time I left Victoria I had grown to love Jersey and have regarded it as home ever since.

Sandhurst meant going to the bottom of the ladder again. However, Britain still had an Empire and we hoped for a life of adventure and travel, probably fighting in numerous bush-fire wars. Suez and Cyprus were in the news and I felt impatient to see active service. The two very pleasant years at the Academy passed quickly. Not being terribly bright, I had to work fairly hard to get into the Royal Engineers, but nevertheless, I had time to make hundreds of new friends and enjoy the lighter side of life. There were the famous Sandhurst rags when we chained the cannon wheel to wheel across the London road. There were parties galore and girls by the score. I now found these more receptive. One in particular, a lady soldier, was more receptive than most and we saw a lot of each other. On the night of her Commissioning Ball I set out with a friend in my 1939 BSA sports car, known to all as Rigormortis. By modern standards it was a lethal device, but in those days bald tyres and defective lights were rather the vogue. It was a crisp clear March evening as, bedecked in black tie and silk scarves, we sped past Frensham Pond. Because the head lights gave out such a poor light, it took me several seconds to realize that my front wheel had mysteriously become detached and was proceeding in front of us towards the pond. Out of control, the car ran down a sandy bank and stopped abruptly in a pool of black mud. Fortunately a convoy of Austin 7's and sundry wrecks belonging to other cadets saw our plight, and within a few minutes we abandoned the BSA and were on our way to the Ball once more, this time seated less comfortably on a spare tyre attached to the boot of an aged Riley. Even so, I was a little late for the dinner and my first meeting with the dignified and upright colonel, whose daughter I was escorting, was not enhanced by my dishevelled appearance and my immediate request to borrow his car. Clearly he thought I was a bad influence on his daughter. I'm sure he was right!

2

TRAVEL AND ADVENTURE

THE huge grey shark swept by like a submarine, its streamlined tail swayed from side to side effortlessly and I was close enough to see every detail of the gill slits. Even underwater I could feel the hair standing up on the back of my neck, my heart pounding and my hands shaking. The ten-pound wrasse, my harpoon still embedded in him, remained jammed in his rock crevice and as the shark faded into the distance, I shot upwards, my lungs straining for air.

On the surface I felt even more vulnerable. What did Hans Hass say? Were not sharks supposed to attack men on the surface whilst they might mistake an underwater swimmer for a fish? I had never met a shark before and this had been a very big one; fourteen, sixteen perhaps eighteen feet. However, in Cornwall I should have guessed it was almost certainly one of the basking variety and unless, by chance, it collided with me, virtually harmless. I decided it was not much fun being the hunted and I felt a moment of sympathy for the rabbits that I sought out in the hedgerows with my clumber spaniel, Lily, and my smelly ferret, Charlie.

The last holidays after Sandhurst were the greatest fun. In Jersey we experimented with nitro-glycerine to create a rock-garden; brewed a lethal spirit that almost blinded a retired colonel who mistook it for his usual Sauterne and nearly drowned ourselves with the converted German submarine escape apparatus. All good things come to an end, and so it was that I found myself gazing up at General Gordon, astride his camel, at the School of Military Engineering at Chatham.

Those of us who became Royal Engineers had gathered here to be instructed in the black arts of sappering. For nine months we built bridges, laid mines, dug trenches, fired demolitions, surveyed roads, drove bulldozers and pumped water.

'By the time we have finished with you,' stated the mild-mannered, pipe-smoking warrant-officer, 'you will be fit to tackle any obstacle in the world.'

Being only thirty miles from the West End, the austere barracks did nothing to dampen our spirits. By now I had acquired a green Jowett Jupiter sports car. It was excellently built, had a fine turn of speed with torsion-bar suspension which enhanced its cornering. I enjoyed trying to beat the record from Eros to Gordon's camel.

My twenty-first birthday party was celebrated in a cellar in Gray's Inn Road. It was a well conducted orgy and so impressed were the police, when inevitably they arrived, that they returned later, off-duty, to join in the fun. Although some senior officers regarded us as an irresponsible gang of immature idiots and told us so frequently, there were others who tended to encourage our exploits.

'Sappers,' we had been told, 'are all mad, married or methodist,' and there was certainly a number of Royal Engineer officers who lived up to this reputation. Such men, we noted, were often well decorated and would have blushed had they heard some of the legends told of their deeds. It was they who encouraged us, possibly because they felt that even we might invent some fiendish engine of war or act irrationally, but courageously, on the field of battle. Mess nights beneath the portraits of Gordon, Kitchener and Napier reminded us of the illustrious heritage of eccentric generals. Determined to live up to our reputation, we derailed an army train by accident and blew up a row of washbasins in the officers' mess. The authorities were amazingly patient, although we drove one instructor after another berserk. 'There has never been such an ill-behaved course,' stated a chief instructor. But discipline and self-control did not seem to go with independent thought, and the practical application of unconventional ideas.

I managed to get a posting to a field squadron on active service in Cyprus, and at the end of the course we had six weeks leave, which I determined was not to be wasted. My girl friend from Sandhurst days was now in Singapore and her letters gave vivid descriptions of Malaya and, with my deep-seated desire to travel, I decided to go on a private expedition to the Far East. Forty-two days were quite enough to get there and back. A friendly MP said he knew someone in the Royal Air Force who might help, if I would carry out a few despatches. Thus, early on a July morning, I boarded a glittering silver RAF Comet and set off on a trip that did not turn out quite as I had planned.

Flying at forty thousand feet we crossed the Mediterranean to make our first stop at El Adem. Stepping out into the blinding sunlight, we were struck by a wall of hot dry air. The heat was incredible and I could not imagine how men had fought and lived in such a temperature for years on end, but scattered over the surface of the desert were numerous burnt-out tanks and wrecked vehicles as reminders of their efforts.

Engine trouble forced us to spend an unscheduled night-stop in the sticky heat of Bahrain, before crossing the Indian Ocean to Ceylon. At lunchtime on the third day, the dark-green Malay Peninsula appeared from beneath a mass of cumuli and we came in low over many off-shore islands surrounded by fishing-boats. On arrival at RAF Changi, we heard that a revolution had broken out in Iraq and RAF planes were temporarily banned from overflying that country. Indeed we had been the last plane through. I thought how lucky we had been, not even pausing to realize that it also meant that I was cut off. My time in Singapore and Malaya was spent in a brief look at some very ordinary stretches of primary jungle, sampling the night life and underwater fishing. There was certainly plenty to see beneath the waves, and we met barracuda, ray and even one small shark.

After three weeks I sought to arrange my return home, only to be told that there was no likelihood of an RAF flight in the foreseeable future. The civil air-fare was approximately £350, a sum beyond my wildest dreams, so I volunteered to act as a groom to a consignment of horses being flown to India or as attendant to a couple of dozen monkeys intended for Hamburg Zoo. But both plans failed. So I turned my attention to reaching England via America.

The American consul in Singapore was sympathetic and helpful. He said that if I could get to Clarkfield in the Philippines, there was always a chance that the United States Air Force might give me a lift to the States. Fortunately the New Zealand Air Force had a regular flight to Hong Kong via North Borneo and Clarkfield. Thus it was that I found myself, drenched to the skin in a leaking Royal New Zealand Air Force Bristol Freighter, butting through a heavy tropical downpour over the South China Sea. Eventually we reached the jungle-clad mountains of the Philippines and later dried out in the officers' club. The resident Royal Air Force liaison officer explained my plight to his taciturn opposite number.

At last the heavily built American major spoke: 'You've got a problem, boy,' he said, drawing hard on his cheroot, 'but maybe we can help. You come to the party tonight and tomorrow we'll figure what we can do.'

In the morning I learnt that the first difficulty was for a non-United States national to remain on the air-base for more than seventy-two hours without contravening some greatly respected regulation. The resourceful Major Harry had solved this even before I met him at 07.30 hours.

'You've just become a United Nations observer,' he exclaimed, passing me a large cup of black coffee. My 'papers' bearing the crest of the House of Commons impressed our allies far more than they had the Royal Air Force.

'We always try to help guys on a special mission for the Pentagon,' said one officer, 'and I guess that's the sort of duty you're doing.' I did not contradict him, and whilst my new-found friends worked hard on my behalf, I tried to keep out of their way by practising at the Rod and Gun Club and going on manoeuvres with the Air Police, a highly mobile unit of American and Philippino servicemen, responsible for the security of this enormous base.

Throughout my stay the residents overwhelmed me with kindness, but after ten days I was still there and, despite all their efforts, one or two items of red tape still blocked my progress. It was at the end of the morning, when the office staff was packing up for lunch that Liz, the quiet secretary whom I had been chatting up in the outer office, asked me if I would care to come to her twenty-first birthday party that night. I accepted gladly, but she had left before I realized that I knew neither her surname nor where she lived. Hearing my predicament, Major Harry gave a low whistle and then very slowly said, 'Man, you've just struck gold. That secretary is the general's daughter.' I arrived at the residence wearing my tropical dinner-jacket to be greeted by the commander of the 13th Pacific Air Force in his braces. A huge hand gripped mine as he skilfully manipulated a barbecue spit with the other. To the strains of Sinatra, this senior officer told me with relish of the wonderful times he had enjoyed in London during the war and of the close friends, many of whom he was certain I should know, he had left behind in Britain.

'How long are you staying, young man?' he said, filling my glass with a liberal quantity of *Old Crow*. I told him that I seemed to be there indefinitely and he promised to sort it out in the morning.

The fifty-six sets of orders that I was handed next day authorized me to travel from Clarkfield Air Base, Philippines to Burtonwood, England via Travis Air Base, California and Dover Air Force Base, Delaware. It was stated that this was necessary in the military service and was authorized under an Air Force regulation, which was eighteen letters and figures long. The first lieutenant who handed me the papers looked unhappy, and when I enquired the cause, he said that having taken them to the great man for signature, he had been ordered to sign them himself. I consoled him by pointing out that my movement-authority to get me to Clarkfield had been signed by my girlfriend. He shuffled off unconvinced with the hang-dog expression of a man under sentence.

It was a long flight to the States in the comfortable Constellation with stops at Wake and Guam Islands, where thanks to the thoughtfulness of the general in sending a signal, I was ushered into the VIP lounge and entertained royally at both places. I could only assume that the wartime parties in London must have been very good ones.

On arrival in Honolulu the aircraft was diverted to the civil airport, where an impressive array of grass-skirted girlies and Hawaiian bands greeted us. However, on discovering that we were not the anticipated tourist flight from San Francisco, they disappeared, grumbling, into the night.

The last leg of the journey to the States was passed in oblivion, thanks to a monumental party on Hawaii. As a result, I was feeling slightly jaded when we arrived late at night at Travis Air Force Base, California. To my dismay and concern, I discovered that the general's liberal supply of signals had dried up and no-one had ever heard of me. However, there was a plane flying east in two days' time and if I cared to stay at the officers' club for a couple of nights at ten dollars a time, I could catch that. Stringent foreign currency restrictions and the total inadequacy of a second lieutenant's pay had reduced my ready cash to three dollars, ninety-five cents, hardly sufficient to keep oneself in essential body liquid for forty-eight hours. At this point a kindly negro sergeant mentioned that, even as we spoke, there was an RAF bomber on the runway.

A corporal in faded battledress looked up from beneath an array of air recognition-placards and said in laconic cockney, 'Bust fuel pipe, be here for at least a fortnight,' thus dashing my hopes of a quick flip home in the belly of the Vulcan.

However, the sergeant remembered something else. He had seen a giant C130 transport arrive that night *en route* for New Mexico and, what was more, the pilot was an RAF officer on secondment. Flight-Lieutenant Hicks was sipping grape-juice at the bar when I acquainted him with my problem. Surprisingly he seemed delighted to meet another Briton and readily agreed to add me to the load of pineapples he was flying to some highly secret destination in the desert. Soon after take-off I climbed into a bunk and slept soundly until we reached a place that really sounded like the wild west – Albuquerque.

On landing I was invited to join the crew for breakfast and Hicks persuaded his merry men to part with all their loose dollars in exchange for my cheque. Whilst we were doing this a man in white overalls came over to our table and asked about the C130's radio. Without paying him much attention, the radio operator said it was 'all fine', but that the aircraft was open if he wished to inspect the set. The crew then went off to change, leaving me to finish my coffee.

The white overalled technician returned and coming straight up to me said in an angry tone, 'That radio's not working and you know it!'

I looked up in bewilderment and tried to explain that I was not a member of the crew.

'How in hell's name am I going to speak to the President of the United States if that set's no good?' he demanded.

It was all nonsense to me, but I said, 'Well, Flight-Lieutenant Hicks will be back shortly and perhaps he can help you.'

The man stormed off, clearly very angry, muttering that I was a spy from Russia. When Hicks got back I said, 'That chap was here about the radio again – he wants to speak to the President of the US.'

'Oh well,' said Hicks, only mildly interested, 'I expect he'll come back.'

Obviously the whole matter was of no importance and due to my lack of comprehension of American terminology and vocabulary, quite above my head.

At the flight operations desk they attempted to get me a lift eastwards, and whilst we were enquiring about aircraft timings, the overalled gentleman reappeared, as Hicks had said he would.

'I want to speak to the President,' he boomed at the sergeant who was helping us.

'You wait your turn, man – jeez sit right over there and wait your turn.'

The man turned puce with rage, went over to a drinking fountain and pressing the knob, yelled, 'Get me the President.'

Conversation in the flight operations ceased. Even Hicks looked surprised and the desk sergeant said, 'Excuse me, sir, I think we may have a problem.' He picked up the telephone and said, 'Air Police.' The man was still in consultation with the President (down the water pipe) when the white-helmeted police seized him.

'Who is he?' I asked Hicks.

'Oh! just some poor fellow escaped from the local lunatic asylum and broke into the Base.'

There were no USAF flights going east that day, so I decided to buy a ticket to Denver in Colorado where I was told I might pick up a flight to Washington next day. I thanked my friends and was about to leave the air base when the desk sergeant thrust me a piece of paper, 'You'll need that to get out of the main gate,' he said, 'our security is pretty tight here.'

Outside the civil airline office, legs crossed and smoking a pipe, sat the first Red Indian I had ever seen in the flesh. He eyed my brown shoes, long stockings, khaki shorts and stared fixedly at my officer's cane.

'How,' he grunted after a long silence.

Unconsciously raising my hand in the sign of peace, I replied, 'Very well, thank you,' and went inside.

Having got a ticket I sat in the shade awaiting the plane. The Indian watched me, sucking and puffing at his empty pipe. The temperature rose. At last he spoke again.

'What that stick for?'

Could I say a symbol of authority, a British Army tradition, we exchange them for a baton on promotion to Field-Marshal or the bloody dress regulations say I've got to carry it?

'You may have heard of General Gordon?' I enquired.

The Indian nodded solemnly. Perhaps the Americans had a Gordon too, better be careful what I say, he probably butchered the Blackfeet or whatever tribe this gentleman belongs to, I thought.

'Well, General Gordon led an army of Chinese soldiers many years ago. A stick like this was the only weapon he ever carried in battle. The enemy believed it to be magic and it so inspired his men that they never lost a fight.'

The Indian nodded, 'Plenty good wood,' he grunted.

On arrival at Denver, I followed the usual procedure of telephoning the nearest USAF Base. In this case it was the Air Force Academy. Within minutes a car arrived. A major ushered me into an office to await the arrival of the colonel. Coffee was produced, my papers checked and we began talking about England, which he claimed to know well from the war.

'Say, who won the FA Cup last year?' he asked.

I am not a keen disciple of football and simply could not remember.

'How about the cricket? How's the Test Match going?' he went on. I said I only played rugby and he looked a little disappointed. Suddenly the door burst open and a large, red-faced man in a short-sleeved shirt and Bermuda's stepped in.

'Well, what do you think?' he demanded.

'Oh, I think he's genuine,' said the major.

The colonel, for that was who the newcomer turned out to be, pumped my hand and apologized for the 'interrogation'. 'Can't be too careful, can't be too careful,' he emphasized. 'Now James here will see you have all you need and we'll hope to get you on that flight tomorrow. Any friend of General Morman's is a friend of mine.'

'Hurray for General Morman,' I thought as I showered, prior to tackling a giant T-bone steak with James. Unfortunately James had arranged for me to attend an all-night orgy at the nearby nurses' home and so I was not in the best condition as I stood waiting for the next plane. I decided *Old Crow* really lived up to its name!

A buckskin-clad, sixgun-toting sheriff with two bloodhounds arrived to hunt for a deaf-mute child, lost in the Rockies. Someone introduced me.

The sheriff, with a grip like a gorilla, shook hands and said, 'Howdy, partner.'

'Do you think you've a good chance of finding the boy?' I asked.

'Yep,' he drawled. 'If the bears don't first.' Everyone around nodded and muttered, 'bears'.

We were still discussing the bears when the plane arrived. It was a special, plushly furnished aircraft of what appeared to be the Presidential Flight. The occupants were mainly a US Army golf team returning from a tournament in Canada. They had a high-stake poker school in progress, but declining their offer of a game, I decided to sleep off the effects of *Old Crow*. Next to me sat an enlisted man, reading a comic.

'Do you golf too?' I asked.

'No, I'm going home on special furlough,' he replied.

'Oh! compassionate leave,' I said.

'Yes, you might call it that,' he replied. 'My papa attacked moma with an axe last night.'

'Really, how awful, I am sorry, is she badly hurt?' I asked.

'Yep, I guess so, he chopped her head clean off, darn it,' he said sadly.

At Washington the general's signals had done their stuff and I was taken on a conducted tour of the capital by night, before flying on to Macquire Air Base, near New Jersey. With luck I would arrive in UK two days before the troopship left for Cyprus. I sent a telegram to my depot regiment and settled down to write my diary as the four-engined transport lifted off on the first leg of the flight over the Atlantic. We had only been airborne for some twenty minutes when I noticed dense black smoke pouring from an engine. No flames were visible and the aircraft was behaving normally. In the next seat was a USAF pilot, already dozing quietly. I watched the smoke. Ought I to say something? Obviously it was nothing unusual, because the transport was full of airmen who showed no concern, but was this because like my neighbour, they were already asleep?

The smoke was getting worse, my neighbour grunted, so I seized the opportunity and said, 'Sorry to trouble you, but could you tell me what the purpose of the smoke is?'

Joseph N. Beerbecker, Jnr., opened one eye and glared out. 'Chrrrrist,' he gasped, 'we're on fire!'

The loudspeaker system cut in. 'This is the captain speaking. We have a malfunction in one of our starboard engines. We are returning to base.'

As we rolled to a halt, great columns of foam jetted onto the engine stifling the fire. We returned to the building to await the next flight, which I learned would be the same aircraft in two days' time when they had changed the engine! That afternoon a plane was leaving for Paris which would be better than waiting another twenty-four hours. A helpful movements officer said that he would try to get me transferred and went off to see a more senior officer for authority. A few minutes later he returned with an uneasy expression. 'The major says you've to see him,' he said.

The major, a harassed man, who looked as if he carried the troubles of the world in his brief-case, flicked through my papers.

'The 13th Pacific Air Force can't issue orders for you to travel to England,' he said, his voice rising.

The phone rang – he answered it – 'You're —,' he started, but the phone rang again, and whilst he spoke the light on a silent red phone glowed.

Two aides bumped heads as they seized it. 'Yes, sir,' they said four times and put it down. It was obvious that war was about to break out, so apologizing for being a nuisance, I gathered up my papers and was backing out, when the major screamed, 'Not so fast – I know what you are – you're a deserter – and those orders of yours are no good here.'

The movements officer looked embarrassed. 'It's been a busy day,' he said.

'Do I look like a deserter?' I asked him.

'Well, I couldn't say as I've never met an English deserter,' was his slightly unhelpful reply.

I felt very much like Alice in Wonderland. However, I guessed that the overworked staff officer would be off-duty next day, if he had not suffered a coronary beforehand. I was still on the passenger list of the original plane and, keeping well out of sight, hopped aboard at the last minute.

Our only stop was at Goose Bay in Labrador, when contrary to my expectations, I was not arrested. It was bitterly cold and sleet was falling, as still clad in my khaki shorts and shirt, I walked over the tarmac to the transit lounge. A befurred figure shuffled past with a trolley. He stopped suddenly, spun round, looked at me and said slowly, 'Gee, you must be British.'

The long Atlantic flight was passed in a series of lively card games with a sergeant of Hungarian extraction and a captain from the Middle West. When we got to Prestwick I found that by chance a USAF Dakota was going down to Burtonwood.

As I climbed aboard the pilot said, 'This gooney bird's got a sick engine. You'd better put this on,' and he handed me a parachute, but we arrived safely. The pilot couldn't understand my profuse thanks, and there wasn't time to tell him the story of how the USAF had devoted so much time to getting a very junior officer twelve thousand miles to catch a boat.

The band was playing on the quayside as I staggered up the gangplank with numerous items of hastily packed luggage. I waved goodbye to my parents, remembered to shout a brief word to my father about a parking summons that I would not be there to receive and bumped into several chums from Sandhurst days.

'Hello, Blashers – you look brown, where have you been?'

'Oh! come and have a beer and I'll tell you.'

In Cyprus I was fortunate to join a field squadron commanded by an energetic and unconventional major, who gave his subordinates a free rein with the minimum of supervision and the maximum support. Our regiment was housed in a tented camp on the foothills above Limassol. My troop consisted of fifty-four sappers, mostly National Servicemen with no great love of the Army, but they were a tough, spirited gang who worked like beavers and got into trouble continuously.

'Why did you throw the NAAFI juke-box at the manager?' I said to one of my sinners.

'Well, sir, I put a five-piastre piece in and nothing happened. "You've been done", my mate Sapper Gaze told me – at that moment up comes the manager bloke, so I hands him juke-box to see if he can get me five piastres out.' The manager, allegedly struck by a flying two hundred pound juke-box, was in hospital with multiple injuries.

We usually supported one or more infantry battalions, and roared about in our own little fleet of trucks and armoured vehicles, armed to the teeth with a large variety of weapons and explosive devices. Like all small units acting independently on active service, we had our fair share of adventure.

One dark winter's night a patrol discovered a hole that had been cut in the rock surface of a mountain track. Obviously it was intended that a mine should be inserted into this at a later date. It was decided to booby-trap the place to give the EOKA bomber a rude shock and I was ordered to produce and lay a suitable device. Accordingly, I fashioned a fiendish little bomb and placed it in position. I was aware that if it did not function, someone would have to remove it, so I marked the place with a strand of green plastic-coated wire, bound round a fir tree five paces away, and then made a detailed sketch map of the area.

Unfortunately, when the campaign ended some months later, I was not far from the site, and being the nearest sapper, was ordered to dispose of the device. It was long after dark when we reached the area. There was now no need for secrecy, so we drove up the moonlit track. Since my last visit, a great many heavy trucks had used the road and the surface was now hard-packed and unbroken. To make matters worse, I could not see any sign of the green wire on a tree. Nevertheless, using the map, I found the area and my driver, Lance-Corporal Cutler, began to search with a mine-detector.

'Nothing,' he grunted. 'Not a thing, sir.'

'Not surprising,' I replied, 'There's very little metal in it anyway and we put it eighteen inches down.'

However, there was one slight depression that fitted my bearings and distances, so I ordered the vehicle to back off a few yards and whilst Cutler held the torch, I probed the soil. It was solid rock, but suddenly my prodder penetrated something rather soft.

'I think we have it,' I murmured. 'Feels like the edge of the hole that the terrorist cut in the rock.'

Cutler's face was as usual expressionless. We had been through a number of anxious moments together and he never showed any emotion.

Digging through the soil, my fingers felt a small slab of rock about the size of a large book.

'It's under here – I remember this stone,' I remarked.

'Ah ha,' said Cutler and sniffed loudly.

The wind rising from the Mediterranean sighed in the fir trees and I felt a shiver of excitement run down my spine as my finger-nail touched something metallic.

'Must be the release switch,' I thought. 'Now I've got to get hold of the tongues and the end and hold them together whilst Cutler lifts the slab. Then he inserts a safety-pin and, hey presto, we are home and dry.'

But I couldn't get at the tongues, the soil around the bomb was packed like rock.

'Not worth fooling with this,' I said. 'Let's blow it.'

'We haven't got much explosive left, sir,' said Harry. 'Used most of it on that job this morning.'

He went over to the vehicle where Rampling sat listening to the radio set.

'Have yer dun?' said Rampling.

'Not yet, though he's found it, and if you can get off your arse, I'll see if we've got a stick of P.E. left,' I heard Cutler say.

A moment later he returned holding one miserable four-ounce stick of the yellow almond-smelling explosive.

'That's all there is,' he said, handing it to me together with a detonator and a length of safety fuse.

'Oh! well, that should do it,' I replied and tamped the charge carefully into the hole above the bomb. We sheltered round a bend in the track whilst the fuse burned. Two thousand feet beneath us the Mediterranean glittered in the moonlight and the lights of the coastal towns twinkled amongst the olive groves.

The explosion was not very loud, and as soon as the debris had stopped falling, I walked forward to the crater. The stone slab had gone and there was no evidence of the bomb. Funny, I thought, would have expected to see something. I bent down and thrust my hand deep into the warm soil at the bottom of the crater. About six inches down I felt the coarse texture of a length of fuse. So there were remains. I lifted the fuse; it stuck; I pulled, and to my horror Cutler's torch revealed a hideous string of mechanism, fuse and explosive dangling from my hand. Our charge had failed and as I watched the buckled tongues at the end, the release switch shifted a fraction of an inch. They were only held by the glutinous soil and now released, were opening.

'Down!' I yelled and pitched the whole thing over the cliff. The explosion shook us both.

'You all right, Cutler,' I said.

'Sir,' said Cutler.

'Have yer done then?' said Rampling, when we got back to the Land-Rover.

Rampling was one of the most amusing and yet courageous National Service soldiers I ever met. A born comic from Preston, where his mother made confectionery, he was my batman and the troop medical orderly. I reckoned that even if a chap were dying, Rampling would make him laugh.

A great man came to the regiment one day to talk to the troops about the situation and questions were invited. The CO had expressed his wish that it should be left to the soldiers to ask the questions. Seated in an open-air cinema, we heard HMG policy explained in simple terms by the erudite politician. Finally, he smiled confidently and sat down.

'Now I am sure some of you would like to ask a question,' beamed the CO.

Rampling, spokesman of the most rebellious, was on his feet at once and enquired whether HMG was concerned about the leaky tents in which most troops in Cyprus had spent the winter.

The RSM scowled, the subalterns smiled, the CO whispered in the great man's ear and the great man gave a long-winded answer, touching on the Defence estimates and the temporary nature of the campaign, which did nothing to rebut the insinuation of incompetence in high places. The audience growled menacingly.

The education sergeant then put an intelligent, well-worded question which the great man enjoyed answering and, to show it, said, 'That's a good question, Sergeant.' But his pleasure was interrupted by Rampling's Lancashire tones.

'I've got another question I'd like to ask,' he said. 'Me mates and me sometimes studies *Hansard*.' And then, reading from a scrappy piece of paper, he quoted a recent rather vicious attack on British policy on Cyprus by the Opposition and enquired whether our lecturer would care to explain in more detail what the Government's rather inadequate reply had meant.

The great man rose slowly and to give himself time to consider an answer, repeated the question and made a weak joke about how well-informed our men seemed to be. His answer was not at all convincing and the audience made it clear that it was not satisfied. Thankfully an easy and clearly predictable question followed. The morning was getting on and a good lunch awaited us in the mess.

The CO started to say, 'Well, if there are no further questions . . .', but Rampling had another, and this time the soldiers applauded as he spoke out. They were enjoying watching a political figure getting a roasting.

'Why is it that we National Servicemen chase all over the hills, day and night trying to catch bloody terrorists and when we gets one, you put him in a comfortable camp, which we usually have to build, and pays him twenty quid a week of British taxpayers' money?'

A cheer went up and the speaker mopped his brow with a clean white handkerchief. His explanation of British justice, and the need for proof in courts of law did not satisfy the men and several obviously wanted to carry on the debate. But the CO wisely and quickly thanked our guest and ushered him off for a strong gin. Rampling was carried shoulder high to the NAAFI.

A few days later I had been on reconnaissance in the Troodos mountains. My party consisted of the Land-Rover, driven as usual by Corporal Cutler, and the Daimler armoured scout-car, driven by Sapper Oran, with Rampling as his crewman. We rounded a bend and saw a Royal Marines Commando vehicle parked on the verge. The driver was punching out the remains of a smashed windscreen and an officer was tying a dressing around a gash in his forehead.

'What's wrong?' I asked, pulling up beside him.

'I wouldn't go through that village if I were you,' he said, indicating a cluster of red-roofed buildings that nestled in the foothills beneath us.

'They've got the road barricaded with huge earthenware jars and when you try to move them, they stone you to blazes from the roof tops,' he explained.

'Did you open fire?' I asked.

'No, not a man in sight, usual trick, just women and children.'

To avoid the village would mean a detour of over sixty miles and I had another job to do that evening.

I explained the situation to my handful of men and said, 'Oran, you lead the way in the armoured car. If the road is blocked, don't stop, just smash straight through. We'll be right behind you in the Land-Rover.'

'Good luck,' nodded the Commando officer, as we sped off down the dusty road towards the village. We were still half a mile away when the chanting of 'Ee–oo–ka, Ee–oo–ka', reached our ears.

Cutler pulled on his goggles and I drew my revolver. Turkeys, dogs and chickens scattered as we roared into the narrow street, flanked by the vine-bedecked coffee shops. Not a soul in sight. At the narrowest point in the road, an unbroken line of red earthenware jars formed a solid wall.

'Keep going,' I roared, as I saw the brake lights on the armoured car flicker, but Sapper Oran needed no encouragement and with a loud crunch, hit the jars. The Daimler disappeared momentarily in an explosion of pottery, olive oil and grain, which cascaded across the street. The bits were still falling as we followed through the gap. On the roofs I saw astonished faces peering down at the mess.

We sped on and were still in the village when, to my consternation, Oran stopped. At once I realized why. Somehow we had taken the wrong turning and were now at a dead end. There was hardly room to turn round, but as I leaped out, Rampling was out too directing the driver.

In record time we were facing outward, but Cutler said, 'Here comes trouble,' and I saw a huge crowd of villagers moving slowly towards us up the street. My stomach felt very queasy and I remembered the awful stories of exactly similar incidents when troops had been caught by hostile crowds. There were four of us and at least a hundred of them. The crowd was silent, grim-faced, determined. Not a man in sight. Just dark-skinned women in the traditional black dress of the Cypriot peasant. The fact that we had just destroyed a large amount of their winter store of olive oil and grain did nothing to endear us to them. Their leader was a wrinkled old woman, who carried an axe in her bony hand. They awaited her orders; she knew she had us cornered and like a cat with a mouse was enjoying the scene. Even if we fired, we couldn't stop more than half a dozen before they seized us. My only other thought was to charge them with the vehicles. The consequences were too horrible to contemplate.

'You must disperse or we shall open fire,' I said in as stern and authoritative voice as I could manage.

The old woman, standing twenty-five yards away, spat a long

stream of filthy green phlegm in reply. She looked at her comrades
and said something I did not understand.

'Oki,' they roared in response and edged nearer to us.

'Here, will you hold this, sir,' said Rampling, thrusting his rifle
into my hand.

'What on earth . . .,' I began to ask, but he was already ambling
towards the crowd.

He reached the old crone and looking forever like an English
Bobby on duty at a football match, placed his hands on his hips and
said loudly, 'You can't do that there here, Mom.'

The witch looked bewildered.

'Come on, I'll take ruddy axe,' said the lad from Preston and,
grasping the razor-sharp weapon, turned to the crowd and waving
them back said, 'Now I've got to get back to camp for ma tea, so if
you'll just clear the road, we can all go home.'

To my astonishment, they obeyed.

'OK Harry, come on,' yelled Rampling and signalled us forward.

'Tata, sorry about the oil jars, but thou shouldn't park them on
busy highway, you know,' he grinned, a he leaped aboard the
armoured car.

We got almost fifty yards before the crowd recovered from its
surprise and ran screaming after us with sticks and stones. However,
thanks to the cool courage of this extraordinary soldier, we escaped
any serious damage.

Back in camp two hours later I called him over, 'You did well,
Rampling – thank you very much,' I said.

'Ay, it was good laff, wasn't it,' he grinned and shuffled off to
persuade the cooks to give him a late tea.

Years later, as an instructor at Sandhurst, I tried to impress on the
cadets how fortunate they were to lead men who would be un-
troubled by disaster, unflattered by success, who would face adver-
sity and danger with the same cool courage, sparkling with a unique
brand of ready wit.

3
SEA, SAND AND SURVIVAL

'I EXPECT you are wondering why I asked you here this evening,' said the commissioner, raising his gin and tonic.

'You said you were interested in discussing an underwater project,' I remarked.

'Yes, that's quite right.' His eyes twinkled and without pausing, he said, 'Have you ever heard the legend of the great port of Paphos?'

As the warm evening darkened and the crickets began their nightly overture in the garden of the residence, I listened intently to Ivor Williams, Commissioner of Limassol, outlining with Welsh fervour his theory about an extensive port that had once existed at Paphos in the south-east corner of Cyprus. His servant came and went, soundlessly refilling our glasses and it was late when he said, 'Well, there it is, my boy, a great mystery, do you think you could solve it?'

'I can have a jolly good try,' I replied with genuine enthusiasm.

So it was that in August 1959 I stood with a group of National Service soldiers in the Paphos museum, whilst the assistant curator told us the history of this famous area. The soldiers shuffled, sniffed, coughed and scratched; archaeology was not a subject close to their hearts.

'So you see, each year many, many ships came from all over the Mediterranean bearing young maidens.' The men's eyebrows raised.

'He's on about skirt,' whispered a lad from Leeds, waking Mr. Harringay, 1955 with a prod in the ribs.

'Ough!' grunted Sapper Robins, taking an instant interest in the lecture.

'The young women were unmarried,' explained the curator, 'and it was necessary that they should be virgins.' Even Rampling was awake now. 'They left their ships at anchor in the port and walked up through a place we call the beautiful gardens, where they worshipped and made offerings with terracota figurines. At Kouklia there was a great temple, in the centre of which was a fifteen-foot phallus – this is a model of the original,' said the curator as he tapped a black monolith on which he was leaning. Then, with a wry smile, he added, 'It is said that so many maidens came to be initiated that some had to wait here until the winter.'

'Bet there weren't no shortage for t'ordination in them days,' muttered Rampling.

Our mission sounded simple. The underwater section of 33rd Independent Field Squadron, Royal Engineers, would explore the sea-bed off Paphos, with a view to establishing possible evidence of a large port or harbour. Complete with a hundred-ton flat-bottomed and open-decked Royal Engineer 'Z' Craft, thirty-five soldiers, piles of underwater diving equipment, plus an eager Army Public Relations Officer, the expedition arrived at Paphos. The introduction of a spot of ancient sex into the task was a splendid catalyst and the men set about their work with considerable enthusiasm. Thus, for a few weeks during four summers, the army surveyed the sea-bed and brought up tons of pottery, marble, glass and metal.

One of our earlier finds was the wreckage of a man-o'-war, whose carronades lay scattered in shallow water a mile off shore. It was whilst lifting these that we came upon the monster of the Moulia Reef. We had just raised the last of five large cannon, the wind was freshening from the south-west and I decided to have a last look round in case we had missed anything. Flipping along over the rocky bed, I came to a ravine and peered down. Something smooth, grey and round, like a metallic cylinder lay at right angles across the sandy floor of the cleft. I turned round slowly. 'What on earth is that?' I thought and jack-knifing my body, I slid down into the rock.

The undersea gorge was larger than appeared from the surface, towards one end it opened up and I found myself staring into a low cave. The cleft was simply a large crack in the roof. The grey cylinder now looked about twelve inches in diameter and got thicker as it disappeared into the gloom of the cave. Grasping the rock, I pushed myself down and under the ledge. For a few moments all seemed black, then as my eyes grew accustomed to the dark, I perceived a movement. A small cloud of sand billowed up. To my left the cylinder moved, or I should say twitched, and at the same time, the floor of the cave slid forward several feet. Still puzzled I stared in and it was another few moments before I realized I was hovering between the roof of the cave and the back of a giant sting-ray. An arm's length in front, I could make out the gentle mound of its head, behind me stretched the huge tail that had first attracted my attention. It was very large and I could only hazard a guess that it was ten feet from wing-tip to wing-tip.

Why did it stay so still? Perhaps it had been stunned by our explosions earlier that day. Hardly daring to breathe for fear that the rattle of my valve would disturb the creature, I inched backwards from the black hole. Before I reached the ravine it twitched again, but at last I was back in the light and speeding to the surface.

'What's that in the crack?' shouted Lance-Corporal Jones, who had been watching my descent.

Tearing out my mouth-piece, I yelled back, 'The monster of the Moulia Rocks – it's a bloody great ray.'

Only a couple of evenings before, we had listened to the fishermen of Paphos telling us of a terrible sea monster that lived on this reef, destroying their nets and even threatening their boats.

'If you can kill it,' they promised, 'we'll buy every soldier a beer.'

'Prepare me a five-pound charge of plastic explosive,' I ordered, 'and tell Christos to come and see the monster, we'll need him to give evidence if we're to get that beer!'

Christos, one of our Cypriot boatmen, swam over and donning a mask, kicked his way down to the monster's lair. He came back ashen and convinced. Five minutes later the sea erupted in a white plume as the demolition charge detonated inside the cave. Thus ended the monster, but we never got our beer.

'It is far too big to be killed by you,' laughed the fishermen, in spite of Christos's evidence.

In August 1960 I returned to England, purchased a splendid .375 Magnum big game rifle and got married! The rifle was intended for an expedition I was planning to Ethiopia that autumn. Alas, almost at the moment of our departure, a revolution broke out and although it was quickly put down by the Emperor, it was not thought prudent for British officers to be wandering in that part of Africa for a while.

My other acquisition, Judith, was an excellent swimmer and became the general manager to the underwater expeditions, which now went on almost continuously. Our work at Paphos had produced conflicting conclusions. One Cyprus newspaper claimed we had discovered 'the Eighth Wonder of the World', but archaeologists who came to examine the huge pile of artefacts, made conflicting statements and then disappeared, leaving us to scratch our heads.

Frankly, I was not convinced that we had proved beyond reasonable doubt that the great harbour had ever existed. The real problem was that none of the archaeologists could dive and therefore everything had to be brought to the surface for them to examine. On one trip to England I had spent days in London trying to find someone with expert knowledge, who could dive, but without success.

I was due to return to Britain in December 1961 and therefore I decided to have one last really thorough look at the area to see if we could unravel the mystery. The sea-bed was littered with the rubbish of the centuries and the museum was overflowing with our discoveries, but alas, the splendid carronades we had raised from the Moulia reef in 1960 were now rusting relics.

However, in July 1961 I launched the most ambitious expedition to date. Titled Operation Aphrodite II, it consisted of a task force of boats, vehicles, light aircraft and the faithful Sapper flagship, Z *11*. Almost a hundred soldiers and civilians were involved. The Royal Navy made some preliminary soundings for us and the RAF flew special sorties with infra-red cameras.

The people of this quiet corner of Cyprus were awe-struck by the incredible effort the British, who had now given them independence, were putting into solving some ancient legend. The press was also interested and the expedition needed a special Public Relations section to deal with the growing number of enquiries.

I felt very conscious of the need to show some success for all this effort. It was rather like being on a mountaineering expedition. To completely satisfy sponsors, one had to reach the summit. But in this case, I did not know where the summit was or even what it looked like.

The expedition officers, Judith and I were sitting on the quay sipping our third cup of coffee. Greek music echoed from the bar, overhead the cloudless sky was alive with twinkling stars. On the deck of Z *11*, the divers were turning in with the usual ribaldry that is the hallmark of the British soldier.

'Excuse me, sir.' The powerful figure of Corporal Wickens bent over the table.

'Hello, Corporal Wickens,' said Judith. 'Would you like some coffee?'

'No, thank you, ma'am, I'm trying to give it up!' he said and continued, 'I have a police officer here, sir, who would like a word with you.'

That sounded ominous – the new republic might be touchy about

such things as parking a 'Z' craft without lights or perhaps Sapper
Grimshaw had gone berserk in Ktima. In fact, there were two policemen.

'Pull up a chair and join us,' we said.

They sat down, the barman brought cold beer and we toasted
each other. After a long pause, the larger of the officers said slowly,
'Do you know the legend of the great gun?'

I did indeed. The story was simple. When the Turks had ruled
Cyprus, they had stationed a garrison in the square fort on the
harbour wall of Paphos port. It was said that on top of the battlements they placed a large cannon. This artillery piece was able to
hurl a ball to any part of the town and thus the Greek-Cypriot
inhabitants lived under constant threat. Eventually a revolution
took place and the Greeks managed to capture the castle, after
butchering the Turkish garrison. In the end the revolt failed, but
when the Turks returned to Paphos, they found the gun had gone.
With customary efficiency and ruthlessness, the Turks took numerous
prisoners and in an effort to discover the whereabouts of the cannon,
tortured them to death, but they never discovered where it was
hidden.

Naturally everyone thought that the gun had simply been lowered
over the battlements into the water, and on previous expeditions we
had made exhaustive searches of the sea-bed beneath the walls of
the fort. We had found a few cannon balls, but no gun. To throw a
shot into Ktima, it must be a sizeable piece and would probably
weigh several tons. Not an easy thing to move overland. If the gun
was not in the immediate area of the fort, the Greeks had probably
dragged it away into the town, but then it was most likely that the
Turkish inquisitors would have found it.

Another expert, I thought, who knows the exact location of the
gun and for a few pounds will tell us.

'Well, what's the story,' I said, passing the policemen the dish of
salted nuts.

'I have seen the great gun,' said the younger officer, looking very
serious.

'Where?' I enquired, still sceptical.

'It is near here on the other side of the headland, very close to the
shore,' he said. 'I can show you the place, sir.'

'All right,' I said. 'We'll have a look at your spot tomorrow, when
can you accompany us?'

'I am off-duty tomorrow afternoon,' replied my informant, 'I'll come to the jetty then.'

It was four o'clock when the reconnaissance party boarded the tug and we set out on yet another quest for the long-lost cannon. Rounding the headland, we followed the constable's directions and headed in to the beach.

'Getting pretty shallow,' cautioned the helmsman. Fifty yards ahead the waves rolled over a reef.

'We can't go in much closer,' I said over my shoulder to the policeman. 'Where do you reckon it is now?'

'There,' he said, 'just beyond the rocks.' His finger pointed at the line of black shadows. The tug rolled in the gentle swell.

'That'll do,' I said, 'we'll swim in from here.'

With a splash, half a dozen divers equipped only with masks, breathing-tubes and flippers, jumped in and fanning out in an extended line, twenty feet between each man, they began to swim slowly towards the shore. I was not very hopeful of finding anything. For about ten minutes we searched. There was nothing to see but bare rock and sand.

Corporal Jones' excited voice rang out above the sound of the waves. 'It's here, it's here,' he yelled, 'a damned great gun.'

And there indeed it was! At first, all we could see was the breech sticking up about eight inches above the sand. It was lying in four feet of water, and within a few minutes we had uncovered two feet of it.

'What a monster,' said the Public Relations Officer, who had come to see the fun. 'How are you going to lift it?'

That was the problem. The cannon was buried in deep sand at an angle of forty-five degrees. To landward and seaward, there were low reefs. We couldn't bring the 'Z' craft over it and as I guessed it must weigh at least two tons, it was going to need some pretty good lifting tackle to move it.

I walked on to the beach and looked around. Just inland rose the massive natural rock slabs in which were carved the Tombs of the Kings and running down from them was a narrow track. This track was obviously very old and made a relatively smooth path through the rock formations. Did the Greeks drag the gun down this path, I wondered, and then somehow push or float it out to its hiding place?

Mr. Takis, the museum curator, suddenly appeared, running down the path. 'Is it true?' he shouted. 'Your radio operator tells me that you have found it.'

Top left and right: The invalid carriage cannon – and its end

Above: School CCF, Victoria College, Jersey

Right: Setting out on my first expedition!

Above: With my parents at Bisley

Left: Judith and I explore Scotland

Above: Early morning within sight of the Zelten Oil Field, Libya 1963. *L to r:* Dr Hendrick Forss, David Southwood, David Hall (our leader) in foreground

Right: Exploration Aphrodite. Our first finds

Below right: Raising cannon from a wreck on the Moulia rocks, Paphos

Above: The Blue Nile. Tisisiat Falls – dry season

Below: The Tisisiat Falls in full spate

'Well, we've certainly located a big gun,' I replied, 'but until I can get it out, it's difficult to say if it is the one in question.'

'How will you do that?' asked the excited archaeologist.

'We'll blast a channel through the inshore reef. Meanwhile Corporal Osgood will bring his recovery vehicle ashore from *Z 11* and try to get it over the headland to this point. Then we'll run out the winch-cable for divers to fix to the gun, then heave-ho and it should be like pulling a tooth,' I explained.

'Wonderful, wonderful – I must go and telephone the director in Nicosia – and the newspapers,' said Takis, rushing off again.

So it was at dawn next day that our divers laid the charges they had spent the previous evening preparing. A heavy swell made the work difficult and several sappers had to be treated for lacerations after being swept against the reef. On the shore Corporal Osgood and his REME fitters had got the massive Scammell recovery-vehicle to the site and were already running out their cables. *Z 11* lay two hundred yards out, providing communications and refreshments. By nine o'clock we were ready to fire the first set of charges; the police cleared the area and the fuse was ignited. Suddenly, low overhead, came an Army Auster aircraft containing several senior officers who had flown down to witness the operation. It banked sharply over *Z 11* and came straight over the beach. Frantically, I waved it away.

With a dull roar, the charges exploded, sending a column of spray straight upward at the Auster, which, none the worse for a drenching, flew straight on! One more bang, then the cable was fixed and the winch took the strain. The demolitions had done the job, and in a few minutes the crowd of onlookers could see the great black, iron cannon in the surf. Eight feet long and weighing 2.2 tons, our prize was carried by the Scammel in triumph to Paphos port. That night the Cyprus radio credited us with solving the legend, but I knew that to leave the metal exposed to the air would ruin it in no time, so we lowered it into the harbour to await the construction of a special preservative bath.

Eight years afterwards Judith and I went back and walked amongst the ruins on the headland. Some spectacular finds had been made on land since our expeditions. We had been camping only inches above a wonderful mosaic floor of a villa, I discovered. But although Paphos had gained much in its knowledge of the past, the situation of the present had greatly deteriorated. Now Turks and Greeks lived behind barricades, and the houses bore the signs of the civil war. Takis found me in the crusader castle overlooking the harbour.

'Welcome, welcome,' he said, embracing me. 'Have you seen your great gun? It is mounted in a place of honour on the quay.'

We strolled into the little port and at once saw the gun, mounted on a carriage in front of the Cyprus Navy Headquarters. I raised my camera. A sentry rushed over.

'It is forbidden to photograph military weapons,' he explained politely.

'Things have changed,' apologized Takis.

Elsewhere in Cyprus we had made other discoveries, but, of course, there was the military side to diving that usually meant hard work under difficult conditions. One morning the telephone in the office rang. It was the military port office.

'John, we're in trouble,' said the commandant. 'Some idiot has just let our mobile crane run into the harbour. It's effectively blocking the slip and we've no crane big enough to lift it.'

It seemed the only way to move it was to pass a cable beneath and then partly sink a 'Z' craft on either side, fasten the cable to them and refloat the craft. The only snag was that the machine was lying in liquid mud.

Securing the crane's jib to the dockside, Sapper Ellis and I slid into the chilly water. I took a hose-pipe to enable me to 'tunnel' through the mud. Ellis handled the steel-wire cable which we were to pass beneath the machine. The mud closed about us as we felt our way through the tangled mass of struts and cables. It was pitch black.

Communicating by a system of hand signals, we descended slowly. When we reached a more solid lump, I hosed it away. I guessed we were right beneath the crane when I felt a slight increase in pressure on my ears. My depth gauge was invisible, but I realized at once what was happening. The crane was sinking deeper into the mud, pushing us down beneath it. I stopped moving and held by breath. I heard the clatter of Ellis's valve stop also. The slow, relentless movement of the steel-work was obvious. Only our efforts beforehand had masked it. Why on earth is the crane moving? I thought to myself, but now was not the time to sort that out. We had to get out of this death-trap with all speed. I tried to go forward, but came upon an impenetrable barrier that was probably a wheel. The choice was to go down and try and come up beyond it or go back the way we had come. At least I knew the way back was clear, and in an

instant I decided that was the way out. The mud was getting thicker
and movement against it was an effort. I reached out to Ellis and
gave the signal for 'going back and up'. He seemed to understand
and I felt him move away. Inside my suit, I was sweating with the
effort of forcing my way through the clinging mud. My demand
valve seemed to be giving me more air than I needed, probably the
mud was affecting it.

I was still clutching the hose, although I had rather forgotten
about it. Now it was vital for survival. Suddenly the crane gave a
jerk which frightened me stiff and made me realize that I must move
faster. I slid one shoulder under the hose and passed the nozzle down
towards my feet, then gripping it between my knees and hands, I
began to tunnel backwards, following my lifeline. Something tightened around my thigh. It felt a little like a small octopus that had
taken a fancy to me when working on a wreck the previous week, but
I couldn't move against it and as I struggled, it tightened. I felt it,
coarse and rough. It was simply a loop of rope that I had stuck my
foot through. Laboriously I went forward, freed my leg and started
back again.

It seemed like minutes, but was probably only a few seconds
before I found my nylon cord rising. Feeling above me all the way,
I began to ascend. Once I hit a loose cable and a surge of panic
returned – was I still under the crane? The water was jet-black and
I saw nothing until I surfaced. As the mud drained from my face
mask, Ellis came into view beside me.

'You OK, sir?' he said.

'Yes, but I'm not sure I'd like to repeat that!' I replied.

'Sorry about that,' shouted the port officer. 'One of the strops
slipped on the jib, but you'd have been all right – we had another on
anyway.'

'Thanks for telling me,' I murmured into my mouth-piece. We
got the cable under at the second attempt and I went home. Judith
was waiting.

'Come on,' she smiled. 'Don't look so fed up – let's go underwater
fishing this afternoon.'

Our diving activities in the Mediterranean were not restricted to
Cyprus and I was also able to examine the ancient harbour of
Apollonia and Leptis Magna during visits to Libya on training
exercises.

However, it was not the African coast-line that attracted me, but
the desert. The desolate, magnificent Sahara had not changed in four

thousand years. The population was still largely on the coast or around such water sources as Lake Chad and the Nile. The maps still said 'relief data incomplete'. Those words were like a red rag to a bull.

Libya stretched over five hundred miles deep into this wilderness; all one needed was time, a few Land-Rovers and fuel to be able to explore areas where few, if any men, had trodden before.

We quickly learned to navigate by sun compass, de-bog vehicles with pierced metal planks called sand channels and mend every possible breakdown on a Land-Rover. Our forays into the dun brown waste-land were enlivened with visits to oil-rigs, where rare and glorious hot baths, ice-cold beer and inch-thick steaks were readily available. The oil men had not yet penetrated deep into the desert, but they always seemed glad to see us at their lonely, but well-stocked camps.

Resupply was always the main headache, and many of our ventures were only possible through the generous assistance of the US Air Force, who provided both parachute resupply and on tactical exercises, simulated attack by jet fighters.

Around Tobruk we were concerned with clearing routes through wartime minefields. Although many of the mines were rusty and useless, some of them were in an extremely unstable condition. Rumours of Rommel's gold, tunnels full of Nazi loot and even a U-boat laden with precious metal trapped in its undersea pen, were rife. Already professional treasure-hunters were arriving and two ex-German soldiers had been blown up in the huge underground ordnance depot that lay beneath the headland only a few weeks before. Deep in the desert, oil prospectors were also discovering war relics, and one of the most extraordinary was *Lady Be Good*.

It was a dark night during the last war when a United States Air Force Liberator, nicknamed *Lady Be Good*, was returning to Benghazi from a bombing mission in Italy. It appears that a powerful, high altitude tail-wind blew them back across the Mediterranean in record time, and as the North African coast-line was blacked out the navigator failed to see it. The result was that at a time when they should have landed, they were several hundred miles deep into the desert and flying over the Sand Sea of Calensio. When their fuel finally ran out, they managed to make a crash-landing on a stretch of flat sand between two huge dunes. A wing broke off, one man was injured but the aircraft did not catch fire and most of the crew were little the worse for their experience. Believing themselves to be only a

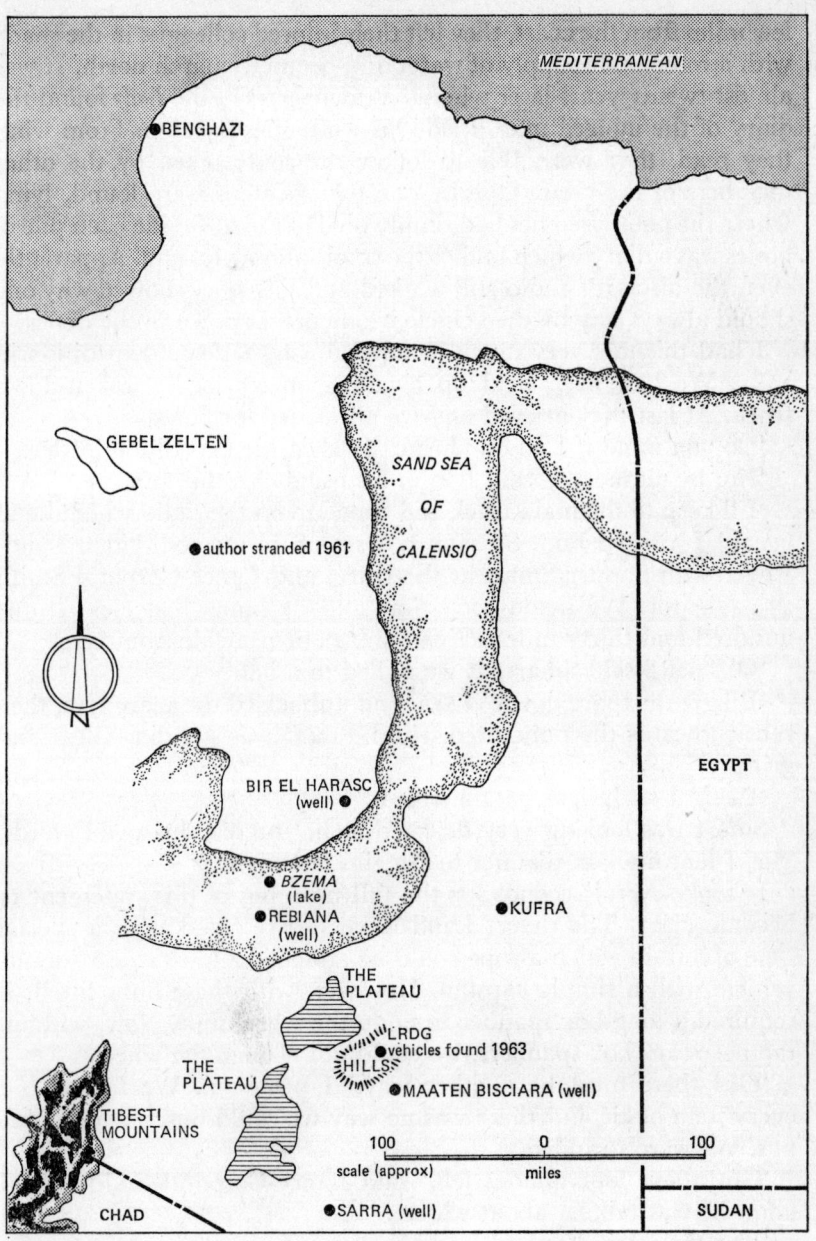

Eastern Libyan Desert

few miles from the coast, they left their injured colleague in the shade with a reasonable supply of water and began to march north. It was almost twenty years later when the discoverers of the *Lady* found the diary of the injured man beside his whitening skeleton. From what they read, they were able to follow the route taken by the other members of the crew. One by one the skeletons were found, lying where the poor wretches had simply died of thirst. Beside each pile of bones was a diary which told of the tragic and awful end. Apparently even the aircraft's radio still worked and this story showed why one should always stay by the vehicle if one breaks down in the desert.

I had this tale very much in mind during a desert expedition in 1961. We had been held up awaiting spares for a broken-down truck. At last they arrived and we all turned for home.

'Do you mind if I go on ahead?' I asked the expedition leader.

'No, by all means,' said Bob in his usual cheerful tone.

'I'll keep to the main track and come up on the radio schedules as usual,' I assured him. So saying, I set off in my well-laden Land-Rover with Sapper Smart at the wheel and Lance-Corporal Smith as navigator. We made good time and by lunch had cleared one hundred and thirty miles. *Hissss!* went our nearside front tyre.

'Oh, hell!' said Smart, as we pulled to a halt.

'I'll get the spare down,' I said and unbuckled the spare tyre, then ran it towards the punctured wheel. Smart was standing silent and grim.

'Well,' I said, 'let's get on with it.'

Smart was looking very dejected as he uttered the awful words, 'Sir, I lent my box spanner to Higgins last night.'

It took several seconds for the full meaning of this statement to become clear. The desert Land-Rovers were fitted with a special type of hub to which a rope could be attached and thus provide the vehicle with a simple capstan. However, with these hubs fitted, it required a long box spanner to undo the wheel nuts. Now, without the necessary box spanners, we could not change the wheel.

'Oh! there must be another way,' I protested. We turned out every item of kit, but there was no way we could unscrew even one nut. We were stranded.

'Got about four gallons left,' said Lance-Corporal Smith and I knew he was talking about water.

'Plus the water bottles,' I added.

Silently and trying to avoid unnecessary activity, we laid out the fluorescent air identification panels in the form of the emergency signal, prepared the flares, made a shelter projecting from the side of the Land-Rover and crawled beneath it. Our radio was not working terribly well and therefore it was no surprise when we failed to make contact at dusk. After the scorching heat of the day, the blissful cool of the night was a welcome relief.

After the first flush of panic, I had wanted to call Smart every name under the sun. However, eight hours later my anger had subsided and I concentrated on trying to evolve a plan that would save us. We had broken down on the edge of the mile-wide track and it was quite possible that the convoy would find us. But they only had to be five hundred yards eastward and they would pass behind a low ridge, missing us completely.

The night passed with one strange incident. Lying in the open grave I had dug in the sand, I awoke to hear a rattling metallic noise nearby. There was no wind, yet when my eyes opened to peer out across the desert bathed in moonlight, I could see nothing. That's strange, I thought, and there it was again. I instinctively drew my Walther pistol from my bedroll and, thus armed, prepared to meet whatever it was making the noise. Raising myself on my elbows, I scanned the moonlit desert. From behind a low hillock, one of our discarded tin cans rolled into view. It was rolling over and over as if being pushed by a strong wind, but the night was still and there was nothing visible pushing the can. As I pondered this, the can suddenly stopped and then rolled back the way it had come. Must be going mad, I thought. Then it changed direction and came towards me.

'My God, a haunted tin can, probably something they put in the rations.'

The shining object was only ten feet away now rolling this way and that, when I raised my pistol. The sharp crack rang out in the still air, the bullet threw up a spurt of sand about a couple of inches from the can, which instantly accelerated away. I fired again. The can stopped rolling and, to my amazement, a desert rat hopped out – clearly annoyed at having his feast disturbed.

Awaking at daylight, I rose stiffly from the sandy bed. The radio still remained silent and although I went through all the drills a dozen times, I could get nothing; altering the setting of the skywave aerial didn't help either. However, just in case others could hear us, I sent an SOS signal giving our position. The sun was well above the horizon when I gave up fiddling with the knobs.

'What shall we have for breakfast?' said Smith.

'I don't mind,' I replied, 'but let's have it quickly before the heat hits us.'

Lying under the shelter I made a mental check of our emergency actions. Flares ready, ears alert for noise of aircraft or vehicles, air identification panels out. Remaining water, now down to two and a half gallons, carefully stowed in the shade. All other sources of liquid checked, we lay in silence, the beads of sweat grew on our filthy skin and turned into rivulets which ran into the sand. God, how we smelt. On the move we had not noticed it, but now it was becoming unpleasant to be near anyone else. Somehow one s own odour was bearable, almost fascinating, but anyone else's was disgusting. Sleep was impossible, so I tried to read, but a voice in my head kept saying, 'There must be a way out.' Rather like shipwrecked sailors on a raft, I mused. It's the waiting that is the worst.

Then an idea struck me. If we could catch some desert rats, we might live a little longer on the liquid their bodies contained. I began to consider ways of doing this.

'Water, sir?' said Smart, handing me a plastic cup of luke-warm fluid.

'What precious stuff this is,' said Smith. 'We always take it for granted in Blighty – just turn on the bloody tap and there it is.'

At noon the sun was right overhead, and to reassure ourselves we took a fix with the bubble sextant. It simply confirmed that we were about one hundred and twenty miles south of the coast. The nearest water was seventy-five miles away. We discussed walking out, but we realized this was hopeless. Stay with your vehicle, was the great cry and we all knew the story of *Lady Be Good*.

Smart was looking very sorry for himself. After all, it was his fault we were in this predicament. But then I had asked if we could go on ahead and alone. Corporal Smith was truly without any blame and looked the most cheerful of us all. We delayed lunch until mid-afternoon to avoid working in the full heat.

'These boiled sweets certainly help to lessen the thirst,' I remarked.

Smart passed me another, and I began to remove the paper. We all heard it together, like a distant rumble of thunder, but with a note that rose and fell.

'Three-tonners,' yelled Smart. 'It's the convoy, I knew they'd find us.'

In a few seconds the flares were streaking upward. I still couldn't see the trucks, but the noise of their engines was quite clear. They must be just the other side of the ridge. An awful feeling gripped me –

would they miss us? Corporal Smith was already tearing towards the ridge, when I heard another engine and spinning round, saw a Land-Rover bearing down on us. The goggle-clad faced grinned.

'Having a spot of bother?' our rescuers enquired.

I think we all learned a lesson.

Some feel towards the desert as others do to the sea – it can be beautiful and fascinating and it can be cruel. The desert Arab is usually an honest and religious man. I say man, because the women of the Sahara are hidden from the eyes of the foreigner. Thus their characteristics, their emotions and personalities cannot be judged by us. Women's Lib is a far cry in the pure Moslem world. I found that many of our people believed that they could communicate just by shouting loudly in English. This I deplored and set about trying to learn Arabic. My standard was never very high, but it was sufficient to talk with the tribesmen, to understand their feelings, difficulties and ambitions. They responded with wonderful hospitality and guided me on several difficult journeys.

We had the most hilarious dinner parties. At the height of one a space satellite appeared overhead and mine host, the Mudir of Rebiana, asked how we had succeeded in putting a new star in the heavens. It was several hours later before I completed my explanation of space travel. I was eager to get to bed as we had an early start next day, but the mudir pressed me with further questions.

'Tell me,' he said, 'did you win your battles against the Italians?'

It was now 1961 and I explained that we had won the war in 1945.

He seemed pleased and said, 'That is good, come, I shall show you something, left here in my safe keeping by your soldiers.'

We strolled to an outhouse. He jerked open the double doors and by the light of my torch, I saw a motor-car. It was a British Army Humber Estate car. The faded yellow paint still clung to its body.

'Where on earth did you find this?' I exclaimed in genuine amazement.

'Oh, some of your men left it here many years ago,' replied my Arab friend. 'I said I would hide it until they came back. It needs a repair, I think.'

After three and a half years in the Mediterranean area, I did not relish my return to Britain. A posting to the Junior Leaders Regiment of the Royal Engineers filled me with horror.

Before taking up my new appointment, I found that the Army had volunteered me as a temporary instructor at an Outward Bound

Mountain School on Lake Ullswater.

'I'm a diver, not a climber,' I protested to the Outward Bound executive, who briefed me in London. 'I know absolutely nothing about mountains.'

The kindly grey-haired gentleman in the dark suit looked sad. 'Oh dear,' he said. 'There does seem to have been an error, doesn't there, and we are so desperately short of instructors.'

I glowered unhelpfully. Dammit, I was not going to act as a wet nurse to a bunch of fourteen-year-olds.

'Do you know what Outward Bound is about?' he enquired.

I admitted I had very little idea. For an hour that cunning fellow lectured and appealed to me. In the end I felt that to refuse to help him was second only to high treason and said I'd go with a good grace. He was an expert in public relations!

Thus it was in the bitter January of 1962 that I trudged around the Lake District, trying to prevent twelve young boys from smoking, talking after lights out and reading pornographic literature. The only way to do this was to work the little blighters so hard that they practically fell asleep on their feet. As part of the process there was a rather insane tradition at the school that demanded you rose before dawn, stripped naked, ran through an acre or two of woodland onto a wooden jetty and plunged into the freezing lake. There was a limit to everybody's patience, I explained to the warden. I would be lashed helpless into a mountain-rescue stretcher and dangled upside down over a thousand foot drop. I would survive without cigarettes or whisky for ten days. I would collect moss and lichen on the nature trails and even press flowers in books, but I quite categorically refused to be seen belting down a woodland path in my birthday suit in pursuit of a dozen naked little boys.

The warden was disappointed and thought me unreasonable, but I stood my ground. I agreed that if it would satisfy him, I would enter the lake in military uniform and with dignity! So, next day, I waited whilst long lines of youngsters, hell bent on improving their character, dashed screaming into Lake Ullswater. Then, at a regulation quick march, dressed in full combat kit and filled with at least four swigs of illicit cherry brandy, I marched off the jetty. I felt I had registered my protest and won my point.

By the time I returned to the Junior Leaders Regiment at Dover, I had some fixed ideas on training young men. I believed that above all else their training must be interesting, inspiring and realistic. Unfortunately this meant that a certain amount of risk was inevitable.

Too many officers seemed happy to take the easy way out, too many had umbrellas ready to put up as soon as a nonsense occurred. As a result the training exercises did not greatly appeal to the young soldiers. Given a free hand, I managed to organize an invasion of Jersey. A co-operative lieutenant-commander in the Royal Navy agreed to take us over in his Minelayer – HMS *Plover*, said to be the slowest ship in the Navy. All my chums on the island were persuaded to provide enemy and friendly partisans. A qualified pilot was required, who knew the treacherous waters around Jersey. My father, a Jerseyman, then in his sixties, was still a reserve Army chaplain. With his spiritual hand at the helm we could not fail – he became the pilot. We almost sank our assault craft; three boys were quite badly hurt, three rifles were lost and one was not recovered for many years, but it was a tremendous exercise and my Junior Leaders enjoyed it greatly.

More exercises followed, including one with Gurkhas as enemy. Our non-commissioned officers cheered up the lads by saying, 'Don't worry, boys, they only cut yer ears off on training.'

Not everyone agreed with my methods and some thought I took too many risks, but you can't make an omelette without breaking eggs.

4

ADVENTUROUS TRAINING

'No water,' gasped David, his face contorting with amazement.

'Well, not much by now,' replied the tall, young officer with a worried expression.

'My God, we must hurry,' said David in an unusually urgent tone.

'What's the trouble?' I asked, dismounting from my Land-Rover onto the baking sand.

'Those people we are carrying the spare parts for are still out in the desert about one hundred miles north of here. They thought we were going to deliver the goods on our way down, but we believed they would be at the oasis.'

'How could we deliver them?' I asked. 'We didn't even use the same route.'

'Obviously a misunderstanding, but the point is that they only had enough water to last until this morning, although they did have some crates of beer. I'll take two of the cars and leave at once. Will you get the base organized here?'

So saying, my friend and commander, Captain David Hall, Royal Engineers, tucked up his Arab robes and launched the dash that probably saved the lives of three soldiers stranded by their broken-down truck in the open desert six hundred miles south of Benghazi. It was August – the hottest month – and when David, driving and navigating with all his customary skill, reached the scene they were pretty groggy.

On my return to Sandhurst, David had asked me to be his deputy on a forthcoming expedition to Southern Libya. We had been troop commanders together in Cyprus and were old friends. David, tall, imposing and incredibly modest, loved the Sahara and everything about it and was rapidly becoming one of the best-known experts on this inhospitable region. His navigation was first-rate and his planning meticulous to the last detail, but he knew the problems that can beset expeditions in the field and looked to me to act as his chief administrator, procurer and manager, whilst he co-ordinated the full scientific programme we had been set. Still having a great interest in the desert, I gladly accepted.

We arrived in Benghazi and fitted out our Land-Rovers at Army headquarters. With a party of some fifteen officer cadets and scientists, we were to examine a completely unexplored plateau, south-west of Kufra, deep in the Libyan desert. On the map of the area were those tantalizing words, 'Relief data incomplete'.

Taking time to get acclimatized, we motored south, training the cadets in driving and navigation *en route*. We had no idea that the spares which a local unit had asked us to take down to another expedition were terribly urgent or that there were people stranded whose very lives might depend on us. It was therefore a close shave. In the summer a man rarely lives longer than six hours without liquid.

David was one of the finest expedition leaders I have known and he achieved most of his success with people just by being a thoroughly nice person. When we arrived in Benghazi he had suggested that we should all walk down to the beach for a swim. It was about three miles and quite rightly he felt the exercise would help us acclimatize. As we were setting out, a chum offered us a lift in a truck. David declined, saying he thought the walk would do us good. Doubtless because I was feeling idle after a frustrating day arguing with some unco-operative quartermaster at the headquarters, I decided that I really couldn't face the walk and accepted the lift. David didn't say anything, but I knew I had let him down badly and tried hard for the rest of the expedition to make amends. I've remembered the incident with a feeling of guilt ever since.

No sooner had we set up base in the Kufra date factory, inhabited by the largest rats in Libya, than the other expedition suffered another crisis. Its mission was to escort a Foreign Office chap around the oases, and having moved onto Bzema it camped by a picture post-card salt lake. I knew the lake well. What none of us knew was that about ten yards out there existed a hot spring and, because of the climate, the steam was not visible. A soldier, seeking to cool off in the apparently refreshing water, had plunged in and swum into the near-boiling liquid. The burns stretched from his neck downwards.

Once again David led out a rescue party and, of course, Henrick Forss, our doctor, went with him. Henrick, a bronzed, muscular Finn, was just the man for an expedition. He has a great sense of humour and a winning smile that will force you to swallow the most evil-tasting potents. His fund of stories of experiences in many lands are a constant source of interest. One of the best field doctors I have ever met, if anyone could save this parboiled soldier, it was Henrick. How he did it is another tale, but the whole incident became a nightmare, when one RAF aircraft after another sank up to its wheel-axles in soft sand, whilst trying to evacuate the poor fellow who, I learned years afterwards, had survived after months in hospital.

From Kufra we moved south, setting up dumps of petrol, water and supplies as we advanced, to cater for our safe return. Desert and polar exploration have much in common – and, indeed, astronauts will have similar logistic problems. The area will not support life and all resources must come with you. A mistake in arithmetic may be fatal. Much more can be left to chance in the jungle or bush, where water and food are usually available to some degree. On the other hand, the clean, insect-free areas of the true desert are a paradise compared with the jungle, where everything either bites, stings or rots.

The only well on our route was at Maaten Bisciara. The sixty-foot shaft was surrounded by the whitening bones of hundreds of animals, and a few humans, who had no rope with which to reach the water. Here we filled our cans and noticed with interest that the first bucketful of slimy green liquid had numerous living beasties in it. Henrick added a liberal dose of chlorine to kill them and we moved off again. At the first stop I reached for the chargal[1] of water that evaporation had chilled as we drove. Taking a great gulp, I felt as if my teeth would drop out. The chlorine was over-powering.

'For God's sake, Henrick,' I croaked, 'what are you trying to do – sterilize us as well?'

'That is a good point,' roared the grinning medico from his moving vehicle. 'Please tell me if I've been successful when we get back to civilization.'

We had only a vast collection of air photographs to tell us what the plateau looked like and the problem was to identify our position on those photographs. Objects at ground level look quite different when seen from above. However, we had no doubt about finding the massive feature. It was thought to be about one hundred and fifty miles long and fifty miles wide, about the size of Wales.

1. A porous canvas water-bag.

We saw the jagged brown cliffs early in the afternoon, and by nightfall had made camp in their shadows. While David used the theodolite to fix our position, Henrick and I organized the evening meal. I had brought a great many dehydrated and canned foods, knowing that in the desert heat metabolism is reduced and the demand for calories also decreases. Thus I believe it is essential for food to be tasty and easily digested. Ample appetizing meals are important factors in maintaining morale on such ventures. It was unfortunate if anyone disliked garlic because our friendly Finn, convinced of its curative qualities, heaped liberal quantities on every dish. After seven or eight courses we sat around the fire drinking canned beer or gin fizz (gin and lemonade powder). Alcohol, a cause of thirst, was best avoided during daylight, but after dark the temperature dropped to around eighty degrees Farenheit and it felt quite chilly. At this time a few drinks were a good morale booster. Nearby, Martin Williams, our bearded geologist, sat sorting out his rock samples and Roger Breeze, our signaller from Jersey, connected us to Benghazi by morse code.

David's computations went on far into the night, but until he was satisfied that he had our longitude and latitude to within twenty yards or so, he would not give up. In fact, this was extremely important because one of our major tasks was to identify points on the ground from the air photographs and calculate their exact position so that a map could be constructed from the aerial pictures.

On the rock-strewn top of the plateau we found 'paths', possibly made by gazelle, but these all led to the head of a wadi and here Martin pointed to the ground.

'Do you see those stones?' he said.

I saw stones everywhere, but then I realized that I was looking at a circle of small rocks, in fact several circles.

'Hut circles,' he said. 'Men lived in these once.'

Sure enough, we had come upon a village site, probably thousands of years old, but exposed, not buried as it might be in England. Dashing about like excited children we found fireplaces, a bone needle, two or three beads and a great flat slab that had obviously been a grinding board.

'Before the water dried up, this was probably a settlement by a river,' Martin pointed out. We went down to the 'river bank' and there, on the surface, discovered more fireplaces, fish-bones and most important, a piece of pottery. Martin catalogued everything with great care and warned us against indiscriminate digging. Amateur archaeologists can often do untold harm by hurried, inexpert excavation.

One of our cadets suddenly saw a small beady-eyed desert fox watching us from the other side of the wadi. All along his trail there was evidence of his search for food and, of course, moisture. His diet seemed to be beetles, small rodents and snakes' eggs. Not much to support life, but it was interesting that a fully adapted animal could exist in this extreme environment.

Meanwhile, up on the plateau's edge, David had found a large stagnant pool of water in a rock crevice. So it did rain here – but Kufra had not seen rain for twenty years, it was said. We dug holes in the wadi-bed and at the junctions and found damp sand. However, at Bir El Harasc, on the way south, a four-foot-deep hole produced a trickle of grey, but pure water in a few minutes. This was due to the same artisan effect that supplied Kufra.

As the days went by I found some of the cadets had too little to do and after the first flush of enthusiasm for the archaeology, geology and zoology, they needed something else to keep them interested. As second-in-command, I therefore employed them on as many useful jobs as possible. One cadet with unbounded enthusiasm for exploration was Garth Brocksopp, an Australian by birth with a typical tough exterior, accompanied by an enquiring mind and a love of hard work. He also possessed a strange sense of humour. On one sortie he came upon a human skeleton under a rock overhang. Carrying the skull back to camp, he waited until dawn before creeping away from his bed roll, leaving the trophy peering out of the top of the blanket with a note beneath it that read, 'Please, sir, may I go sick?' At the end of the expedition it was only with some difficulty that we persuaded him that he could not drive into Benghazi with the anthropological specimen wired onto the radiator of his Land-Rover. Garth was a good number and we were to see much of each other in the years to come.

Apart from intruders like us, the desert was very largely a still, silent place. We saw few birds, very little wildlife and no other men or even the sign of any since the prehistoric inhabitants had died out. There were no wheel tracks, no footprints and no litter. We buried our garbage religiously, partly for hygiene, but also because it seemed offensive to desecrate this unspoilt world. I disapproved of our vehicles moving in line abreast, because it made more scars in the landscape than line ahead. Yet it was sensible because we could motor in comfort out of each other's dust. I have always felt concern for the exploitation of virgin and unexplored territory and this was to trouble me even more in the future. Nature heals, but in the desert the scars may last a million years.

With these thoughts in mind, I recall one strange incident. David had produced very thorough emergency instructions and we all knew what to do in event of a breakdown. We rarely moved with less than two vehicles and each group had a radio. Light signals were to be used at night and the rule was that you waited until dark then climbed onto the highest ground and fired a signal pistol vertically. Anyone seeing the flare, which would go up about four hundred feet, would take a bearing on it by compass and then fire an answering flare. At daylight a search would be mounted.

It was not unusual for small parties to be detached from the main camp, and on one particular evening we were seated about the fire, downing the customary gin and lemonade powder and listening to · Henrick's thoughts on aphrodisiacs. Several of us suddenly started up, for there to the east, a white flare rose from the featureless plain and dropped back again. A little quickly, I thought, but we got the bearing and fired a reply. There were two parties out, although I was surprised by the direction from which the flare had come. Our groups should have been well north of there. At dawn we used the radio and, to our relief, learned that both parties were safe and, strangely, knew nothing of the flare. We searched the area just in case. It was a flat, featureless stretch of stony desert; you could see for miles. There wasn't even a wheel track. I offer no explanation, but I did read of a similar incident being reported by the war-time Long Range Desert Group (LRDG) near to the coast.

We were all disciples of the LRDG and I thought I knew the history of this crack Army unit pretty well. Previous exploits in the Kufra minefields had caused me to read the accounts of the campaign around the oasis with keen interest. However, we were to have a re-supply run from the plateau to Kufra which was to prove rather interesting.

There were three of us in my Land-Rover, which set out for Kufra early one morning. Quite why we went with only one vehicle I can't recall, but it was an easy run on what was by now a well-trodden trail and we had a radio. In the early afternoon we were bowling along at about seventy miles an hour on flat, hard sand. The cars were always piled with kit and, to make more space, panniers of wire-mesh hung out from both sides. In these we carried our rations, sleeping-bags and personal kit. In the back of the Land-

Rover were fitted a dozen jerricans of petrol. Water, not petrol, was carried in the jerricans at the front – in case of a collision. Smoking in or near vehicles was strictly forbidden for obvious reasons. Boiled sweets were great thirst-quenchers and John, my navigator, turned about to locate our stock in a pannier.

'Fire!' – he screamed the dreaded word. If you stop a moving vehicle suddenly, the flames may come back and – *woomph!* that's the end, but by keeping going, one might just keep the flames away from the fuel cans.

'Where?' I said, looking about for some soft sand to stop by, but for once there was none.

'In the pannier – the bedding's alight!' yelled John.

The wind, such as there was, was blowing from behind so I pulled the wheel over to the left and we stopped gently enough to avoid spilling fuel. In a second, we were tearing out the burning bedding. The other cadet dragged a can of precious water off the front of the vehicle, and placed it in safety, in case the vehicle blew up with all our supplies. Using the pathetic little Army fire extinguisher and some hastily-dug sand, we smothered the fire. The cause was simple. A hard bump had damaged our exhaust and made it point upwards at the bottom of the pannier. Fortunately the only loss was a sleeping-bag, but it had not been a pleasant experience. We repacked, had a few good gulps of water and drove on in silence.

I had wanted to make Kufra by dark, but with the delay caused by the fire, we obviously hadn't a hope. As dusk fell, we reached some low rocky hills, north of Maaten Bisciara, really just big piles of jumbled broken stones. There were numerous narrow passes running through the hills and I chose one at random, which turned out to be a little west of the usual route. The sand was soft, and in the failing light I got us bogged in several times.

'We should be able to get some shelter amongst these rocks,' I said, and my weary crew readily agreed that it was none too soon to call it a day. None of us felt like cooking, so we ate a simple, cold supper, washed down with a cup of coffee. The night was clear and before turning in, I went out with the shovel to commune with nature. Squatting beneath the stars I heard the sound twice. The first time I looked back towards the dull black outline of the Land-Rover.

The second time, I said fairly loudly, 'Just a minute,' for I thought one of the cadets had called out to me.

A few moments later, I returned to the car. 'What's the matter?' I enquired.

John was already asleep, his colleague looked up and said, 'Nothing, why?'

'Didn't you call?' I said.

'No,' he replied.

'Funny,' I yawned, 'must have been the wind,' then I fell asleep.

I awoke very cold just after dawn, bursting to spend a penny. I stood up, rubbing my eyes and shivering in the half-light. I was still only half awake, when my eyes caught sight of something odd. About sixty yards from me was a truck, or rather the remains of one, and all around it were scattered bits of equipment, dark against the white sand. I walked over to the Chevrolet, for even at this distance I recognized the familiar shape of the LRDG raiding vehicle. The debris consisted of cartridges, unexploded grenades and mortar bombs, broken rifles and parts of a machine-gun. Ten yards away, at the head of a low mound, lay a small wooden cross and pieces of wood that had probably made up another. Other similar vehicles were parked along the walls of the pass. Some had engines missing, all appeared to have been blasted apart by a single explosion in the back. A self-destruction charge, I guessed.

We combed the area and high amongst the rocks found a faded canvas British Army haversack containing the rusty fragments of a Kodak folding camera and a toothbrush. Nearby was scattered a pile of empty .303 rifle cases. I believe it was here that the LRDG's T Patrol was destroyed by a force from its Italian opposite number, the Auto-Saharan Company based at Kufra. According to W. B. Kennedy Shaw in his book, *Long Range Desert Group* (Collins), a running fight developed on 31 January 1941 when the Italians, with a heavily armed motorized patrol and three aircraft caught the LRDG advancing on Kufra, in a valley of the Gebel Sherif.

Following the battle, a New Zealander, Trooper R. J. Moore, and three colleagues had remained undetected amongst the rocks of the waterless hills. Almost everything they needed for survival had been destroyed in their vehicle, three of them were wounded and, as all the wells within two hundred miles were either in enemy hands or filled with rocks, the situation seemed hopeless. However, they managed to salvage a two-gallon tin of water and scorning any idea of walking a mere eighty miles north-east to surrender to the Italians at Kufra, they turned and marched south towards the Free French positions, known to be several hundred miles away.

The story of their remarkable and heroic escape over an astonishing distance is a worthy tribute to the soldiers of one of the finest special forces ever raised. Three of the men survived and their leader, Trooper Moore, was found by the French walking steadily after ten days, two hundred and ten miles from Gebel Sherif. He was awarded the DCM for his leadership and courage.

We tidied up the grave, re-erected the crosses, stood silent for a moment, then saluted and drove off towards Kufra.

A week later, its work completed, the expedition withdrew northward. Thanks to David's superb organization and co-ordination, the scientific programme had turned out to be extremely worthwhile. We only had one mishap. Martin had to leave us early to return to his job in the Sudan, so he departed as soon as we neared the coast. His precious specimens were all packed in ration boxes. Before entering Benghazi we went to the beach to clean up, shave off desert beards and make ourselves look reasonably civilized. Somehow poor Martin's rocks, collected so painstakingly under the blistering sun, got tipped out on the pebble beach. We never found them all!

By the time we got back to Sandhurst my plans for a new expedition the following year already filled several notebooks. Having seen enough of the desert for a while, I wanted a change of scenery. I had been appointed one of the adventure training officers and, as such, was responsible for guiding cadets in the organization of worthwhile expeditions, aimed at exercising their initiative, self-reliance and leadership, with, it was hoped, the least possible detriment to Britain's foreign relations. This challenging and interesting appointment gave me all the opportunity to organize a major venture myself.

In 1960 I had planned my abortive safari to Ethiopia. My godfather, Lord Forester, had helped to look after His Imperial Majesty during part of his exile in Britain. I hoped the Emperor would remember this and support my proposal to thin out some of his fauna. However, after much preparation, my hopes were dashed by the attempted *coup d'état*. Thus, although I had never been there, I already had a considerable background knowledge of the country. So it was to be Ethiopia, land of thirteen months of sunshine,[1] mountains, dense bush and deserts that was to be the scene of the next venture.

General Mogg, the commandant at Sandhurst, was enthusiastic and approved my plans, so having asked my godfather if he would

1. The Ethiopian Julian Calendar has thirteen months.

be kind enough to write to His Imperial Majesty, I settled down to raise a few hundred pounds to cover the cost. The mail-bag at our Camberley home got steadily heavier and response was encouraging. In spite of the impending arrival of Emma Jane, Judith was determined to come with me. Meanwhile I continued with my other military duties at Sandhurst. I know of no other establishment in Britain where so many charming and helpful people are gathered. It is truly the cradle of the British officer and, indeed, of many officers of foreign armies. Its scenic grounds disguised the intensely professional training that was undergone by almost one thousand young men on a two-year course. All had been carefully selected for the studies intended to equip them, in the words of the academy motto, 'To Serve to Lead'.

A comprehensive academic syllabus combined with military training to earn Sandhurst the reputation of 'a second rate university where the OTC had been allowed to run wild'. Although I did teach Military History, my main instructional duties were on tactics. Cadets were first given theoretical training in the model rooms, where Dinky toy tanks and symbolized units could be moved about with little chance of making some costly and irrevocable error. It was here that I was the unwitting perpetrator of a near-tragedy. The chief instructor was to lecture on the nuclear battle and asked me if I could make a miniature atomic bomb that could be exploded on the model to indicate the arrival of a missile.

'Certainly,' I replied, 'a small charge of loose powder fired electrically should do the trick.' So, pouring the contents of six large army fireworks known as thunderflashes into a flowerpot, I disguised it with a paper house and connected it by cable to a firing-switch on the lectern. I explained the firing procedure to the chief instructor, who seemed delighted with the device and felt sure it would impress several visiting officers, who were to attend the lecture.

As I was to be away the next day, I wedged a round tin lid firmly in the top of the flowerpot in case anyone should knock it over before it was required. However, I instructed the model room clerk to be sure to remove this obstruction before the lecture. Unhappily the clerk was taken ill that night and did not report for duty next day.

When some seventy officers and cadets had seated themselves on the tiers of chairs overlooking the cloth model, the chief instructor began.

'Before you, gentlemen, you see the 1st Battalion the Loamshires and their vehicles,' he stated, indicating a cluster of Dinky toy tanks and plastic symbols.

'They are holding the ridge that runs east–west across your front,' he continued, his pointer stabbing at a sausage-shaped bump, where the hessian had been raised with balls of newspaper.

'The enemy, the 2,322nd Motor Rifle Regiment of the Fantasian Army is here,' he said, dumping an impressive pile of ominous-looking red tanks at the edge of the model. 'They may use nuclear weapons at any moment.'

Allowing the full impact of his words to sink in, he paused for a moment before pressing the concealed firing button. The effect was devastating: with a blinding flash and a deafening bang, the innocuous looking 'village' in the centre of the battlefield exploded. Several cadets were struck by toy tanks and plastic soldiers. Shrapnel from the flowerpot peppered the audience and the colonel seated in the front row had the fluff scorched off his battledress trousers by the resultant fireball. The mushroom cloud of dense white smoke rose quickly to the ceiling, then, like nuclear fallout, descended to fill the room with acrid fumes, which instantly choked the shell-shocked spectators. Coughing and spluttering cadets hurled open the windows, whilst the stand-in model room clerk, a civilian of timid appearance with unquestionable initiative, seized the stirrup pump and extinguished the burning hessian.

It was ten minutes before the smoke cleared sufficiently to allow the lecture to continue. There can be no doubt that the demonstration was a success, but I was not asked to repeat the performance. However, playlets almost worthy of a West End theatre were a regular feature in the model room instruction.

Outside training was much more serious, but had its lighter moments. Exercises were made more realistic by the presence of a cardboard tank, mounted on a frame of angle iron and bicycle wheels. It was propelled by a hefty guardsman and carried a home-made breech-loading gun which fired thunderflashes, and a machine-gun which could shoot blank ammunition. Mobility was somewhat limited by ditches, and on steep slopes the guardsman, bent double in the bowels of the infernal machine, struggled and groaned, whilst I sat in the turret operating the armament. Having no brakes, it ran out of control down hills! Minefields sown with pyrotechnics were laid about the defensive position, but often the devices went off prematurely when officers' dogs rampaged through the position.

Sandhurst encompassed every conceivable type of activity. One of my responsibilities was the pistol club, where I was able to put over my own ideas to aspiring marksmen. An aspect of the training was the combat pistol course. This was a course designed to teach cadets to engage fleeting targets under battle conditions. It was extremely realistic and one of the noted marksmen was a young man called David Bromhead, whose good shooting was to be useful in the years ahead.

Meanwhile preparations for the 1964 Sandhurst Ethiopian Expedition were progressing well. In order that the officer cadets should make a worthwhile contribution to science, they had to be trained to catch and preserve the various specimens required. Under the direction of some of the British Museum (Natural History) staff we pursued adders and grass-snakes over the Army training areas and caught small rodents in box traps. One over-enthusiastic cadet, trying to anaesthetize a shrew held by a colleague, drove the hypodermic needle clean through the animal and paralysed his friend's arm for several hours.

In early August we set out. One party which included a number of overseas cadets went ahead on the first available RAF aircraft. It flew to Aden, leaving the rest of us to follow a week later after the end-of-term Sovereign's Parade. The Aden brigade commander offered to find useful employment for the early arrivals while they were in the colony and despatched them up country to see some action.

At one small fort a group of dissidents opened fire from some distant hills. As the garrison took posts, bullets pinged and ricochetted amongst the grey stone sangars. The range was at least a thousand yards and no-one could see the enemy. Very suddenly the machine-gun on the watch-tower opened up with uncanny accuracy, flushing the tribesmen from their position and sending them scampering away amongst the rocks.

'Jolly fine shooting,' commended the commanding officer, who happened to be visiting the fort. 'Who's on the gun?'

'One of the Sandhurst cadets,' replied the company commander.

'I must congratulate him,' said the colonel, climbing up the tower.

As he reached the platform where the cadet lay behind the machine-gun, he said, 'Don't move, please – I just wanted to say what good shooting that was; glad to see they're teaching you so well at Sandhurst.'

'Thank you, sir,' murmured the cadet turning about, his ebony face and flashing teeth set in a broad grin.

Slightly taken aback, the commanding officer asked, 'Which regiment are you joining?'

'Oh,' smiled the young man. 'I'm not in the British Army.'

Arriving in Aden at midnight a few days later, I was surprised to be greeted by an impressive array of rather worried staff officers, who hastened to explain the terrible oversight that had caused them to employ a member of another Army in the cause of what local propaganda would call 'British Imperialism'. I promised to talk to the cadet.

'Oh! I enjoyed it,' he said when I explained the problem, 'but our President will never know!' Then he added rather wistfully, 'I suppose I can't get the campaign medal now?'

On arrival in Addis Ababa I found my godfather's letter had paved the way and we were invited to the palace. His Imperial Majesty, Haile Selassie I, stood erect behind his desk. One by one we entered and shook his outstretched hand, murmuring '*Votre Majesté*', and giving a short, formal bow, as we did so. There was something very powerful about the tiny figure, who could only have been about five feet two inches high. His alert, brown eyes seemed to penetrate my innermost thoughts. Not a man to be misled, I felt. Closely cropped wavy hair led down to a grey moustache and a short, neat beard and his skin, a light brown colour, was paler than many of his countrymen.

In Addis Ababa I have heard him described as the mouse with the jaws of a lion. His gentle, kindly appearance did not mislead me. I knew that I was standing before one of the most powerful Christian warrior kings the world has ever known.

'How is your godfather?' The soft voice, speaking in perfect English, took me by surprise.

'Very well, Your Majesty, and he sends you his good wishes,' I spluttered.

'He has a beautiful house in Shropshire. I remember the rhododendrons in flower very well,' mused the Emperor. I was amazed how much he remembered of his short war-time stay at Willey Park.

'What do you wish of me?' he said, becoming more formal and addressing us through his interpreter.

'Permission to collect scientific specimens in your country, Your Majesty,' I replied.

His answer in Amharic was made without waiting for the interpreter to translate my request. 'His Imperial Majesty says it shall be so and he will send with you a liaison officer from his army.'

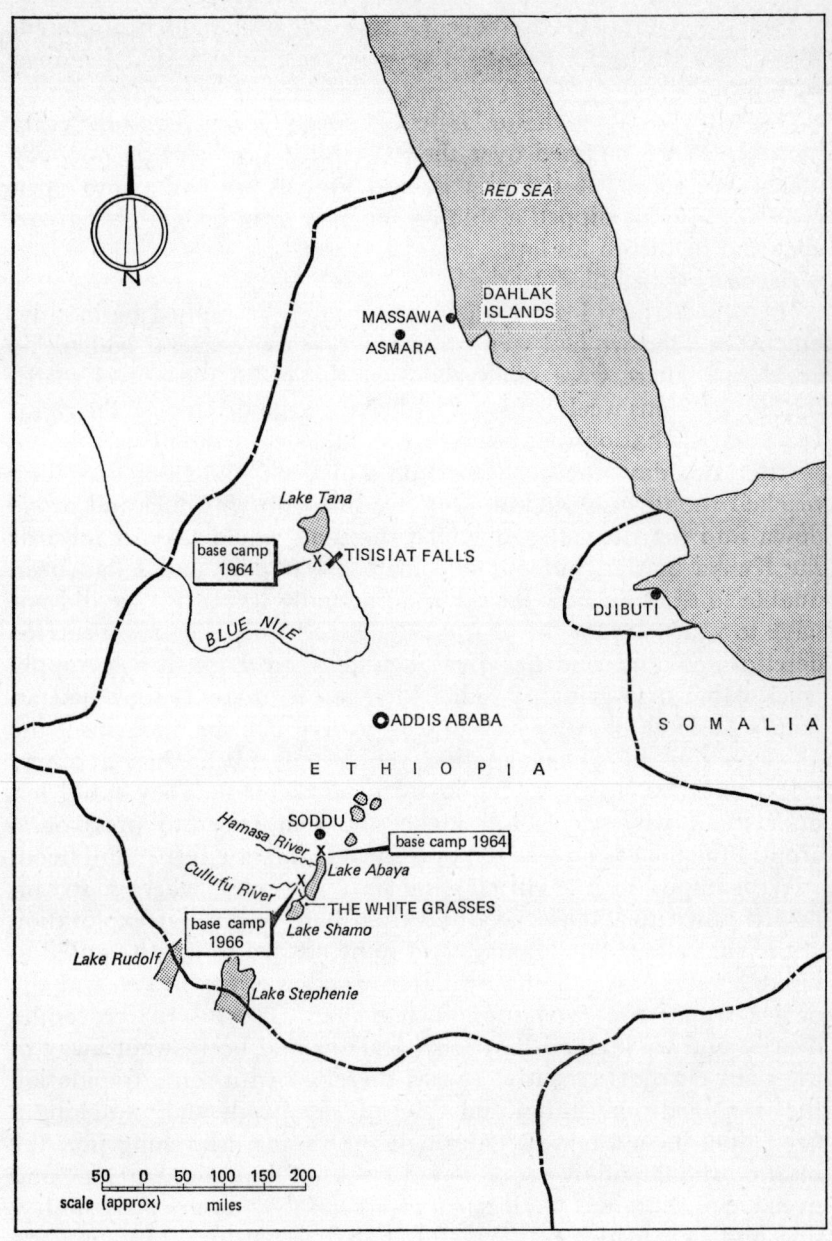

Ethiopia

We bowed out of his presence. Outside one of the cadets muttered, 'Well, he's the nearest thing I've ever seen to a deity.' I agreed with him.

Captain Marcos Berhanu Haile sat silently beside me in the early morning as we bumped over the waterfilled pot-holes on our way south. We soon left the city behind and as we came into open country, Marcos slipped a shining revolver from beneath his great-coat and held it in his lap.

'Expecting trouble?' I asked.

'In this country I always expect trouble,' he replied ominously, but by evening we had seen nothing worse than several bad traffic accidents. There were relatively few vehicles on the gravel roads, but the previous week Ethiopia had changed to driving on the right. It appeared that only half the drivers had heard the news!

After two days the good road on which we had been travelling reached the town of Soddu. Here we filled up with fuel and drove down into the rift valley. I hoped the road would take us towards the Kenya border, but our information was poor and I had been unable to discover how far the road actually went. But we did not have to wait long for the answer. Quite suddenly the gravel surface deteriorated and our heavily laden one-ton Land-Rover supply truck came to a grinding halt, axle-deep in mud. It took half an hour's pushing, shoving and towing to free it from the grip of the black cotton soil. Then another vehicle got stuck, then another. Local villagers stood looking at us in amazement. They could not understand why we should make so much effort to press on – around the next bend was the bridgeless Hamasa River in full flood.

We camped in a small clearing near the road, where a stream flowed down to Lake Abaya and from here began our exploration of the rift valley. The Hamasa had to be crossed so we attempted to build a raft. Alas, all the available wood was too heavy and the device would not even support one man. There were crocodiles nearby and we learned that some Italians had been swept away in the swift currents recently. It was therefore with some trepidation that we piled our clothes and rifles on our heads and, clutching a fixed line, inched our way through the rapids. Marching into the bush on the far side we soon found tracks of lion, pig, antelope and hyena. Splitting into small parties we each took an area of country-side and began to seek the animals that the British Museum had listed.

It was mid-afternoon when Johnnie Johnson, our camera-man

and ornithologist, spied the greater kudu browsing in some trees a quarter of a mile away. A short, easy stalk got me to within two hundred yards, but it was not possible to get any closer and so taking very careful aim, I sent a high velocity round crashing down the valley.

Breathless I reached the antelope. It was down but not dead. Oh, hell! I thought, Why did I have to shoot it at all? My second bullet killed it instantly and in order to take a perfect skin for the museum, we worked with great care. It was not a pleasant sight and soon the trees around us were heavy with hideous black vultures. Various parts of the body were required to be retained and the skull was removed intact. Inside the beast we discovered a complete foetus, apparently of considerable biological value, which we preserved in formalin in a large plastic tub. Finally we cut a haunch for our supper and then stood back to allow the vultures to clean up. Johnnie and Garth Brocksopp filmed the revolting sequence, which was of ornithological interest. Carrying the bloody items back across the Hamasa that night was a little worrying. We knew that the crocodiles were supposed to go for blood!

The local governor, His Excellency Wolde-Semait Gabre Wolde, was a most progressive man. Educated in Britain, he was striving to build up the province, and with determination and energy seemed to be doing a good job. He was always very helpful and so I was delighted to be able to do something for him.

'There's a lion killing all the cattle in a village near here,' he said when visiting us one day. 'I should be grateful if you could get rid of it for us.'

So that afternoon we set off in a Land-Rover to the area in question and met a local guide. He was dressed in a blue sports jacket and loin cloth; in one ear was a large gold ear-ring, indicating that he had killed a lion single-handed. Following him closely, we soon came on fresh spoor, which led into dense bush. Marcos and I were ahead with the guide. Two cadets, David Bromhead and Andrew Penny, came some ten yards behind us.

After a little time we came upon some thick bushes. From these came the sound of a low cough or grunt and the guide gesticulated wildly, shouting, 'Oola, oola!'

He pointed into the bush. I could see nothing, nor could Marcos. Turning, I made a silent sign to David to discover if he could see anything. As if to answer me, he flung up his rifle and, at the same moment, a great yellow shape leapt over me!

'What on earth . . .' I gasped.

'A bloody great lioness,' shouted David, whose knowledge of lions and Africa was much greater than mine. 'She was looking round one side of the bush, whilst you looked round the other,' he said.

The guide and Marcos were already in pursuit, but our quarry had disappeared and after a fruitless search, we headed back for the Land-Rover.

'Well, at least we saw it,' said Andrew. At that moment the parked Land-Rover came in sight.

'Look on the track!' said David in an urgent whisper. We all stood rooted to the spot. For there, by the vehicle, lay the lioness, stretched full length in the evening sun. A few feet away in the grass two cubs could be seen playing.

Cunning old thing, I thought, she's doubled back. I raised my rifle, but the sight of this beautiful beast and her young was too much. We sat down cursing that no-one had a camera. Even Marcos, an experienced hunter, agreed we should not kill her, so we decided to have a cigarette and then, if she had not moved, we would try to out-flank her and reach the Land-Rover.

But our plans were changed by the appearance of an Ethiopian shepherd boy strolling nonchalantly up the path towards us, completely oblivious of the great cat obscured from his view. Jumping up, Marcos yelled, 'Ambessa, ambessa!'

The boy stopped with an expression of surprise. He saw nothing wrong and then peering round the Land-Rover, caught a glimpse of the hind quarters of the lioness. Like a Walt Disney character, he leapt into a tree and scrambled to its highest and rather precarious branch. The lioness eyed him with mild interest.

'Keep together, safety-catches off, and we'll walk towards her,' I said, trying to sound confident. We were twenty-five yards away – which is not far when one remembers a charging lion can do a hundred yards in four seconds – before she moved. Then, with a yawn, she stood up and ambled to the roadside. The guide clearly thought this was the moment and flung up his rifle, but luckily his shot was wild and in a bound the lioness and her cubs had gone.

'You are extraordinary people,' said the governor, shaking his head sadly. 'How would you feel about killing a fox in England that had taken all your chickens and left you with nothing to eat for four months?' I felt like explaining the British attitude to foxes, but we apologized for our failure and went out to cull some bush-pigs that were destroying crops. After all, no-one minds shooting an ugly beast!

The thorn scrub was teeming with pig and, as you could rarely
see more than thirty yards, there was some sporting shooting to be
done. I managed to get close to one small herd and shot a good
eating-size sow, when unfortunately the bush all around erupted
with pigs, running in every direction in mad panic. Tek Negussie,
a handsome Ethiopian cadet, pushed my wife up a tree to save her
from one – a deed which she has never forgotten and, as a result,
regards all Ethiopians with the uttermost gratitude.

Elsewhere, Marcos had shot, in the nick of time, a monster boar
that had ambushed him and our other lady member, Kay Thompson.
Kay, ever an intrepid woman, was left sitting on the carcass with
Marcos's pistol while he went for assistance to carry the beast out.
He was gone several hours, night fell, and the pig twitched once or
twice but Kay was still sitting on it when we eventually reached
her. She did admit to smoking several cigarettes! Kay was also
rather good at finding snakes, and our collection of deadly reptiles
grew daily.

There was one part of our mission which was of great importance.
The British Museum had charged us to find Osgood's swamp rat.
Only one specimen of this strange black-and-white rodent had ever
been collected and, as that was in America, the British Museum
badly needed one of their own. Photocopies of a picture of the
creature were reproduced and distributed all over the suspected
locality, which was near Lake Tana, in Gojjam, north of Addis
Ababa. Thus it was to here that we journeyed for the last part of
the expedition. Through the driving rain of the wet season, we
headed up into the highlands. Around us, the bleak plateau was
populated by tall, proud Amharas, who lived in neat, round huts
called tukuls.

The only real break in the scenery came at Shafartak, when we
reached the Blue Nile Gorge and in a short space of approximately
three miles dropped four thousand feet. We lunched in the warm,
dry air at the bottom and watched the Blue Nile, heavy with brown
silt, swirling by beneath the bridge. Climbing back on to the plateau,
we drove to Debra Marcos, the capital of the province of Gojjam.
There we were guests at the governor's palace and were treated to
a gigantic feast of raw meat, enjerra and wat. Enjerra, the traditional Ethiopian food, is unleavened bread, with the appearance
and consistency of a grey sorbo-rubber bath mat. The wat is a very
hot meat sauce.

The governor, dressed in tweed jacket and cavalry twill trousers,

plied us with *Black Label* whisky and was extremely hospitable. That
night I lay awake listening to the raw meat and whisky churning
over in my stomach and also in Judith's!

'What did you think of the Blue Nile?' I asked her.

'Not very blue,' was her sleepy reply.

'No-one has ever really explored it, you know. There are supposed to be some terrible rapids and the world's most aggressive
crocodiles,' I continued.

She yawned.

'I wonder if it could be navigated with rubber dinghies,' I mused.
Judith said nothing, she was already asleep.

Our base camp was set up in a community centre by the Picolo
Abbai River, said to be the origin of the Blue Nile or Great Abbai,
and it was to here that the local people came in response to our
offer of fifteen dollars reward for an Osgood's swamp rat. We
combed the countryside for the rodent, laid hundreds of traps and
dealt with dozens of snakes, antelopes, small mammals and birds
that were brought daily to our camp. Many were indeed interesting
and we purchased these, but there was no sign of Osgood. We had
failed and felt miserable about it.

On Lake Tana our fishermen had been very successful and made
a fine collection. Our dispirited band of rat-catchers needed an out-
ing, so we all went up to Bahadar, partly to fish, but also to view
the famous falls of Tisisiat, where the Blue Nile tumbles one hundred
and fifty feet into its narrow gorge. The mist thrown up by the falls
may be seen for miles, hence the name Tisisiat – Smoke of Fire.
Standing on the opposite bank I watched the great river cascading
over the polished black basalt. Above the roar of the boiling water,
the fish eagle called and brightly coloured birds flitted amongst the
luxuriant green growth that swayed gently in the drifting clouds of
spray. The power and majesty of the river was awe-inspiring.

'I know what you're thinking,' said Judith, who had been watching me.

'Do you?' I smiled and said slowly, 'It might be possible with
rubber boats.'

On the way back to Addis Ababa we paused for lunch at Debra
Libanos, a well-known Coptic church on the edge of a great gorge.
Johnnie, ever ready with his binoculars, suddenly raced back to the
cars.

'There are some very unusual monkeys on the cliffs down there,'
he said excitedly. 'I'd like to film them if we've time.'

'Yes,' I replied, 'by all means. I'll come down with you.' So saying, we ran to the edge of the gorge and about two hundred yards away, I could see a large number of big, chocolate-brown monkeys.

'What do you think they are?' I asked.

'Gelada baboons,' said Johnnie, watching them intently. 'Very rare and only found in Ethiopia.'

Already I could hear the whir of Johnnie's Bolex and for thirty minutes he watched these strange creatures. The males looked like little warriors, with dark-brown capes and a flaming red patch on their chests. They bared their teeth to defend the families, who scurried away with their young into the rising mist. The resultant film was excellent and so interesting that the BBC considered using it for television. However, having kept it for a while and noted what there was to be seen in Ethiopia, they sent their own expedition. Without any good reason, we felt just a little bit cheated.

On return to England we took our specimens to the British Museum. Everyone was delighted with them and I had just started to apologize to the mammalogist for our failure to obtain Osgood's swamp rat, when he cut in.

'After you had left, we looked into the whole question of Osgood rather more carefully and we've decided that in fact the rat he discovered in Ethiopia is exactly the same as one that is found in the Congo, so it isn't really a rarity after all. It was just an unusual distribution.'

I stared in blank amazement at the man. How could I tell him of the days and weeks spent searching every inch of the swampy bog-land around the source of the Blue Nile? How could he understand the hundreds of man-hours that had gone into the quest? How could he understand our own terrible feelings of failure at not discovering the mythical rat after all?

Ethiopia had one or two hidden tricks that did not emerge until later, when eight of us got malaria in spite of taking the regular dose of paludrin. Nevertheless, the expedition was considered highly successful and immediately I began planning a follow-up. The following year I had to do my staff college exam, but in 1966 perhaps I could get beyond the Hamasa.

The Sandhurst Ethiopian Expedition of 1966 was designed to be a joint service affair. Over fifty officer cadets of many nations and scientists would take part in a study of the archaeology, veterinary and zoological aspects of the area. I wanted to get into the rift valley between the Hamasa River and the Kenya border.

As adventure training officer I had my busiest time in the summer term. We had some twenty expeditions going off to various parts of the globe, and as their date of departure grew nearer, so the urgency for administrative arrangements to be finalized grew greater. The scene in my office at Sandhurst must have appeared somewhat chaotic as cadets staggered in and out with animal traps, underwater equipment, mountaineering gear, rifles and mosquito nets. There was very often a good piece for the local press and the *Camberley News* had a habit of ringing me on Monday mornings to enquire if there were any interesting stories. On one particular day when they telephoned, I had to confess that nothing of any special interest had happened in the last week. As I was speaking my yellow Labrador bitch, Kinder, waddled in through the open door. To my amazement, she was carrying a stuffed mongoose in her mouth.

On the telephone, the reporter was saying, 'Are you sure there is nothing we can write a piece on?'

'Well, my dog has just brought in a stuffed mongoose,' I replied, laughing.

'Where did she get it and what does it look like?' said the newspaper man. He was most anxious to take a photograph of this unusual sight, although he admitted that they were very short of news. Kinder, terribly pleased with herself, continued to waddle round and round the office, making snorting noises. In no time at all the reporter arrived, together with a photographer, and took copious pictures of the idiotic dog parading up and down on the lawns. I had no idea where she had found this trophy, but I imagine that someone had given it to her as a joke.

'What are you going to do with it?' asked the reporter.

'Oh! I'll probably stick it up on the training area and teach cadets to recognize animals,' I joked.

The next day I left for Aden to make arrangements for a number of expeditions that were setting out that summer. When I returned a week later, the academy public relations officer greeted me in great excitement and explained that, following the use by the *Camberley News* of the story of my dog and the mongoose, almost all the national press now wished to descend on Sandhurst and photograph the expedition in a mock jungle on the training area. They supposed that I would have sewn the woods with a liberal quantity of stuffed animals.

'But I only said that as a joke!' I protested.

'Never mind, but now you must see that you carry it out. It will

Above: Alan Calder,
flying his Army Air
Corps Beaver with
great skill, kept us
supplied on the Blue
Nile

Right: I hold the
Sunday service at
Debra Marcos

Nigel Sale during our climbing training before the expedition

The assault boats leaving the bridge at Shafartak

The two amicable
Ethiopian bandits

Dr Derek Yalden
(zoologist), John
Fletcher, and Colin
Chapman (zoologist)
ascending the side
of the Blue Nile
Gorge

Jim Masters (*left*)
and Joe Ruston
taking the expedi-
tion's flagship
Kitchener through a
Blue Nile rapid

Above: A dinghy shoots the cataracts above the Tisisiat Falls

Below: Where Ian Macleod died in the Northern Gorge. Roger Chapman steadies John Fletcher on the rope

be a wonderful thing for Sandhurst,' ordered the PRO.

For several weeks I searched desperately for stuffed animals and, in the end, all I had located was one leopard's head, a pair of pottos and the original mongoose. It was a warm June Sunday afternoon when the press descended *en masse*. I had laid on all sorts of interesting demonstrations. A special raft was constructed and used to ferry a Land-Rover over the lake. A light mortar fired a line and grapnel into the dense vegetation on one of the islands. This was to demonstrate how we proposed to get a rope over a crocodile-infested river. The fact that the grapnel broke away from its cable and landed in Camberley was fortunately missed by the press. But it was all to no avail, they simply wanted photographs of the stuffed animal safari. We duly obliged and bewildered cadets crawled through the trees, looking for the stuffed leopard and the pottos. The following Monday almost every national newspaper gave wide coverage to the exercise, which strangely, the staff at Sandhurst regarded as a good thing to enhance the Army's image! Also, to my great surprise, funds began to come in and help to make the expedition solvent. So perhaps Kinder's mongoose had been worth while after all!

The expedition main base was to be established at the southern end of Lake Abaya, near the developing town of Arba Minch on the floor of the rift valley. At this point, the valley is extremely narrow and clearly defined. It is almost exactly four thousand feet above sea level, with mountains rising in steps on either side to a height of over thirteen thousand feet. The valley contains many lakes, swamps, and areas of dense jungle. In 1964 I had noticed that the flora had changed rapidly with altitude and the new expedition was going to encounter areas of scrub, grass land, rain forests and, in the highest regions, a topography not unlike Dartmoor.

It was not easy to obtain reliable weather information, but I made our plans to deal with what I thought would be the worst situation. This I considered to be heavy rain, falling daily on the high ground, with a reduced precipitation in the valley. The result of this would be a rapid rise and fall of the many rivers that flowed into the lake.

The only motor track in the valley ran from north to south along the west side of Lake Abaya, and was bisected by numerous streams and rivers. One of these was the Hamasa that had stopped us in 1964 and as far as I could discover, it had still not been bridged. It was clear that the expedition would have considerable sapper problems and even the purification of water was likely to be a difficult task. Thus I appointed Officer Cadet Bill Bullock as the 'chief engineer' and he formed a small team of potential sapper officers.

The problem of crossing the water-obstacles was the most difficult to solve, and I sought the advice of a good many experts before making a decision. In fact, this was a period of research that stood me in good stead in later years when dealing with the Darien Gap.

One way to get the vehicles across was to fit flotation bags to their sides. These could be pumped up by a small device fitted to the exhaust system. The disadvantage was the vulnerability of the bags and the fact that the wheels of the vehicle hung down into the river and could catch on boulders or rocks beneath.

I also investigated something called the Bubble. This device consisted of a fabric hemisphere connected by a trunk to an industrial compressor, which filled it to slightly above atmospheric pressure and caused it to hover. A vehicle could be suspended on wire strops inside the bubble and provided some directional force could be applied, it should be able to cross rivers by this means. However, the problem was where to put the compressor, and although this method was considered seriously, our friends at the Ministry of Aviation felt the need for more research and development before sending a Bubble to Africa.

There were, of course, various amphibious vehicles, including an amphibious Land-Rover. This had a boat-shaped hull and was driven along by a propeller running off the rear differential. Inflatable bags gave it additional buoyancy. The problem here was, once again, that the wheels hung down into the river and could catch on snags, also it was extremely difficult to get the vehicle out of the river and up a steep bank.

Finally we turned to the well-tried idea of a raft. There were various methods involving oil-drums, ground-sheets stuffed with grass and even tarpaulins wrapped right around the vehicles. Boats were too bulky to carry and so I managed to persuade the Daimler Company to build us a special light-weight, air-portable raft in fibre glass and polyurethane. This was designed by Bill and the material only weighed two pounds per cubic foot. With its cellular construction, it was excellent flotation material. The raft consisted of five pontoons made up of the polythene blocks bolted together and coated with a strong, fibre glass skin. Wheel channels were moulded on top, outriggers were fitted to either side, connected to the structure by reinforced fibre glass tubes. The raft was designed to carry a laden, quarter-ton Land-Rover plus three men. Ramps were provided by using tongued planks of hard wood. The complete raft could be carried on the roof of two Land-Rovers and could be assembled in forty-five minutes by six men. Special light-weight nylon rope of eight tons breaking strain, aluminium anchorages and light-weight blocks were added so that it might be used as a ferry.

We believed that the problem of obtaining pure water could be overcome by using small, portable filter pumps, rather like a wartime stirrup pump. The water sources were usually thick with mud which meant that the filters would need regular cleaning. To ensure that they worked, we tried them out in Farnborough sewage works! Another method which was becoming popular was to use a solar still. This is a method of obtaining water in small quantities by condensing the humidity that exists in the earth onto the underside of a plastic sheet. Eventually the droplets will form rivulets and run down to a point where they drip into a small can.

As scientists we had with us Patrick Morris, a qualified zoologist, and a young vet called Paul Bramley. Our doctor, a civilian who specialized in gynaecology, was from the West Country, and to make our film we had a Territorial Army officer who was also a BBC producer, Geoffrey Boswall. Kay Thompson was our only lady member. In the field we were to be joined by a party of some fifteen local police, who would escort us during the expedition. The bulk of the stores and vehicles had come over from Aden with expedition members from the Parachute Regiment and the Welsh Guards.

When the convoy reached the Hamasa River we were delighted to find that the rains had not been heavy, and this time the vehicles crossed the wide ford with little difficulty and the raft was not required. In the late afternoon of the second day we established our main base camp at the foot of Lake Abaya as planned. The weather was excellent, with a noon temperature in the eighties and no sign of rain. There was only one real problem, the mosquitoes. They rose at night from the lake in their millions and simply devoured us.

We had been in the camp for a few days when, to our amazement, a certain officer cadet strolled in. Our amazement was caused by the fact that he had missed the plane in England, having overslept, I suspect, and we had left without him. Now, apparently on his own initiative, he had got himself all the way to Aden, hitched a lift across the Red Sea on an Arab dhow and eventually come up the railway to Addis Ababa. Here again he had just missed us and so he had managed to beg some money from the Defence Attaché and get a local aeroplane to bring him to Arba Minch. On the way he had discarded almost all that he had. However, he had been entrusted with one of the special water filter pumps, and although his clothes were in pretty bad condition, he still held the pump. It was a wonderful show of initiative and I found it hard to be angry with the lad!

Operating from our base camp we made many journeys up and down the rift valley, and in general found that the people were friendly and hospitable. However, on one occasion, when moving south to see some unique carved, wooden monoliths, we were confronted with what might have been a nasty situation.

We had camped not far from a large village to the west of Lake Shamo. Supper had been served and Kay had produced the ration of whisky for the night. Suddenly the silence around us was broken by the sound of drums from the nearby village. In a flash, Negussie was on his feet and disappeared into the surrounding bush. The drums got louder, but we went on with our work, writing up reports and servicing the vehicles, trying not to pay any attention.

Negussie returned and whispered to me, 'John, I am not happy about the villagers here, the last white men they saw were probably the Italians, who may well have mistreated them. We must go to that village and find out what is happening. Will you come with me?'

It was an interesting experience to accompany an officer on a purposeful patrol, when only two years before I had been trying to teach him the art of patrolling on a Surrey common.

Picking up our rifles, we set off into the night. I earned a quick rebuke when I tripped over a log, but most of our sounds were drowned by the drums which were now almost deafening. Clearly the villagers were getting very worked up about something. At last we came to the stockade and leaving a police corporal and myself to cover him, Negussie went forward to the gate. It was not properly shut, and through the fence we could see a huge fire burning with half-naked figures leaping about and jumping through the flames. Around them the crowd ululated and the drums beat faster and faster. Negussie paused at the gate for a moment or two listening intently. He came from the north and I doubted if he would understand the language these people spoke. Like most Ethiopian officers, he was smartly dressed and even when working for long hours, in the in the rain and the mud, Negussie always managed to look as if he had just come off parade. Suddenly we saw him push open the gate and walk in. The drums stopped at once and the ululating ceased instantly. He held up his hand, his pistol was still in its holster. I could understand a little of what he was trying to say.

'I am an officer of the Emperor, tonight the Emperor's friends are camping near here. What is all this noise about?'

A wizened old man dressed in a leopard's skin shambled forward to shake his hand, and in a whining, pleading voice, talked to him for several minutes. Eventually Negussie nodded, said something in Amharic and turned and strode out of the compound. At once the drums thundered louder than ever and the ululating began again. I must admit I thought it a pretty cool act, for had they been hostile, he wouldn't have lasted long.

'It's all right,' he said, 'they're having a celebration for the return of their chief, who is expected back tonight.'

What I had witnessed only served to increase my respect for the Ethiopian as a courageous fighter, and not once in all our expeditions in that wild land did I ever have reason to doubt the bravery of these hardy people. This was not the only time that Negussie's intrepidity had impressed me. Early one morning he came with Bill Bullock and me to examine a possible rafting site on the shores of Lake Abaya. It was barely light when we left the camp and coming to the water's edge we decided to walk out along a partly finished jetty, to get a good view. I led the way, followed by Negussie and then Bill. We all had our arms filled with oddments of reconnaissance kit and made our way forward by hopping from the top of one timber pile to the next, never more than a couple of feet above the water. Almost at the end of the jetty I looked down and saw what I thought was a large, rubber tyre, with the tread just on the surface of the water.

'Is that a tyre or could it be a crocodile?' I asked Negussie. As if to answer he used a red-and-white striped surveyor's pole he was carrying to press firmly down in the centre of the object. It sank without movement, and as he released the pole, bobbed up again.

'Ah, obviously a tyre,' we all thought and took another pace forward. At that moment, Negussie repeated the process but this time the result was different. With a great roar and a crash a leviathan rose up from the depths. It was a large crocodile and its tail came crashing round to strike the timbers just beneath my feet, sending splinters flying in all directions. At the same time it launched itself at Negussie, who fortunately being extremely agile, leapt to the top of a convenient pile. The beast then turned on me and with his mouth wide open displaying serried lines of yellowing teeth, tried to get my leg. In one hand I held a .303 sporting rifle and in the other I carried more survey equipment. Flicking the safety catch off with my thumb, I thrust the rifle down into the gaping mouth and pulled the trigger. The jaws closed about the barrel as the gun went off. Blood spurted out towards me, and at that moment Bill and Negussie fired their weapons into it. With an awful gurgling sound, it began to slide back into the water.

'Hold it quickly,' yelled Negussie, and before we could stop him, had seized the thing by the tail. It took us nearly an hour to get the carcass of the reptile ashore and finally we carried it back to camp in triumph in a Land-Rover. It was a salutary lesson and one I'm not likely to forget. It brings out the old maxim that the crocodile will very often attack after you have stepped over him and not when you are about to. Frankly it was as close as I want to get to one.

We had other narrow escapes. On one occasion Negussie, who is perhaps accident-prone, almost trod on a large python that was sleeping on some grass right in front of him, and during one hunt I suddenly found myself aware of an incredibly strong, strange smell that seemed to make my eyes itch. I had not really given it a thought until Komo, my faithful bearer, screamed out a warning, 'Ambessa!' and a lion loped away from behind some nearby bushes. I suppose the scent affected me as that of domestic cats, to which I am allergic.

The scientific side of the expedition was going well. The archaeological team under the Sandhurst Naval representative found signs of early historic occupations to the north of Lake Abaya. Our veterinary surgeon did some valuable work sending samples of monkeys' blood back to the Imperial Central Laboratory, Addis Ababa, in connection with the spread of a yellow fever epidemic that was sweeping to the south of the country. The zoologists also had great success with everything from fish, to snakes, to large mammals, and Patrick Morris's field laboratory had the appearance of a witch's cave.

Two attempts were made to ascend the 13,780-feet Gughe mountain. The first was frustrated by incorrect local information, the second by heavy rain in early September. However, the party did manage to reach the fabulous Bonchie Valley at ten thousand feet after two and a half days' march with mules. It was an incredibly remote area; the region was unpoliced, which was a rare occurrence in Ethiopia. 'The soil is so productive that the people never quarrel,' was the explanation given by an official. Those who had struggled twelve hours a day through slushy mud along precipitous mountain paths breathing rarified air, could think of better reasons; but when reached, it was a memorable sight; not deliberately laid out but very pleasing to the eye. Each farmer's tukul had its own clump of bamboo sweeping up to the sky, its patch of false banana trees and a natural lawn of the greenest grass imaginable.

Meanwhile in the valley our reconnaissance teams had located an area of grassland alive with large game animals. It was reported that there were zebras, hartebeest, rhone and greater kudu. There were also said to be lion and giraffe. The area was known locally as the White Grasses and had obviously remained a pocket of game because it was so difficult to reach. Behind it rose a steep escarpment, on the other side was the lake and elsewhere there was swamp and rivers cutting it off from the rest of the country. It was part of our programme to survey new areas for wild life conservation and clearly we must have a look at this district. The only problem was how to get there. However, we believed that this could be done if we could cross a difficult little river called the Cullufu. Thus I decided to launch Operation Rubicon.

The plan was to move one party by vehicle south, ferry them across the Cullufu and then they would make their way up a track which we believed would take them up to the area of the grasses. A second party would cross Lake Abaya by boat and proceed on foot. All the stores and provisions for the game survey team would go with the Land-Rover. The raft was quickly constructed at the river and in no time we had got the vehicle across.

We were relieved to be safely over the water, because it was at this site a few days earlier that we had witnessed a horrifying scene. Standing on the bank, we were looking for a suitable place to raft across. Downstream, some hundred and fifty yards away, a large herd of native cattle had been brought down to water. Suddenly a great commotion occurred. The cattle gave startled tongue and scrambled back up the bank from the river, as the herdsmen rushed down, screaming and waving their spears. For a moment I was mystified by the sudden uproar. What on earth was wrong?

The centre of attention seemed to be a great white bramah bull, which now stood with its tall heavy horns raised at the water's edge. His legs were deep in the mud and he seemed to be struggling to draw something out of the river. Even at this distance I could see the muscles of his powerful body contorted in effort.

'He's got something in his mouth,' gasped one of the cadets.

Through my binoculars I could now see there was something, but it was not in the bull's mouth, it was round it – it was the jaws of a huge crocodile. Very slowly, remorselessly the reptile was dragging the animal into the river. We had a rifle but at that distance, with the demented herdsman dashing round the struggling beast, I dared not fire.

If we could have crossed the river, we might have saved the bull, but the sight of the massive croc did not encourage anyone to try a quick dip at that point. While we watched impotently, the reptile won the dreadful tug-o'-war and with its thick, squat legs working like pistons, and its scaly tail thrashing the water into a foam, it pulled its victim into the shallows. Suddenly the bull was down, the froth turned red and still kicking frantically, the stricken beast disappeared in the turbid brown stream. The rest we could imagine. The croc would place the carcass in its underground lair or beneath a rock on the riverbed, until it had putrefied sufficiently for its liking.

The narrow and little-used track was barely wide enough for one Land-Rover and it was fortunate that we had a small supply of dynamite with us to get rid of some of the larger boulders that blocked the path.

By evening we had reached the area and made camp on the open plain in the darkness. We cooked our meal by the light of torches and turned in for the night. After an hour or so I was woken up by the sentry; he could hear noises all around him. Sure enough, listening, I could hear them too. It took me a moment to realize that they were great herds grazing on the grasses round about us. By torchlight we could see hundreds of pairs of eyes watching us. We left a lantern burning and went back to sleep. At dawn we were greeted by the most rewarding sight, of the herds moving down to water and we moved our own camp to the area of a small river. Here we carried out a game survey and head count of as many of the beasts as we could. They were not particularly timid and it seemed unlikely that they had ever been hunted. Therefore we were afraid of killing any ourselves lest they should be scared away from this area for all time.

The collection of smaller animals went on unabated. Indeed in the world of zoology they are probably more important because they are least known. Everyone who had a spare moment was sent out to try and catch frogs, toads, mice and rats and our collection grew accordingly. One soldier who was particularly good at it won high praise. I just could not understand how he collected so many frogs. Every day he turned up with bucketfuls and yet he didn't seem particularly tired or worn out by his efforts. It was long after the expedition that I discovered his method. It was quite simple! He would go down to a native village in his Land-Rover with a copy of *Playboy*. As soon as the local men had gathered round him, he would open the centre pages and let them have a quick peep. He would then close the magazine quickly and say, 'Three frogs, one look.' Thus encouraged, the natives would rush off to collect as many frogs as they could and come back for another view of the centre page.

I had not planned to return to Addis Ababa until about 5 September, but on 24 August very heavy rain fell, turning the ground into a quagmire and I became most concerned that this might be the beginning of the rains for this region. We watched the skies and the barometer anxiously, but the next day there was more torrential rain and the parties working in the bush had great difficulty in moving anywhere. The resupply vehicle could not get through to the outlying patrols, and all around us the dry sun-scorched soil became a marsh. The Cullufu River was now a thundering cataract, roaring between the jungle-clad banks. Overhead the sky was permanently dark and the chilly nights were illuminated by brilliant lightning. The incessant rain continued for days, turning minor streams into swollen torrents and the rivers into floods. Vehicles and people floundered about their tasks as best they could. On the night of 27 August I decided that we must pull out, otherwise we should be completely cut off for the rest of the rainy season.

At the Daimler ferry, as we called the rafting point on the Cullufu, the river was still a raging torrent, making use of our raft extremely hazardous. A tree-footbridge we had made was partially submerged and one of the officers was swept into the turbulent water whilst trying to cross it. Fortunately he managed to seize a tree trunk, but was in imminent danger of being carried downstream to the crocodile-infested area and then to a stretch of rapids. It was only the prompt action of Guardsman Cox of the Welsh Guards that saved his life, and later Cox was awarded the Queen's Commendation for Brave Conduct. One by one the bedraggled parties struggled into base camp. They all told the same story – heavy rain and deep mud – we simply had to get out and across the Hamasa before we were too late. We struck camp at dawn on 31 August and packed our sodden tentage and equipment into the vehicles.

At 21.00 hours we reached the Hamasa River. It was running

too high and fast to be crossed, so we parked the vehicles on high
ground and the expedition settled down to sleep. The engineers set
up a river watch – everyone was at fifteen minutes' notice to move
and suddenly, at 23.30 hours, the level of the water began to drop
noticeably. At midnight the order was given to prepare to cross, and
the engineers, with safety lines, waded through the swirling waters
to the rocky northern bank. The crossing had been planned while we
waited, and in the inky blackness, it was truly surprising that all
went so smoothly. The sappers recced the ford whilst armed guards
kept watch for crocodiles. Guide lines were run out and a safety
rope was put downstream. Using pick and shovel, we improved the
exits and approaches and then everyone waded through the rushing
water to the far side, leaving just the driver and one man whose
job it was to hold the hose pipe onto the exhaust system in the
vehicle. Everyone wore a life jacket. Shortly after midnight the first
truck moved slowly into the torrent. We all kept our fingers crossed,
but its winch rope had been paid out in advance so that it could
drag itself out if necessary. However, the big vehicles went through
with little trouble and it was only when the smaller Land-Rovers
tried that our problems began. Most of them stalled in the mud and
water when it got to about three feet deep, but the sappers, struggling
in the foaming river, were ready with the winch ropes, and as soon
as a vehicle was seen to be in trouble, they attached lines and the
three-tonners heaved the smaller vehicles out. By 03.00 hours everyone was across.

The expedition was over, but we still had to get all our zoological
specimens back to England. Although we had done our best to
preserve them adequately, the presence of some large, slightly
putrefying reptiles in a hot, stuffy aeroplane *en route* from Aden to
UK did not endear us to the RAF, and one of the planes was caused
to make an unscheduled landing at Malta when the stench became
overpowering. There can't be many pilots who can claim to have
been forced down by a crocodile!

On our return to Addis Ababa we had been greatly honoured to
receive an invitation to meet His Imperial Majesty once again. This
time the invitation was for everybody and I wondered whether the
court realized how many of us there were. My problem was to get
the cadets in and out again in some semblance of order. Normally
this would not have presented any difficulty, but it is traditional in
Ethiopia to bow to the Emperor three times. Once when you enter
the door, again half-way up the red carpet towards him and finally

when right before him. He may then extend his hand and greet you. On leaving his presence you are required to repeat the process in reverse, bowing once before him, once in the middle of the room and once finally at the door. No problem, you may think – for well-drilled officer cadets of the three Services, but there is one difficulty in that His Imperial Majesty tends to have the odd lion or cheetah strolling around the throne room and I could imagine a terrible international incident might result if an officer cadet, walking backwards, should fall over one of these royal beasts. I consulted Tommy, one of the Ethiopians working at the British Embassy, who told me how I could overcome this.

'You will notice,' he said, 'that Ethiopians cast themselves down very low when they bow to the Emperor, almost pressing their foreheads upon the carpet.'

'Yes,' I said, 'I have noticed this.'

'Then you too must bow very low,' was Tommy's reply, 'as by so doing, you'll be able to see between your legs and notice if there are any lions lying in your path.'

The reception went splendidly. His Imperial Majesty made us very welcome and talked in both French and English to many members of the expedition. Finally, as the audience was drawing to a close, he turned to me and said softly, 'I do hope you will come back to my Empire and make another expedition.'

I said I should be delighted and asked if he had anything in particular that he would like me to do.

He gave a wry little smile and said quietly, 'Why not explore my Blue Nile?'

5

THE BLUE NILE

THE mile-deep gorge that cuts through the highlands of north-west Ethiopia is the home of the infamous Blue Nile; here this great natural feature cuts its way across the mountain fastness and leads the river to spill out into the sun-soaked plains of the Sudan. Until 1968 it remained virtually unexplored, although the actual source lies in a bog south of Lake Tana and is not difficult to reach.

From my research I learned that the first Briton to view this spring was the adventurer James Bruce. Visiting Ethiopia in 1711 he wrote of 'people who anointed themselves not with bear's grease or pomatum, but with the blood of cows, who instead of playing tunes upon them wore the entrails of animals as ornaments and who, insteading of eating hog meat, licked their lips over bleeding living flesh.' For my part, while seeking the elusive swamp rat, I had tramped many miles, and been eaten alive by mosquitoes in this region.

The stream that flows from this spring becomes the Little Abbai, which, it is said, flows through Lake Tana and becomes the Great Abbai or Blue Nile near the town of Bahadar. Personally I doubt this theory, but it is a common one with rivers said to rise beyond a great lake.

For its first eighteen miles the Blue Nile is wide and shallow, flowing through swampy water-meadows and around numerous islands. But there are long stretches of dangerous white water and several small waterfalls.

At Tisisiat the river suddenly drops over the second biggest falls in Africa. There the huge volume of water is compressed into the narrow sheer-sided gorge and for almost one hundred miles the river races through this cleft in the earth before the valley opens out and becomes less severe. However, the river is still at the bottom of a great gutter in the Ethiopian Highlands and ten thousand feet above it towers the cloud-swathed Mount Chokai. From here on, the river alternates between rocky cataracts, dangerous shallows and stretches of flat water populated by hippo and large aggressive crocodiles.

Mosquitoes, insects and disease, as well as rumours of radio-active gas, kept the Ethiopians away from this inhospitable world.

As far as I could tell the first attempt at navigation was made in 1902 by an American big-game hunter who brought three specially designed steel boats from Britain. However, after only three miles these were swamped in a cataract and the expedition was abandoned. In 1905, a Swede called Jesson came upstream from the Sudan. He could only get his boats to the Azir River, where he met hostile natives and marched back to the Sudan. Later he reported that it would have been suicidal to attempt to force a passage in steel boats over the rocks and rapids.

In 1926 Major R. E. Cheeseman, the British consul in north-west Ethiopia, tried to follow the course of the river on foot. His survey work was invaluable but, owing to the great difficulty he experienced in moving along the banks of the gorge, he was soon forced up on to the high plateau.

In 1955 a small party of Germans attempted to canoe down the river. They had with them a number of ladies who, by all accounts, were very attractive. However, crocodiles are no respecters of persons. The canoes were attacked and the party driven from the river.

One of the best-organized expeditions, I discovered, was mounted in 1962 by the Canoe Club of Geneva. Six very tough and experienced canoeists set out in two large Canadian-style boats. They started, as have many expeditions, from the Blue Nile bridge at Shafartak and after a great effort they reached a point near the Sudan border. There they camped on an island and whilst asleep were attacked by bandits. In the fight two men died, but the rest managed to escape in one canoe.

The next attempt was by Arne Rubin who became the first man to travel along the Blue Nile from Shafartak bridge to Rosiares. During our research we corresponded with this plucky Swede, who in 1965 had navigated this stretch in a Kleeper canoe, alone! It was a splendid achievement. The next year he returned, with a friend, to attempt the upper reaches of the river, but after fifty miles of hair-raising adventure their canoe was smashed and they were forced to walk out. There were other expeditions and in March 1968 a small team, mainly from Britain, attempting the river in rubber boats came to grief after eighteen miles, with the bottoms torn off their

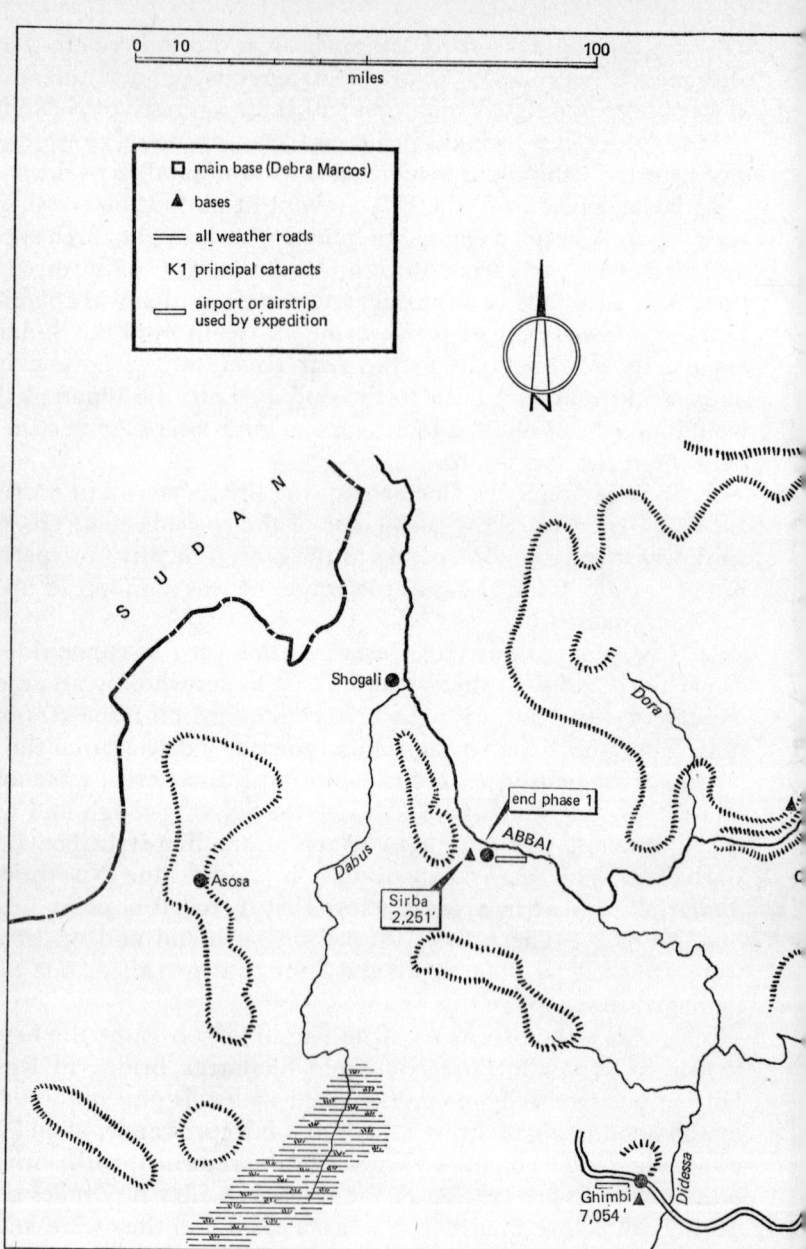

□ main base (Debra Marcos)

▲ bases

═══ all weather roads

K1 principal cataracts

airport or airstrip
used by expedition

S U D A N

Shogali

Dora

end phase 1

ABBAI

Dabus

Asosa

Sirba
2,251'

Ghimbi
7,054'

Didessa

The Great Abbai

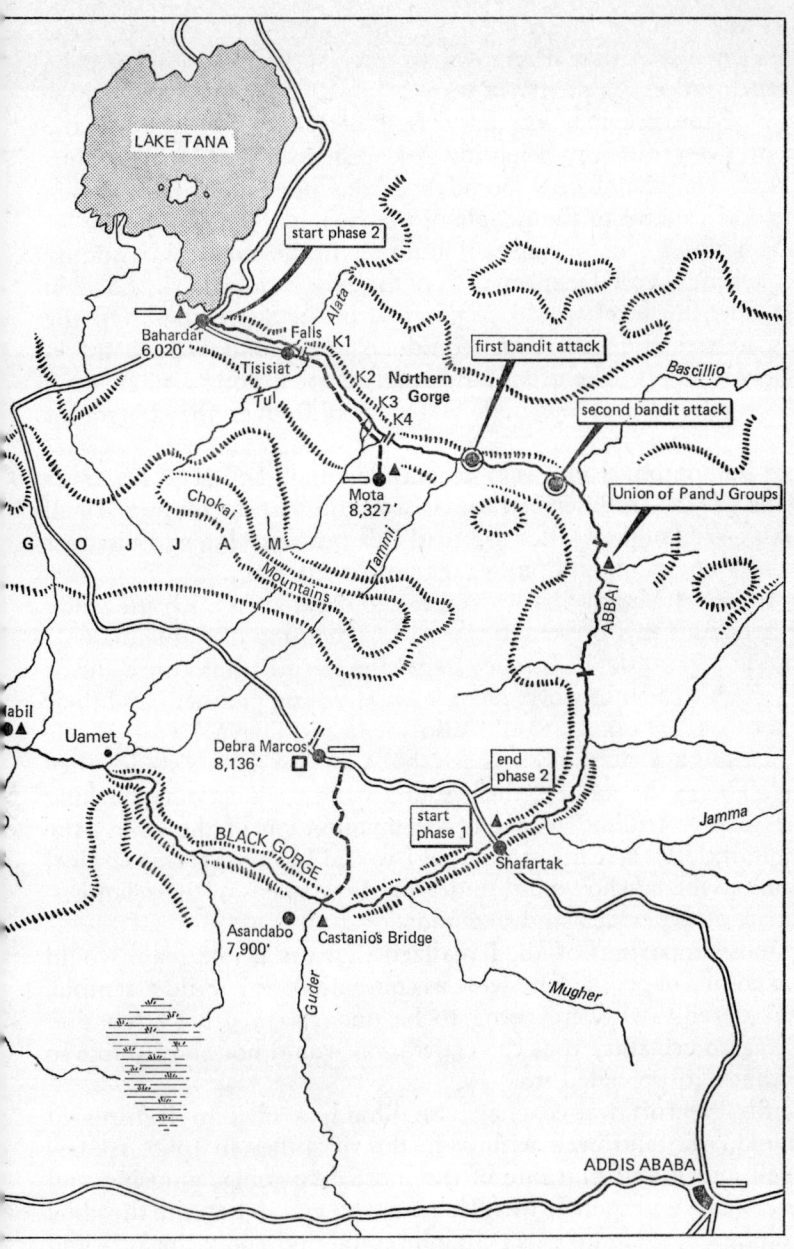

LAKE TANA

start phase 2

Bahardar
6,020'

Falls

Tisisiat

Alata

K1

K2 Northern
K3 Gorge
K4

Tul

Mota
8,327'

Chokai

G O J J A M

Mountains

Tammi

first bandit attack

Bascillio

second bandit attack

Union of P and J Groups

ABBAI

Nabil

Uamet

Debra Marcos
8,136'

BLACK GORGE

end
phase 2

Jamma

start
phase 1

Shafartak

Asandabo
7,900'

Castanio's Bridge

Guder

Mugher

ADDIS ABABA

craft. It was a salutary warning to us, and studying the reports of the disasters I realized that if one was to navigate this river it must be done when there was plenty of water.

None of the previous explorers had been able to examine the banks or carry out any scientific research, so we hoped that our expedition would not only be adventurous but would be of value both to science and to the people of the region.

Up to eighty inches of rain falls annually in the mountains, mainly in the summer, and I expected that the Nile would be in flood in August and the level would begin to drop in September. On the plateau at this time the rain would be heavy and vehicle tracks extremely difficult. The great advantage of attempting a navigation at this time was that the high water should cover the dangerous rocks.

Chris Bonington, who was to accompany us on behalf of *The Daily Telegraph Magazine*, described the area as 'the last unconquered hell on earth'. We laughed when we read this but were later to discover that it was not so much of an exaggeration after all.

His Imperial Majesty had asked me to organize a scientific study of the area and this presented me with something of a dilemma. It would cost a great deal of money to get the scientists into the difficult region, enable them to work, keep them alive and get them and their specimens out again. It would also mean sending a lot of people there just to back them up and see that they got the assistance they needed. To get the money, the resources and the necessary backing for the project we had to catch the imagination of the army, the press and industry. At the same time I would have to recruit service-men and civilians who would understand the needs of the scientists, and their idiosyncrasies and demands.

But most important of all, I realized that the whole team would have to consist of people who were as compatible as I could assemble, for undoubtedly we were going to be under very great stress and there was no certainty that the expedition would not end up like so many that had preceded it.

My first recruit was Richard Snailham, a civilian lecturer at Sandhurst, who had been with us in the rift valley in 1966. I knew him well and found him one of the most easy-going, amusing and likeable men I had met. It was Richard who was to become the chief Nilographer, reading up everything he could find about the area and helping to write the various prospectuses and begging letters that we had to put out to gain sponsorship and support. He would also write the official history[1] of the expedition and act as treasurer.

My second-in-command was to be Nigel Sale, then adjutant of the Royal Green Jackets. I had known him for some years and believed that this thorough, slightly serious and very efficient officer was just the sort of chap I needed to balance my own character.

One of the most important people would be the chief engineer. Here we required, not a fresh-faced, Sandhurst-trained subaltern with bags of enthusiasm, but an experienced, bold and imaginative sapper who would be prepared to tackle any obstacle with the minimum of resources and manpower. For this post I selected Jim Masters, a quiet forty-year-old officer from Somerset whom I knew I could depend on at all times. We had served together in Cyprus and I respected his depth of experience and expert knowledge.

To organize and lead the White Water team I chose Roger Chapman, whom I had known as an instructor at Sandhurst. Roger, a captain in the Green Howards, was a rugged north-countryman who possessed boundless vitality and dogged determination. It was he who would have the unenviable task of navigating the most difficult stretches.

The scientists would be led by Patrick Morris, a highly resourceful and efficient young zoologist who had also accompanied us in 1966. Ever the devil's advocate, I valued his practical nature and advice on many matters.

As information officer I needed someone with an outstanding memory, a methodical mind and a quick brain. Lieutenant Martin Romilly, then a student at the Royal Military College of Science, fitted the bill.

I had always feared taking girls on an expedition for the distraction and problems they might cause, but I had no hesitation in adding Kay to our list. She would as always be the energetic general manager, pouring oil on troubled waters and writing blissful little notes to cheer our sponsors. Barbara Wells, a scientifically-oriented secretary to a diamond merchant, was our only other lady member.

In total the team would consist of seventy servicemen and civilians from Britain and Ethiopia and the scientists were to include an archaeologist, an ornithologist, a veterinary surgeon, the medical officers and a host of zoologists.

My plan was to set up a base at Debra Marcos roughly at the centre point of the expedition area. From here we could radiate outwards attempting to navigate the river, first from Shafartak to Sirba,

1. Richard Snailham, *The Blue Nile Revealed* (Chatto and Windus, 1970).

when the water level was at the highest. On that phase we should use army aluminium assault boats powered by forty horse-power outboard motors.

For the second part of the expedition we needed boats that would stand up to the tumbling white water in the narrow gorges at the head of the river. Arne Rubin told me he believed that only inflatable craft could survive these terrible conditions. So I planned to navigate the head of the river with special rubber boats.

Re-supply would be by small overland parties dragging mules through the mud on the high plateau, before descending into the baking hot gorge. More supplies would arrive by parachute from a Beaver aircraft of the Army Air Corps. Helicopters had been considered, but I soon discovered that they would prove too costly in fuel and maintenance and the altitude would affect their performance.

Some of the army members were to be from the Royal Military College of Science at Shrivenham where we planned the project. Here lived our patron, Major General Napier Crookenden. The general was the energetic and fiery commandant of the college and his active support was to prove especially valuable. There were other generals, other senior officers and senior scientists who helped, and somewhere in all their hearts there lurked the glimmering flame of adventure, and they had the imagination to see that what we were attempting might just succeed.

Shrivenham was an ideal place to launch an expedition. Judith and I moved into a tumbledown camp near by, took over a host of buildings and together with a Lance-Corporal Henry of the Royal Engineers, who had volunteered to accompany me, we made up the expedition headquarters. The excellent scientific and technical facilities at the college were soon put to good use. A computer was used in design problems and the fluids laboratory staff kindly reproduced a simulated section of the river, complete with an adjustable cataract. Here we would create various wave-formations and test different types of model boat. One day I came to see how the experiments were progressing.

'Splendidly, splendidly,' enthused the white-coated assistant. 'There is only one problem.'

'What's that?' I said.

'The cataract works perfectly and the boat goes down the centre, but it always turns over!'

For advice on the animals I went to the Natural History Department of the British Museum.

'The hippo won't give you any trouble,' said the bearded zoologist, 'providing of course you keep about half a mile away from them.'

I hastened to explain that we were on a river which in places was not more than fifty yards wide.

'Ah well, there you have a problem,' he said. 'The answer is to avoid them in the mating season.'

I enquired when that was.

'That's a good question,' he said, reaching for a leather-bound book. For a moment there was silence. Then he looked up at me over his thick-rimmed glasses. 'Perhaps you'll be able to tell us the answer,' he said.

'What about the crocodiles?' I asked. 'Aren't they supposed to be the largest and most dangerous in the world?'

'Oh, they will all probably be well up the tributaries or downstream in Sudan at the time of the high water,' he explained confidently.

I thanked him for his good advice and strode out into the sunlight of Kensington, deep in thought. At least my rubber boats should be safe from crocodile attack on the upper reaches.

Months of training and preparation now followed. Every spare moment was taken up by the expedition. The commandant at Shrivenham was very co-operative and, although his instructors did not generally approve of the fact that I was allowed so much time off, I was able to devote my efforts to selecting the equipment and the team and to the thankless task of raising £15,000 in cash. We tested boats on the wild rivers of North Wales and in the sandy areas of Aldershot we trained with pack-horses. Boats were selected, boats were rejected, boats were modified and finally with days to go boats were packed. Under the eagle eye of the quartermaster, Captain Buck Taylor, a mass of stores was prepared in an old hangar at the camp.

Undoubtedly a great many people thought we were mad and, although some said so publicly, the majority smiled benevolently. After all, with sponsors such as the British Museum (Natural History), the Royal Geographical Society, *The Daily Telegraph* and numerous organizations, firms and individuals it was clear that a very large number of people had faith in us.

In March 1968 I was able to visit the river and carry out an air reconnaissance. Flying in a small single-engine aircraft I went with John Blower, then chief game warden of Ethiopia, and the expedition's senior military officer, Lieutenant-Colonel Philip Sheperd RA, and flew, as Alan Moorehead had done some years previously, the length of the gorge. It was certainly impressive. We were seeing it in the dry season, and, although I observed whole regiments of crocodiles rushing into the water as the aircraft roared overhead, there did not appear to be any impassable obstacles in the river itself. We returned to England in time to explain the whole thing to Her Majesty the Queen and His Royal Highness Prince Philip during their visit to the Royal School of Military Engineering at Chatham.

Very sadly my mother, one of my staunchest allies and supporters, died suddenly in the April of that year. Apart from the usual family upheavals, the expedition problems seemed to multiply, but whenever I became depressed I forced myself to go on – because that is just what she would have advised.

By the end of July we had completed our preparations, raised the money and found that funds were barely sufficient. Indeed an overdraft was necessary and, through the kindness of a sympathetic manager, we secured an emergency fund of up to £5,000 from the National Westminster Bank at Camberley.

At the eleventh hour a personal disaster struck. During boat training in Wales I fell heavily on to my right knee. Within a day it was swollen and excruciatingly painful. 'Rest it for a month and then start taking gentle exercise,' said the doctor. I acquired a stout walking-stick and a supply of crepe bandages and prayed hard.

Flying in a large chartered civil aircraft we reached Addis Ababa on 31 July. Philip Shepard had come out a few days earlier and had worked extremely hard to pave the way. He had an enormous task, and in the short time had achieved administrative miracles, but the main problem was in obtaining customs clearance, which despite promises by various authorities had not been done.

However, help was forthcoming, and with the aid of the United States Mapping Mission and various Ethiopian government departments we were able to move our personnel and stores to Debra Marcos on 2 August. Here we set up the base in pouring rain. Flying ahead of the main column I went forward with our chief pilot, Major Alan Calder in our Beaver. We reached the grassy airstrip above the town at the same time as a tropical squall. High winds and rain clouds were sweeping across the flat green landscape as Alan fought with the controls and tried to land. Six times he made his approach and six times pulled away again at the last minute. Fuel was beginning to run low and there was not enough to get us back to Addis Ababa.

'Here we go!' he yelled through the intercom as we went in for the seventh time. Ahead, strolling slowly across the strip, a herd of white cows appeared, Alan swore, and the next moment we were over the top of the cattle and with a bump our wheels hit the ground.

At once we felt the full force of the crosswind swing the Beaver from one side of the strip to the other. Fortunately there was nothing in the way and in one hundred yards we had taxied to a halt. The true violence of the storm was now apparent, for as we tried to open the doors, they were almost wrenched off in our hands. At the end of the airfield there was a silver-and-orange helicopter of the Ethiopian Army Air Corps. Alan taxied over, and in spite of the rain I climbed out to meet our allies. Huddled inside the cabin of the 'chopper' were half-a-dozen soldiers, some of whom I noticed had bandaged heads and limbs. The pilot, a young Amhara in a bright orange flying-suit, grinned and slid open a small panel of perspex.

'Good morning,' I shouted above the noise of the wind.

'Hi,' he replied with an American accent, 'Who are you?'

I explained that we were a British Army Expedition, come to make a scientific study of the Blue Nile.

'Gee, I thought you were reinforcements,' he explained. 'Say, don't you guys know there's a war going on?' He pointed to the wounded soldiers whom he was about to evacuate when the storm abated.

I had heard that there was some minor internal problem in the province of Gojjam but I had not been informed of the serious nature of the conflict. It seemed that the people of the region had risen up with one accord against what they considered the dastardly imposition of something called income tax. Clearly we had some sympathy with the rebels. But, in protest, they had turned to killing the tax collectors and now the army were trying to sort out the rebels. We had landed in the middle of a small civil war.

As soon as the rest of the party arrived I went down to visit my old friend the governor. I had last seen him four years ago in his mud-walled palace in the town. On arrival at his offices, I noticed how very few people were around. There was not even a guard on the main gate. Walking up to his office, I found the door open and to my surprise I saw a corporal of police seated at the governor's desk smoking a cigar.

'Ternastling,' I greeted him.

He looked up equally surprised and said in halting English, 'Good morning.'

'Where's the governor?' I enquired.

'He's gone,' said the corporal, 'and I'm going too.' He hastened to explain to me that the town was soon to be attacked by some three thousand armed rebels who were out for the governor's blood and indeed the blood of anyone connected with the civil administration.

'Well, before you go,' I asked him, 'will you be so kind as to let me have some letters that I can send out to the various chiefs to grant us assistance and passage through their tribal areas?'

'Ah yes,' he said, 'I have these here,' and to my astonishment produced a sheaf of letters which he proceeded to stamp with the official rubber stamp. Messengers were sent for and each one was handed a letter for an appropriate chief. Bowing their way out from the corporal's presence they made off at high speed into the hills. I was given more letters of authority and assured that all would be well.

Returning to the camp I explained to the bewildered expedition that we had arrived in a very hostile area, and that the town was likely to be surrounded by a large number of armed tribesmen hell-bent for blood, who would undoubtedly sack it and having done so might turn their attentions to us.

'Ah well,' said phlegmatic Buck Taylor, 'We'll build a zoriba, that'll keep them out.' The zoriba, all of two feet high, was made of thorns and I noted with interest that even the small boys who plagued our camp had no difficulty in hopping over it. The effect was undoubtedly intended to be psychological.

Now we must make the final preparations and do a great deal of air reconnaissance before we moved down to the river. Obstacles had been photographed with polaroid cameras and I used these pictures at the various briefings. Mules and donkeys for the re-supply teams had been made available as a result of the governor's letters, stores were packed, the aircraft flying schedule was detailed and all was made ready. The die was cast.

A member of the expedition had acquainted his old friends in Addis Ababa with our plans which so horrified them that they pleaded with me to abandon the attempt. 'You'll all be killed, you've no idea of the power of the Nile,' they said, but then, like so many of our would-be advisers, they had no first-hand knowledge of the river.

The plan was that the scientists and their immediate supporters should move along the river in boats, In addition another group under Nigel Sale was to march to the river through the Didessa Basin and carry out a game survey *en route*. Because of the river-conditions necessary for safe passage, the first part of the expedition would be from the Blue Nile Bridge at Shafartak to the missionary air strip at Sirba. Having successfully completed this phase, the teams were to be reorganized to explore the river from Lake Tana back to the original starting point at the Blue Nile Bridge. At the outset the river was too low, and I knew that I must wait until the water level had reached what I called the ten metre datum point. We had determined this after several air 'recces' along the length of the gorge. On one particular day I had noticed that there was sufficient water throughout the entire length of the first part of the river, and on this day the water level at a particular spot was ten metres deep. Therefore I knew that whenever the water level at this spot was ten metres deep there was a good chance that the entire course could be navigated. In fact I believed that it was safe for us to travel when the height was between nine and eleven metres. Should there be any appreciable rise or fall, then we must simply pull in, make camp and wait.

To determine the height, we fixed a surveyor's banderole at the water's edge whenever we arrived at a stopping-place. Then, the relative rise and fall was noted. This was a rough-and-ready guide, but in fact it proved extremely successful.

On 5 August the river party began to assemble with their boats and equipment at the bridge. Two days later the thirty-two of us, in four light-alloy assault boats, started on the voyage to Sirba.

At my final briefing of group leaders, I stressed the importance of maintaining the initiative.

'Don't wait for opportunities to arise,' I told them. 'You must make them and seize them. I've given you the broad outline of the plan and you know my instructions; now you must act accordingly. Radio communication may well cease, so don't wait for orders.' They were experienced men and I had every confidence in them.

It was early in the morning, and after a damp and stormy night we rose cramped and stiff to wash at the river-side. I noticed a certain nervous tension and people did not speak much over breakfast. The boats had been made ready the night before and the launching went smoothly. One by one the green metal craft nosed out from the shingle bank into the current. The moment it caught us, we were swung down river and it took all the power of our motors just to keep us stationary in relation to the bank. There was no question about it, we had insufficient power to return, even if we wanted to. It was rather like going to the moon; once you had blasted off you had no alternative but to continue to the end.

As the sun filtered into the gorge, spirits rose and people waved exuberantly to their friends watching from the bridge. Looking up at the towering cliffs, I said a silent prayer and then turned to the problem of navigation.

Each boat carried eight persons and approximately five hundred pounds of stores. We soon found that the engines were wonderfully reliable; fortunately the first day was a fairly easy one, which gave our helmsmen chance to gain some experience before the difficult going that lay ahead. The boats were made of alloy and had double hulls filled with polyurethane foam. They looked rather like green pointed boxes. Jim Masters, who had discussed the design with the Duke of Edinburgh at Chatham, had modified them in various ways. Across the bow was a canvas dodger, which we hoped would keep some of the water from the breaking waves out of the boat, and along the gunwales were wooden splash-boards. Extra buoyance was provided by sausage-shaped yellow inflatable fenders. The craft were filled with radios, flat-topped kit boxes, fuel and scientific stores. Our personal gear we carried in rucksacks, stowed under the dodger. Wedging ourselves in, we sat cocooned in our life-jackets, sweating profusely in the growing heat and enjoying the scenery.

The boats were named after various distinguished men connected with the Nile. The flagship was *Kitchener*, who, although he had died at sea, was a famous sapper and had done some good stuff at Omdurman in 1898. Another boat was called *Wingate* after the Chindit leader who had led Gideon Force against the Italians in Ethiopia in 1941, and who had crossed the Blue Nile on several occasions. We considered naming a boat *Gordon*, after another sapper, but as he had died within sight of the river under attack by hostile tribesmen we decided it might be tempting providence!

The first obstacle facing us was the Black Gorge. This narrow, steep-sided cleft in the black basalt rock, started some fifty miles from the bridge. I knew it continued for another fifty miles, and throughout its length contained numerous cataracts. From the air I had noticed that these occurred where bedrock caused a ridge in the river-bed, and that the gorge usually narrowed at this point.

In the first morning, travelling at about eight knots, we passed between wooded slopes alive with bird-life and broken here and there by red sandstone cliffs. Tributaries came in from the highlands and occasionally an island divided the river. Storks, heron and even a small leopard watched us with interest and curiosity from the sandy beaches.

The Black Gorge came on us suddenly. It towered up from the fifty-yards-wide river, its sides a tumbled mass of jet-black rocks, rounded and polished by the action of water and silt. The speed of the river increased and the only sound now was the hiss of the water on the rocks and the roar of the outboard engines.

Beneath our hull the stream surged and sucked, and at the sides we could see the pressure of water was causing the flow to reverse its direction. Driftwood was floating everywhere and deep whirlpools were common. Suddenly we experienced a feeling like descending rapidly in a lift, and realized in horror that one of these giant whirlpools was actually drawing the boat downwards. Before we had time to utter a word, Joe Ruston, the young Naval officer, had opened the throttle and was trying to drive us out of the seething mass of brown water. He succeeded, but not before many gallons of it had come pouring over the transom.

We approached the first major cataract with an uneasy feeling. Suddenly the river appeared to have gone still and the current had slackened, but ahead we could hear a distinct booming and could see the river was rushing towards a brink beyond which I could see nothing. *Kitchener*, my flagship, edged its way forward and was suddenly gripped in the irresistible pull of the rushing brown water. As we came to the edge we peered over and saw the water pouring down a slope, in a V-shaped formation. At the foot, some hundred feet away, a huge 'hydraulic wave' rolled and tumbled. I had no idea how tall it was, but beyond this I could see more large waves, coming in from the sides of the gorge and adding to this V-shaped impression. We all felt very uneasy, and I could feel butterflies beating in my stomach. Now we were racing down the slope and I heard Jim Masters shout, 'Hang on.'

With a crash we struck the wave, or perhaps I should say it struck us. Brown water poured over, drenching us to the skin and at that moment Joe gunned the engine for every ounce of power. We tilted up at a crazy angle and then were through. The mass of whirlpools and waves beyond the first hydraulic hurled us about as if we were a cork in a tempest. For the next few minutes we baled frantically to be prepared for the next cataract.

Bucketting through the rapids, we were extremely conscious of the immense power of the mighty river. All the boats had their anxious moments. One was disabled by a drifting tree and had to be chased downstream by the other craft. Another was almost lost in an especially difficult rapid, but thanks to the skill of our helmsmen we soon began to enjoy the journey. Contrary to expectations, we saw few crocodiles in the Black Gorge. Those there lay dormant on the sandy beaches, isolated by the turbulent brown water that rushed through the cataracts like a stream of liquid cement.

For days we cruised along, negotiating cataract after cataract. Stops were made to permit the scientific team to go about their work and, at the same time, allow the engineers an opportunity to service the engines. Occasionally, the river level dropped or rose alarmingly and we were forced to come into the bank to wait until it resumed a satisfactory level.

Our first camp was made at the junction with the Guder River, and while our scientists ranged about the sides of the gorge we came upon our first bandits. Two tall upright bronzed men stalked one of our patrols for several hours until the leader, Garth Brocksopp, tiring of the game, reversed the process and herded them down to our camp. Attired in old Italian Army tunics, festooned with accoutrements of leather, worn over faded loin cloths, they spoke no English. On their right shoulder they carried a heavy blanket and in their left hand a five-foot staff. On the other shoulder was slung a heavy Russian rifle (circa 1898), almost certainly captured at the battle of Adowa. Their hair was anointed with rancid butter which smelt revolting.

Taken off guard, I couldn't think of anything suitable to say to a couple of apparently amicable bandits. So I offered them a Mars bar. They eyed it suspiciously, as a pair of black carrion crows might examine an unusual but possibly tasty morsel in an English field. I urged them to eat and eventually one of them shot out a long scrawny set of fingers and grasped the confectionery. He smelt it without expression and handed it to his comrade who did the same. They looked at each other and then at me and nodded their approval before handing the bar back again. I broke it in half and gave them a piece each, at the same time eating some myself. They tasted it with care and then again nodded their approval, and so I gave them the rest of the bar. At this point the doctor arrived, and seeing him carrying his medical kit one of the bandits said, 'Cannunie.'

'I think they want quinine,' said Nigel, 'but I'll give them some paludrine tablets.'

In the middle of the interview Lieutenant Telahoun Mekonnen, our liaison officer from the Ethiopian Navy, came in from a reconnaissance up river. Immaculately dressed in his uniform he stepped ashore and on sighting our visitors his jaw dropped noticeably.

'I must speak to you,' he said, and leading me to one side explained that it was his painful duty to shoot these men immediately. Could I lend him my gun as his own pistol had not yet arrived from Naval headquarters.

I felt sorry that we should need to despatch our two visitors so soon, as it was quite possible we would learn much about the river and the flora from these two wanderers in this lost world. Tilly insisted that he should shoot them, and one of our police guides urged him to take off their ears to return as evidence to Addis Ababa. But, in the end, I prevailed on him to spare us the embarrassment of an incident so early in the expedition. The two policemen who had accompanied us from the bridge looked positively terrified of our visitors, and I noticed that the swarthy bandits regarded our other Ethiopian friends with nothing short of contempt and scorn. Anyway it was time to sail, so I took the opportunity of shaking them both by the hand and giving them some old plastic bags. They bowed politely and thanked me in Amharic.

Our only other contact with the bandits had been the previous day when Ato Mamo, a local chieftain who had befriended us, asked Nigel to remove a splinter of metal that was embedded in his forehead. Happy to oblige the medical officer enquired how it had got there. It transpired that the chief had discovered a small metal cylinder in a field after the war and deciding he needed a new plough-share had heated it up on a fire. He did not have to wait long for the shell to explode and the result was the splinter in his forehead. With impressive skill Nigel removed the foreign body and plugged the man full of penicillin. Ato Mamo in his gratitude told me he knew the bandits of the area well – were they not his friends, and in some cases I suspected, his family.

Speaking through an interpreter he said, 'Now you shall go on your way unmolested.' With suitable dignity I thanked him, privately considering the whole thing was grossly exaggerated. How wrong I was to be proved.

Those who attempted to scale the walls of the gorge found it like climbing a never-ending ladder in a Turkish bath. Water was only plentiful at the top and bottom and two water-bottles had to replace a great quantity of perspiration. The sixty-degree slopes were covered in broken, loose rocks concealed by elephant grass up to twelve feet high. Occasionally snakes slithered across the path, but in this dense

vegetation few animals were seen. Both men and mules were eaten
alive by swarms of ants and insects.

At Uamet the valley began to open out and for the next sixty miles
the going proved easier. However, the number of crocodiles and
hippo increased and we were ever on guard. To be quite truthful,
only one crocodile actually tried to bite a boat, and I felt that this
was very much in self defence! We were making excellent progress.
The weather was warm and fine and spirits were high. But I knew
that this was not a river to be trusted and that ahead lay the Western
Cataracts.

Before entering this dangerous stretch of water we made another
prolonged stop for scientific evaluation. Our camp was very much a
gipsy encampment! Shelters were built of groundsheets stretched on
poles and we slept on Li-los or Mother Earth. The zoologists were
elated at their discoveries, but poor Mansel Spratling, the archaeologist, had nothing to interest him and looked more downcast each
day.

Using our radio, we sent our requests and Chris Bonington's press
reports out each night. He complained, with justification, that there
was nothing exciting to report. I sympathized but promised that the
worst was still to come.

Due to a particularly bad bout of Ethiopian red tape, much of our
rations were still impounded in the customs shed. We were therefore
urged to make those that we had with us last, and, to eke out the
food, everyone hunted whenever possible. However, in the wet
season, the Blue Nile Gorge is almost devoid of game, which seemed
to have migrated to the high land. But the smaller animals were
abundant, and one evening we were walking back along the bank
when Hilary King, one of the young zoologists, suddenly saw a long
black snake slither across the path. With a cry he hurled himself upon
the reptile and quickly caught it in the approved manner behind the
neck. In seconds he had popped it into the snake-bag which he
always carried about his waist. With the beast writhing in captivity
we returned to camp. Having injected it through the canvas and
killed it the zoologists then debagged their specimen. There was
much mirth when we discovered that it was not a harmless constrictor but a young cobra!

Always interested in wildlife I found the collecting fascinating and
watched with interest as finds including soft-shelled turtles, monitor
lizards and brightly coloured bats were produced. Guinea fowl were
seen in abundance, but usually they made off long before we could

get within range. Because of the food shortage there was often an argument between scientists and soldiers as to whether any specimens should be preserved for posterity or eaten on the spot. Our rations were army dehydrated packs each designed to last one man for twenty-four hours, but we had to make two last for three days.

The pack, which weighed approximately two and a half pounds, was wrapped in supposedly water-tight polythene. It consisted of packets of tea, sugar, milk and coffee. There was an oatmeal block which invariably came in powder form after parachuting. Likewise there were 'biscuits, plain' and a tube of all-purpose lubricant called margarine. The central feature of the ration was a geological specimen named a curry-bar which could only be broken up with the aid of a climbing hammer or a rock. Thus pulverized, it was boiled for several hours and, with luck, produced a stew which you could then mix with a handful of rice. There were tins of cheese that were not the easiest things to open, ubiquitous Mars bars and some vitamin tablets which everyone forgot to take and as a result began to get skin complaints. Salt and the matches came in paper packets which soon dissolved in the humidity, but the secret weapon was the sardine tin. The uninitiated soon learned that to attempt to open this device with the opener provided caused the loss of several fingers. This we believed was inserted to confuse the enemy. The correct procedure was of course to drill a hole in the lid with your revolver! Into this hole you inserted a piece of fluff, usually readily available from 'socks, woollen grey'. By using the entire book of matches it was normally possible to ignite the oil-soaked fluff and to create a lamp, or if necessary a small cooker. By the time you'd eaten the rest of your ration the sardine tin would be red hot, and, as the solder had melted, a sharp tap on the side would remove the lid. If timed correctly this revealed some well-cooked sardines, but, more often than not, the contents were a charred lump. The army victuallers had thought of everything and even provided a few sheets of loo paper, but because this ration caused severe constipation this was rarely necessary.

Our occasional visits to native villages meant that we were able to taste the delights of the Ethiopian highland cuisine. Enjerra and Wat are the staple diet and our stomachs suffered horribly as a result of the highly-spiced raw meat.

The hippo, about which I had been warned, were plentiful. Their shiny grey backs rose like whales from the murky depths, and on one occasion we had a near escape when I ordered the fleet to pull in and

moor alongside a line of black rocks. We were twenty yards away
when the rocks swam off ! However, the hippos were far too busy
with their matrimonial affairs to worry us.

The Western Cataracts had been so named because they were a
stretch of very shallow water spread thinly over a jumbled mass of
igneous rock. During my reconnaissance we had seen this area at low
water and realized the potential danger that existed here if the river
level should drop even a foot. Fortunately the gorge was not steep-
sided at this point and with luck we should be able to portage the
boats around any major obstruction. Jim Masters and his sappers
had brought a vast quantity of blocks and tackle for this purpose.

Our luck held and the water level remained high. But on the first
day in this difficult region, we were cruising at about three-quarter
speed over what looked like an easy rapid when there was an enormous bang on the flagship's hull. With its engine racing wildly, the
boat reared up into the air and then pitched backwards into the
swirling torrent. Quite convinced that we were holed, Jim yelled for
everyone to grab a paddle and we tried to keep the bow pointing
downstream in preparation for the next cataract, only a few hundred
yards away. Already Joe had the motor up out of the water and was
replacing the broken shearpin. The rest of the flotilla came to our
aid, circled around and took photographs, while we paddled for our
lives! However, in a very short time we had power once again and
found that by a miracle, the hull was undamaged.

That night we camped upon a sandy beach jutting out from a
terrace filled with huge trees festooned with hanging lianas. This was
true tropical jungle and was quite different to the bush that we had
been in earlier.

Whilst gathering wood for the fire Mansel, our archaeologist,
suddenly leapt into the air with a shriek of delight. Not a man given
to frequent displays of emotion, he was suddenly tearing round like
a terrier hot on the scent of a rat. The reason for his excitement was
soon apparent, for by sheer chance he had discovered an extensive
river settlement which might be a quarter of a million years old.
Working like a demon, helped by all that could be spared, he had
soon produced a neat set of levels in which he laboured with unrelenting vigour. Back in the main camp the zoologists grumbled.
Apparently we had entered a zone devoid of interesting fauna and
flora and they cared not one jot for the valuable archaeological find.
Reasoning with them, I explained that we must stop for at least
thirty-six hours to give Mansel a chance to do the find justice.

Grudgingly they accepted the decision and the work at the dig went on. On the second night at the camp site the river began to rise and I knew we must take this opportunity to float over the rocks and down to the relative safety of the Didessa river junction.

At the junction we made our camp, for defensive reasons, on a small island, for it was in this area that the 1962 Franco-Swiss Expedition had been ambushed. Now the cliffs had given way to the flatter undulating country of the Sudan border. As we drew into the island Martin Romilly decided to re-zero his rifle. Selecting a convenient tree stump at the river-side he pumped half a dozen rounds at it. This impressed the local Shankilla, who were crouching unseen in the reeds, that we were hostile and they fled in terror. Perhaps it was not a bad thing after all, because it may have been these people or their near neighbours who had attacked the French six years previously. Tilly pursued them and eventually managed to capture one young boy whom he brought back to the camp and, after an hour's grilling, convinced him that we wished to be friends and had not intended to appear hostile. Returning to his tribe the boy came back with the old chief and his topless wives, who were immediately christened Gert and Daisy.

They were all as black as coal, a true Negroid people. Slowly they became more friendly and trusting. The girls were especially amused by the hair on our bodies, they being almost completely hairless. When they saw one member of the expedition who had a particularly fine growth on chest and arms, they burst into hysterics. It was only after considerable efforts at interpretation that we discovered the reason for their mirth was that they had not previously seen, as they said, a monkey that could talk. The Shankilla took us to their villages and demonstrated such well-tried arts as fire-making and the production of an alcoholic drink. They also said that we were the first white people they had seen. Meanwhile Nigel, John Blower and their party arrived from the south. After a gruelling cross-country march they had, almost by chance, managed to find us. Now we were near the end of the first part of the expedition and it only remained to reach the missionary airstrip at Sirba and be flown out to the head of the river to start the last battle. In the early reconnaissance days I had visited this airstrip and been slightly alarmed to be surrounded by two hundred armed tribesmen as we taxied to a halt. However, the rapid use of a Polaroid camera had a calming effect and soon got them all laughing.

Our island, we discovered, was also the bridal chamber of the local hippopotamus, who came up from the river at night and frolicked in the trees. The grunting and squealing were quite alarming and next morning we discovered some huge tunnels that had been carved, quite literally, around the camp by the rampaging beasts the previous night.

On reaching Sirba, we became the first people ever to take power boats down this section of the Blue Nile, but now we faced the difficult problem of extracting the expedition by air from this desolate spot. However in Addis, Philip Sheperd had not been idle and, armed with a good supply of *Black Label* whisky, he had been able to secure the services of the American Army Air Corps. The Beaver would carry out all the passengers and much of the kit, but the boats were to be underslung and flown out by the helicopter. Unfortunately the difficult task was not completely successful and, to this day, an assault boat lies buried deep in the jungle on top of a local mountain. It will be an interesting puzzle for archaeologists in the future.

The withdrawal from Sirba went fairly smoothly, although we had to leave a small detachment with the remaining boats for a few days. Richard Snailham was amongst these and indulged his sociological curiosity by wandering amongst the Shankilla. He always saved up his oldest clothes and wore them out on expeditions, thus it was in a pair of ragged shorts and torn shirt, sheltering beneath a tattered beach-hat, that he strode into the village square one evening. The tropical night had settled and the drums were beating loudly, dancers whirled in the firelight and Richard felt himself privileged to have come upon some rare celebration. His curiosity got the better of him and he joined in only to discover when it was almost too late that these were the fertility rites and that he was now in an awkward position from which it might prove difficult to withdraw. His appointed lady was most persistent, Richard on the other hand was playing hard to get and showing that he was merely interested in the music. Eventually one of the braves seized the girl, and in a fury demonstrated what Richard's duties consisted of. Looking suitably offended, the sociologist strode back to camp.

While those of us on the river suffered a certain amount of hardship and nervous stress, it was nothing compared with the conditions that the re-supply teams were meeting in their overland marches. Both north and south of the river, groups led by Gage Williams and Garth Brocksopp were struggling to get supplies forward to us. Using Land-Rovers, mules, and their feet they spared no effort to

Above: Self defence

Right: Northern Gorge, the Blue Nile. David Bromhead, Roger Chapman and Richard Snailham

Below right: Roger Chapman reloads after the second bandit attack

Above: The island where the night battle was fought during the second bandit attack

Below: Mission accomplished

The Blue Nile: Kay
Thompson and
Johnnie Johnson

I present His
Imperial Majesty
Haile Selassie I
with a Chihuahua
bitch at the end of
the Great Abbai
Expedition

Above: The Dahlak Islands. The old prison on 'Devil's Island', Nocra, that became our base

Below: A Dahlak sumbacca

reach us on the river. Whereas the conditions of high water were necessary for navigation, so the rains produced the most awful quagmire. Vehicles became bogged very quickly and the mules staggering along the paths with their heavy loads had a terrible time. One mule was drowned crossing a fast-flowing river, another fell over a cliff. But these re-supply teams were necessary because, although we could parachute down most of what we needed, the scientific specimens could not be taken out by air and these were now being carried out of the gorge by mules. The combination of David Bromhead and Garth Brocksopp in one team guaranteed that there would be a certain amount of hunting. Sure enough, during a period of enforced idleness at Ghimbi, they set about enlarging the mammal collection for the British Museum. David managed to shoot a hyena outside the police station and, although this might not seem a particularly unusual event, it brought people from as far away as fifty miles to view the carcass. The reason for their interest was that the hyena is still regarded, in some parts of Africa, and especially in the western region of Ethiopia, as an animal with supernatural powers. It is said that there are several tribes in this particular area who practice a form of hyena worship. We had already encountered one example of the taboos that surround this hideous animal and his cousin the jackal.

While Nigel had been marching in through the undulating Didessa valley, he had come upon a man badly wounded in a shooting accident. Apparently he and his friends had been out hunting jackal near their village. The wounded man had shot a jackal, but at the same moment, a friend's gun had gone off and drilled him through both thighs and the scrotum. He was in a bad way and Nigel did what he could for the poor fellow, but the villagers would not permit the white men to carry him into the shelter of one of their huts. They believed that he had been shot because the bullet fired by him at the jackal had later been thrown back by magic. The senior medical officer flew to the scene in the Beaver and circled overhead for some time giving instructions to Nigel by radio. Next day they had to leave the man, and later heard with some sadness that he had died shortly afterwards.

There are many interesting tribal stories about the cult of the hyena and I would like to have gone further west into the Dabus region in search of some of these tribes. Garth had attempted to get through but had been forced to turn back by the rains. Perhaps we shall fit it in as another expedition.

The comparative rest I had enjoyed while travelling on the river, coupled with some gentle exercise each day had the desired effect on my knee. I now used the walking-stick from force of habit rather than from necessity. However, the stick had proved very useful when a group of us had been moving with difficulty across an inclined rock-face that led to a sheer drop into the river.

We carried climbing equipment in the boats, but, coming on this obstacle while moving down the gorge, we decided to make our way across it as best we could without sending back for ropes. There were a few crevices to facilitate the traverse and, had we not been carrying rifles and packs, it would have been relatively easy.

I chose a route low down on the face and, moving gingerly with the aid of my stick, edged forward, trying not to look down at the surging brown water a hundred feet below.

More agile, young Junior Sergeant Chris Whitwell chose a higher and more difficult route. Inch by inch we advanced over the slippery basalt and were half-way across when the clatter of a rifle on the rock above made me look up. The Sergeant had slipped. Three fingers of one hand were holding in a shallow crevice at arms' length, whilst his legs frantically sought to grip the smooth stone.

'I can't hold on,' he hissed through lips compressed with effort.

Oh my God I thought. If only we had a rope.

By now his knuckles were white and I looked about desperately trying to find some way of reaching him. The rock between us was featureless. Without warning the boy started to slide feet first and face down towards the precipice. He was gaining speed when he came level with me. The walking-stick was just long enough to hook him between the legs.

'Ouch,' said my catch as he was brought to an abrupt and painful halt. My left foot slipped and for an awful moment I thought we were both going over, but all was well and a few minutes later we stood safely on the far side of the face.

I was worried that we were not all as fit as we should be, mainly because of our confinement in the boats. When I returned to base camp at Debra Marcos the first thing I noted was the altitude. We had risen a considerable height and now were puffing and panting as we strode about the airstrip.

My plans for the second phase of the expedition were already made when I left Sirba. It was only a matter of time for the various group leaders to reorganize and re-equip themselves before we tackled the northern portion of the river.

While we made our preparations the archaeological team had another exciting discovery. On the southern shore of Lake Tana, to the west of Bahardar, they found a small fortress which defended a peninsula from the main land. The moat, ramparts and gate-house were soon revealed from beneath the tangled growth that had gradually crept over them in the passing years. It had undoubtedly been constructed at about the time of the Portuguese arrival in Ethiopia.

The zoologists too had their excitement. Hilary King got himself captured and almost murdered by brigands and, having survived this, made a near-fatal mistake of stalking by night what he thought was a jackal only to discover his quarry was a lion. He was armed at the time with a .22 rifle and two rounds of ammunition!

Meanwhile the White Water team, as they had become known, were anxious to get started. They had quickly formed a small *corps-d'élite* of nine men in three boats and I gave them as much rein as possible, because I knew that they would need all their initiative in the task that lay ahead.

Flying over their route, Alan Calder reported that there were many more crocodiles than we had expected and therefore we decided that Captain John Wilsey should take the one remaining assault boat, and come upstream from the Blue Nile bridge to meet us somewhere near the Bascillio Junction. He could then escort us in his metal boat through the most heavily infested areas.

And so they started. The way ahead of the boats was foaming white water for many miles, but the first day they found fairly easy and exhilarating. However, by that afternoon, they had met the full force of the cataracts and realized that with only paddles they were powerless to do more than keep the boat's bow head on to the waves. At the end of the day, the team were highly elated and, in spite of their experience, full of confidence in the boats. From Bahadar to Tisisiat a road runs parallel with the river and therefore we were able to visit them at night. But from here things changed. The rapids were more powerful than even Roger Chapman had imagined and very soon the team were battered and bruised. To make life more difficult there were parts of the river where it widened out and flowed through hundreds of channels. The problem was to know which one to take. The edge of the river was a swamp with no firm ground for any distance and this meant that setting up camp for the night was a long and a laborious business.

While the team continued downstream, I devoted my own efforts to preparing a new group to meet them at the Portuguese bridge.

They had more than their fair share of thrills and spills and suddenly I discovered some of the White Water team, far from being stimulated, were becoming very frightened. They had divided themselves into hawks and doves – some wanting to go on, others wanting to pull back – and they argued amongst themselves nonsensically. All I could do was to make one or two unpopular decisions and try to help them sort themselves out. Having done this, they then pressed on with much more caution towards the falls at Tisisiat where the boats were roped over.

In the northern gorge the cataracts became even more dangerous and I sent Nigel on ahead to run the re-supply groups, who were now stationed along the lip of the gorge ready to give help when needed. It was soon found that the big problem was that the boats could not stop, and therefore they needed early warning to pull into the bank before a cataract. Then, if there was sufficient water, they would ride it down but if the rocks showed up they had to portage the boat round the side, a laborious and difficult task especially in the bottom of this vertical-sided chasm.

Meanwhile I had flown on to Mota to complete the preparations for the next group. Here I learnt the full story of Gage Williams' capture a few weeks earlier. It seems that the income tax rebels were now in a very ugly mood, and already one of our recce parties had experienced more trouble with them at the Portuguese bridge.

We went down into the bottom of the gorge, in a long, straggling column of mules and men, taking with us fresh boats, engines, stores, weapons, ammunition and everything else we needed for the final part of the journey.

The last few kilometres of the descent was an interesting example of how mules can be used successfully in this terrain. The path was barely wide enough for a man to walk, and yet these sturdy beasts carried on with their heavy loads. Suddenly we came to the edge of a cliff and saw a little path plunging over into the last deep gorge. Going to the edge, I could see beneath me the rickety structure of the old Portuguese bridge. The centre span's masonry arch had been replaced with local timber. As I watched, a small herd of cows were driven across and some masonry tumbled away from the bridge. I was amazed that it had stood so long. There was something eerie about the gorge at this point. It was damp, dark and silent, except for the swish of the water racing under the bridge. We had been forced to come here because it was the only place for many miles where there was a track that led down to the river and a bridge across it, however rickety.

All we had to do now was to set up camp, await the arrival of the White Water team, and then form up the new group to proceed into the most interesting area of all which lay to the south.

Each evening I listened on the radio for the news of the various sections and I knew that the White Water team were only a few miles away. I could tell from their tone that they were very tired and many of them were suffering from infected bites and cuts. I would be relieved to have them back with me as I felt that one or two of them, lacking imagination, were allowing their courage to lead to rashness.

However, at the bridge we had plenty of problems to occupy our time. The tribesmen clearly resented our presence and each day grew more insistent that we should leave. Stores were in short supply and money was running out. I was more than a little worried about the rains, for if they stopped early the river would dry up rapidly, and time was not on our side.

Many of us had persistent sores and the expedition was showing signs of general nervous strain. Whilst working a simple flying ferry across the river I was swept overboard and came close to being drowned.

'Our luck seems to be running out,' muttered one of my friends round the fire that night.

6

A TESTING TIME

IAN's dead,' said Roger. Strangely the words did not surprise me.
'Swept away, nothing we could do,' gasped Chris Bonington.

All around me my group gathered to hear the terrible news. I
took Roger to one side and we sat quietly on a great, black basalt
slab in the shade of the cliffs, while he told me the story. He spoke
in a low voice, his tanned, muscular body glistening with sweat;
he had run most of the way to bring me the news, when he found
he could not get through on the radio.

The story was simple. It was late on the previous day when the
battered and exhausted members of his Team had reached the
Abaya Gorge. Here the mountain torrent carves a thousand-foot-
deep gash in the Gojjam Highlands and cascades down a tortuous
rock-strewn path to join the Blue Nile near the ancient Portuguese
bridge.

The White Water Team had been the nine toughest and most
experienced men I could assemble to tackle the worst cataracts of
the Upper Blue Nile. Their three specially constructed inflatable
boats were aptly named *Faith*, *Hope* and *Charity*.

For several weeks they had struggled against the mighty river and
at last, in the Northern Gorge, they had come upon a stretch of
rapids too fearsome for even these stalwarts. On my specific orders,
they had let the boats go through the raging water unmanned, to
be collected by my own group a short distance downstream, at the
old bridge. The towering, vertical sides of the Gorge had forced
them to march west to find a path that would take them to my
position. Alas, this narrow route had led across the Abaya River.
Now it was a racing brown torrent, swollen by the rains.

Thus in the late afternoon they had started to cross. Sandhurst
instructor and physicist Alastair Newman, known for his nerves of
steel and apparent lack of emotion, had been the first in and, taking

a great leap, had swum with fast, powerful strokes to the far side. He had carried with him a line of climbing rope and, clambering up the rock on the far bank, had called out to send another man across to assist him. It did not look difficult and they were anxious to cross before dark. After all, they knew that I was only a few miles ahead with fresh men, new boats, rations and supplies.

Corporal Ian MacLeod of the Black Watch and Special Air Service volunteered to go next. I had known Ian from years before when I had taught him to swim under water in the sheltered coves of Cyprus. He was a wiry and popular Glaswegian, who was one of our toughest and most resourceful members. As well as being a thoroughly professional soldier, he had a scholarly air about him and was an accomplished linguist. Ian was a man who spoke no ill of any other and a man of whom no-one spoke ill.

He had not been too well, following a narrow escape and bad battering in the rapids near Tisisiat, a week earlier. However, apart from a bandaged knee, he showed no sign of his ailments. It was typical of this rugged Scot that he would always volunteer for the dirtiest job. With a rope lashed securely to his waist, he lowered himself into the rushing water and struck out for the far shore, only some forty feet away.

At first all went well, but suddenly, as he was about to reach the bank, the rope went taut and Ian disappeared beneath the surface. Seconds later he bobbed up. His friends, realizing his plight, gave more slack to enable him to reach the far side, but almost at once it went taut again. The rope was being carried downstream by the speeding current, or perhaps a submerged tree had struck it and was carrying it down. Whatever the cause, Ian was drowning, being held down by the length of rope that he had used as a life-line. On the banks his friends tried to pay out more line so that he could reach the far bank. For a moment it seemed as if he had made it, but then the river washed over him and he disappeared, still fighting for his life.

Roger Chapman was already ripping off his clothes and equipment; someone hurled a semi-inflated lifejacket to Ian, it missed and floated away. Others, realizing that he desperately needed just a few feet more slack line, yelled, 'Cut the rope.' A jack-knife was tossed across the river to Alastair, who stood next to the end of the rope, and he began to saw through the tough fibres. Roger dived in and reached Ian, forcing the drowning corporal above the surface. Still the rope anchored them against the jetting current. Then it parted, and at once the two men spun downstream through the tossing brown waves of the cataract. Roger, fighting with all his massive strength to gain a grip on the bank, could be seen struggling as he was swept along beside the polished, black boulders, his one arm crooked around Ian. The team members dashed along the bank, leaping from rock to rock, trying to keep pace with the men in the water. Now Roger had one arm around a finger of rock and was trying to pull Ian from the water. Still the current pounded them and by now Ian was unconscious. Ahead was a small waterfall, only a ten-foot drop, but with abundant rocks at its base; everyone knew survival chances would not be high if they were swept over this obstacle. Roger's face was red and contorted with effort, Ian's ashen and grey. At this point the vertical sides of the gorge reached almost to the water's edge, and the would-be rescuers were having great difficulty in reaching the men. On the bank where Roger was holding on there was only Alastair and he was moving as fast as humanly possible. On the other side, the rest of the team stood unable to assist.

Suddenly Ian's limp body was seized by some unseen force, and he was dragged relentlessly downward from Roger's desperate grip. In seconds he had gone. Once his head bobbed above the surface, but after that he was never seen again.

Dick Snailham, Chris Bonington, Colin Chapman and Garth Brocksopp summoned every last ounce of energy and raced down the narrowing, boulder-strewn ledge on the far bank, desperately hoping to catch a glimpse of Ian and be able to reach him. It was all in vain. The ledge soon ended and they were forced up the side of the gorge. Ahead they could see the river disappearing into a black abyss, into which the water tumbled with a terrible roar.

Chris Bonington, his voice broken with emotion, said, 'We can't get any further, he's gone.' Gulping in the warm humid air, his companions nodded agreement and all turned back. As darkness fell, they rigged up an aerial ropeway and crossed to spend a damp, cold night amongst the rocks. Their minds and bodies had reached a point of exhaustion, which sleep would barely alleviate. To make matters worse, their location in the deep canyon had prevented radio-contact with the rest of the expedition. Roger knew I was only about five miles ahead, but he also knew that we were virtually captives of the local tribesmen. To the dispirited members of the White Water group, it seemed that the bottom had fallen out of their world. Any hope of continuing the expedition seemed out of the question.

This was the story Roger had told me. Martin, the methodical intelligence officer, had joined us, and I found myself issuing the orders for an emergency helicopter search. I seemed to do it almost mechanically and, after a moment, I realized that my mind was running on two tracks at once. Ian Carruthers, one of the signals officers, was already establishing communications with base and Martin was asking me short, sharp questions, to which I was giving automatic answers, which must have been subconsciously thought out minutes or perhaps days before. The other part of my mind was saying, 'Poor Ian, a search is hopeless.' I remembered my own desperate struggle in the grip of the river only the previous morning. There were the crocodiles to consider and I expected the tribesmen to shoot at any helicopter that was seen hovering over their territory. I finished giving orders and stood deep in thought, looking at the milk-chocolate coloured water, racing under the old bridge.

'Would you like some of my special porridge, surr?' a deep Wiltshire voice asked. It was Corporal Henry, our general factotum/chief clerk/expedition joker. I thanked him, taking the warm mess tin and the unwashed spoon he offered. In his simple way, Henry realized something must be done to bring people back to reality and he had cooked up a great dish of burnt porridge! The other members of the White Water team came in during the morning, exhausted and despondent. The Beaver was overhead by mid-morning and searched the river-bed and the Abaya Gorge. Alan Calder, the chief pilot, spoke to me on the radio and said, regrettably, he could see nothing.

In the early afternoon a small helicopter from the United States Army Air Corps landed on a broad ledge above our camp. This caused a great stir amongst the tribesmen, but we were very glad to see him, and leaving his crewman at our camp, the American sergeant flew me up and down the gorge, travelling as slowly as possible so that I could scan the innocuous-looking water and the banks for any sign of Ian. Once something did catch my eye. It was a football bladder, obviously released from a wrecked Redshank, whose tubes were filled with such bladders as a safety measure. It could only have escaped if the tube had been torn open and this could only have been done by a crocodile. There were several huge log-like reptiles sleeping on the sandbanks.

Turning up the Abaya Gorge, we saw the terrible conditions into which Ian had disappeared and there, still camped on the ledge, were Alistair and Garth. They waved slowly, as if to say, 'It's no good, you're wasting your time.'

We made a final sweep of the immediate area and with fuel running low, turned for Mota. As we rose out of the chasm, the engine gave an unhealthy cough, always a worrying noise in a helicopter. We dropped a few feet and I noticed that the sergeant had started to sweat profusely, although it was quite cool in the aircraft. We were too low for safety, only a hundred feet above the ground, that was now rising rapidly to meet us. The engine coughed again, and the pilot grunted something unintelligible over the intercomm. By his actions I gathered we were going to land. He brought us in on a small patch of grass beside a low bluff, and whilst the rotors continued to thrash around, he sprang out and began to tinker with the motor. Apparently he was soon satisfied with his efforts, for he turned his back to the helicopter, spent a quick penny and climbed in again, grinned at me and gave a thumbs-up sign. We took off and flew up to Mota without incident.

On the bumpy little airfield outside the corrugated iron-roofed town, that nestled amongst the eucalyptus trees, I saw a twin-engined Otter aeroplane. This was also from the US Army Air Corps and had carried the fuel for the helicopter up from Addis and thus enabled the search to be carried out. I thanked the crew for its rapid response to our call, but could give it no good news. Sergeant Tex Matthews was our radio operator at Mota. He was a close friend of Ian and he took the sad news that I broke to him very much to heart. Matthews pleaded to be allowed to go down to the river to search, but it was important to us that he remained on top of the plateau to relay radio messages back to base, and therefore I had to refuse his request.

Time was precious if I wanted another flight before dark, so as soon as the helicopter was refuelled, we flew down to the gorge again, dropping over the lip of the plateau as if it were the edge of a coral reef, into the abyss beneath. More crocodiles were in evidence, but most alarming was the apparent increase in the number of tribesmen gathering about our camp at the bridge. All were well armed and waved their rifles excitedly. Was this the vanguard of the force of three thousand rebels that local chiefs had assured us would attack unless we moved away quickly? I had dismissed this as gross exaggeration, and simply thought it to be a threat to get us to leave their area. I had been sure that they wanted to be rid of the responsibility for us, because whilst we remained in their territory, by tradition we were in their charge. Now I was not so sure, and I began to wonder how long forty of us with our sporting rifles, shot guns and pistols could hold out in the exposed bed of the gorge against an attack by so many rebels. Nigel Sale and his party, with one injured man, were still out in the Abaya region, making their way to the bridge.

The river was running too high for comfort, and I did not want to sail on until it had dropped another two feet. We only had enough boats to take ten men and their equipment. Many of the survivors of the White Water group were injured and sick, and quite unfit to proceed by river. Ahead of us lay the worst crocodile-infested stretch yet, and I wanted John Wilsey to reach the Bascillio Junction with his relief force before I set out to study the one part of the Blue Nile which was unmapped, unexplored and unknown. It would be a difficult enough stretch of water without interference from the rebels and, as we had our last look for Ian, I felt I was sitting on a gunpowder-keg with the fuse burning shorter each second.

By the time we landed on the ledge above the camp, my plan was made. Get the walking wounded, sick and other persons up to Mota as quickly as possible. Gavin Pike, a tough young cavalry captain, who had been with me on two previous trips in Ethiopia, would take these men out. Nine of our fittest would sail on under me to survey the last stretch and meet John at the rendezvous, if he ever got there. I would tell Nigel by radio to make for Mota direct and not come to our camp. All I needed was about four hours to organize this. As I clambered out on to the short grass, I noticed two young warriors with their rifles unslung and pointing vaguely in my direction.

Trying to appear quite unconcerned, I thanked the sergeant pilot for his help and said just loud enough for him to hear, 'I think we've got trouble here, I'll get your crewman up from the camp, but keep your engine running.'

A goat track, a foot or so wide, led down the cliff face to the camp. One of the warriors followed me down.

Mesfin, our Ethiopian Government liaison officer, came to me and said quickly, 'I am afraid that the chiefs say we are all their prisoners and must not move. I cannot do anything more with them.' In camp everyone looked worried and watched with drawn faces. The tribesmen were clearly in a truculent mood.

When in doubt, confuse the enemy! 'Good,' I said. 'Thank you, Mesfin, please tell the chief I have been to Mota and I bear important news for all the tribe, but first I must prepare some notes, then I will come and tell them all about it.' Hoping the interpretation of this white lie, and the ensuing questions, would keep the warriors busy for a few minutes, I seized the confused American crewman.

'You've got problems, Captain,' he said.

'Yes, but with luck you can get out as soon as I start speaking to the tribesmen. Go to the chief of police at Mota and get him to come here as fast as possible and sort out these old gentlemen and their people. You are our only hope, so do all you can. Also, please tell my headquarters what is happening.'

With that, I turned and replacing my beret with my topee, I strolled over to the bridge, and whilst Mesfin interpreted, gave a long harangue about Ian's death, the search, our scientific work, the medical aid I had brought from Mota for the treatment of all ills and how grateful we were to the tribesmen for looking after us. I threw in the names of Haile Selassie, Churchill and Wingate occasionally for good measure and I was still speaking when the helicopter lifted off the ledge and soared back towards Mota. My audience barely seemed to notice; it was not part of their problem.

To endorse the speech, I announced that there would be a sick parade in ten minutes for the tribesmen. Then, grabbing Ian MacLeod's medical kit, I told Corporal Henry to gather together all the spare pills and potions he could find. Together we set up a surgery on the bridge.

The queue of patients stretched fifty yards. They jostled for places and minor punch-ups took place between the warriors to get to the head of the queue. Our meagre medical resources were totally inadequate for anything more than token treatment. Our genuine medical officer was himself sick at base and Ian, who had been our best medical orderly, was dead. Treating the tropical sores and eye disease as best we could, we gave out aspirins for tummy aches and Corporal Henry's remedy for the numerous malingerers was a Horlicks tablet sellotaped to the body over the allegedly painful area. In the case of a particularly unpleasant brave, Henry administered two dozen cascara tablets with a drink of water. He then told the young warrior to run home as fast as possible, lie down and await results! We never saw him again!

As night fell we held a simple memorial service for Ian. We had all lost a good friend. I then gave out the orders for the next day. Gavin would take out the overland column. Nigel had already been diverted. I would lead the new 'P' group, as it was to be called, down river, intending to meet John Wilsey eventually. We would take most of the guns and ammunition from the others. I had a feeling our need might be greater. However, everything depended on the tribesmen letting us go. But I had sent out word to the muleteers of Mota to bring their beasts to the bridge in the morning of the following day.

At darkness the chiefs and most of their followers retired to the top of the gorge, and fortunately there was so much preparation to carry out that our minds were fully occupied until sleep took over.

Once during the night our sentries woke me; a noise had been heard twice on the track above the camp, but the necklace of stone-filled tin cans strung across the path had not rattled. Probably a hyena.

The dawn was cold and damp and, with it, the tribesmen returned. Hardly had the sun reached into the gorge when we heard the sound of a helicopter. The police chief of Mota, Captain Mulena Alamu, strode into our camp, smartly dressed in a freshly laundered uniform, peaked cap, shiny boots, black Sam Browne and bearing a .300 carbine and a revolver. He walked amongst the chiefs, smiling and greeting them; a diminutive figure, confident and authoritative, just like his emperor. He crossed the bridge, spoke with the Begemir chiefs, who had remained on their own side. Then he made copious notes in a large official book. In no time, this efficient law officer had sorted out the problem with commendable tact and diplomacy. I had spoken to him through Mesfin and, as he left, I followed him up the cliff path to the waiting helicopter.

Glancing around to make sure he could not be overheard, he said to me in perfect English, 'It is all right for you to continue, but keep your guns handy and a good watch at night.'

'Where did you learn English?' I said in genuine surprise.

'England,' he hissed, and climbing into the helicopter shouted, 'Tanastalin,' and was gone.

At the bridge we remained under guard. However, following the visit of the gallant captain, we were treated with a new respect and there was no more talk of our leaving or, for that matter remaining, as prisoners.

Miraculously, the mules had arrived on time and the overland party was soon shouting farewell as it started up the steep ascent to the plateau. It did not have an easy journey; ambush parties greeted it throughout the route and, at each stop, there was much argument and discussion before it was allowed to pass. The entire province was in a state of turmoil and the rebels were said to be marching on Mota.

Back on the river, we prepared to sail next day. The Beaver made an air-drop of supplies at 15.15 hours, but many of the items that were free-dropped fell on to rocks and were badly damaged. With foresight, the packers at base camp had placed the whisky inside Bonington's new socks. So at least we were able to wring out the remains of a few precious drops. As Alan circled above, he told me of more tribesmen massing in the mountains around the gorge and said the Beaver had been shot at. We really were in a boiling cauldron, and I was worried about our overland party ever reaching Mota.

However, my first problem was to overcome the fears and anxieties of the team. They had all taken quite a pounding and some seemed apprehensive about the conditions ahead. Reconnaissance by air does not always give a true picture of river conditions, and we had been lulled into a false sense of confidence several times. I knew we could easily manage the conditions ahead, but the team needed a lot of persuading. They had not seen the Army recce boats in rough conditions and, of the six sent from the United Kingdom, only two had been found fit for use. Nevertheless, I had no doubt that these craft would manage the conditions I had seen during my air reconnaissance.

It was 21 September. The temperature at 08.00 hours was seventy-four degrees Fahrenheit and, during the night, we had suffered a moderately heavy rainstorm. We awoke cold and wet on our rocky beds. Our guards were still with us, having spent an equally wretched night wrapped in their voluminous shammas. As I dipped the razor into a mess tin of warm water, a white-and-black fish-eagle pitched its yodelling call into the canyon of the Blue Nile. The river simply hissed and bubbled as it swept on its way. Our sentries, sensing our imminent departure, shuffled nearer hoping for gifts of surplus food or equipment.

Now the team was packing up and was soon ready to move. Joe Ruston and I were to scout ahead in the recce boat *Semper* and warn the two engineless Redshanks of forthcoming hazards. John Fletcher, our outboard-engine expert was helming the second recce boat *Ubique* and with him was our rugged and experienced crocodile expert, zoologist Colin Chapman. *Ubique* would bring up the tail of the little fleet.

The recce boats were both equipped with nine and a half horse-power outboard-motors, which could hold against the current and which enabled them to manœuvre more easily than the Red-shanks. Even so, the recce boats were not constructed as strongly as the Avon craft. If anything went wrong, the recce boats would act as rescue craft; if we were attacked by crocodiles, they had the heavier weapons necessary for defence. Colin was certain that the crocodiles would not attack, but I remembered he had said there were none north of Tisisiat, and one had strolled into our camp above the falls!

Roger was the White Water expert, so I asked him to brief us all on the tactics. He did this with his usual attention to detail, and at 10.30 hours we cast off. The river gave us an exciting ride and, at times, I judged it prudent to bring the fleet into the bank, and rope past a particularly difficult cataract. We shot through most rapids in grand style! Hitting big waves, we were drenched to the skin, but the old recce boats did remarkably well and we soon became very confident in them. Our helmsmen were experts at their job. From the banks, antelope stared at us and birds rose in dismay as we flashed by. The crocodiles were well hidden, for we saw none during the first part of the journey. This I put down to the engine noise driving them to shelter in the murky depths.

High on the hills, we saw white-robed people and heard their shrill cries, as they announced us from mountain-top to mountain-top. At water level the black basalt was so polished that it looked like marble. The river varied from thirty to fifty yards wide and, in parts, was moving as fast as nine knots.

The Red-shanks paddled on steadily, and it quickly became apparent how useful the powered recce boats were in escorting, guiding and towing the paddled craft. In the early part of the day, we negotiated twelve rough patches and only occasionally had to resort to our roping technique.

We were able to inspect a place where Cheesman[1] believed the river had changed course. There was every sign that this happened, but as the water level was sixty feet below the old bed, it must have happened long ago. In fact, Cheesman's original map was correct, but the copies and reproductions showed the river in the earlier course to the north of the great Gumar feature.

As we journeyed on into the most fantastic vertical-sided gorges, the water was moving like a stream of liquid brown mud, hissing between the cliffs. These sheer walls which rose from the water for

1. Major R. E. Cheesman, *Lake Tana and the Blue Nile* (Frank Cass, 1968).

some hundred to two hundred feet appeared to be limestone capped with lava. Towards late afternoon we reached some vertical pillars of rock, standing in mid-river. This gave us an exact position, as I recognised them from the air reconnaissance.

Suddenly I caught sight of a roughly-built dwelling, perched high on the cliff on the Gojjam bank. I had not expected to find any sign of habitation down here and was determined to inspect it. Waving our Ethiopian flag, I signalled the other boats to pull in to the shore. Stumbling along the rock-strewn beach, we tried to find a route up, but while we were doing so, a figure appeared on the cliff top. I greeted him, but he regarded us in silence. Then, without warning, he became agitated and started shouting and waving us away. This I thought unusual as Ethiopians are most punctilious about returning greetings. However, it could be that the lone man lived in the dwelling and thought us to be raiders, although I doubt if many bands of robbers would bother to fly the Imperial Ethiopian flag! As we sailed on in our rock-trench, our voices echoed unnaturally and for some way we were completely enclosed in the massive slot.

A sharp bark to our left drew our attention to a strange sight. Scampering amongst the rocks was a party of hideous grey-coated old men. Or that was what it looked like. 'Hamadryad baboons,' called out Colin. The boats slowed, cameras clicked, the baboons screamed with rage and one threw a small stone, then we were past them.

I had not seen these creatures before and was still making notes about them when Joe said, 'Look at those caves, surely they are man-made?'

To our right were two large openings, situated in the rock face about thirty feet above the water level. At the same time, a small cove containing a stream and some low trees appeared on the left. According to my navigation it was probably the Tammi River.

'Pull in to the beach!' I yelled. The caves were too interesting to miss and it was a good time to stop anyway.

The camp site was the most pleasant we had found so far. The stream had cut a narrow gorge, which ran back some fifty yards behind the beach. The little river formed a beautiful waterfall as it entered the gorge, spurting out from the terrace above. The water was clear and slightly warm. Lichen, moss and ferns grew out from the cliff in profusion. Beneath the trees was a plentiful supply of firewood and a clear area in which to erect our bashas.

Across the Nile the mouths of the two large caves gaped at us, one semicircular and the other triangular. The entrances were partly blocked by a wall of rough stones that certainly looked man-made. There was no evidence of any inhabitants and, as I studied them from the camp in the dusk, I wondered how we could gain access. There was an overhang immediately above the caves and the only possibility seemed to be to climb up from the river-bed. It was obviously a job for our rock-climbers and it was fortuitous that Chris Bonington was here.

While supper was cooking, Garth and David, our military zoologists, went on a lizard hunt. John Fletcher repaired the transom on his boat, which had been damaged during the day. Chris and Roger discussed a plan for getting into the caves on the morrow. Richard Snailham filled several more pages of his note-book. Joe was working on the engines. Alistair, Colin and I cooked up a mess of sardines and rice.

It got dark quickly, but in spite of our exertions, spirits were too high to sleep and we talked for several hours. It had been a good day. After weeks of painfully slow progress, we had covered seventeen miles in five hours and conquered the worst of the rapids below the Portuguese bridge. From now on we should have a relatively easy voyage, although there might be the odd sporting stretch of water to keep us on our toes and, of course, there were always the crocodiles!

Our camp seemed safe from interference as it would be almost impossible to approach it undetected, but there was the usual risk of a crocodile coming up from the river and chewing a boat. With luck we had left the political problem at the bridge well behind us.

I did guard from 22.00 hours until midnight, spending the time writing up my log by the light of a guttering candle. The night was quiet, warm and dry.

My concern now was the crocodiles that I knew lay ahead. On my air reconnaissance I had seen some really huge monsters and certainly many more than we had seen elsewhere on the river. My original plan had gone wrong at this stage, for I had assumed from scientific advice that the crocodiles would move up the tributaries or go downstream when the rains came and turned the upper reaches of the river into foaming cataracts. But they were still here. Earlier I had despatched John Wilsey with his small team and an assault boat to come upstream to meet us from Shafartak. However, I understood that this plan was not working too well and I had not made direct contact with John for several days, probably due to a failure of his radio. But main base had managed to pick him up and told me that two of his forty horsepower engines had blown up under the terrific strain of forcing the rapids. A third engine dropped from the Beaver had disappeared into the Nile when the parachute failed to open. Unfortunately, this load also contained the team's rations and they must now be living partly off the land. Our last spare engine was on its way to them by helicopter. I knew John would not give up and could easily imagine him straining every muscle to get his boat to the Bascillio/Nile junction. With him was our smart Ethiopian Naval liaison officer, 'Tilly' Mekonnen, and one of the best boatmen of the expedition, Warrant Officer Ticky Wright, R.E. It was comforting to know that our relief force was composed of such men.

Base also told me that John had reported an alarming increase in the numbers of crocodiles per mile, and he strongly advised that we should not proceed past the junction without the aluminium assault boat as an escort. Until we met John, I had a simple plan of defence against the crocodiles. First we would try to avoid them, remembering the bite one had taken at an assault boat the previous month. Each boat was to carry a sandbag full of stones for use as a deterrent. Finally, if all else failed, we would open fire and thrash the water with our paddles. Colin, who had been working on crocodile surveys in Ethiopia for several years, did not think they would attack. Nevertheless I would still have the heavy-calibre rifle ready just in case.

I reckoned I needed three days to explore this fascinating area and, with luck, John should have reached the Bascillio by then.

Healthwise we were not in bad shape. Most people's cuts and lacerations were healing or, at least, the infection was not spreading. Antibiotics were in very short supply and, acting as the medic, I found we only had a few Tetracyclin tablets left. My own injuries were giving little trouble; the knee only hurt occasionally and I could dispense with the walking-stick. My torn hands were of more concern. Nylon rope had cut through to the bone during my earlier rescue from the river and some infection had set in. I could feel the warning signs of pains in my elbow-joints and armpits, but with constant cleansing and dressing, I hoped to keep going for another week.

Heavy rain fell while I was asleep. At dawn the baboons' barking chorus roused us from our beds. We eagerly ate the breakfast prepared by the last sentry and then started to explore the caves. Joe lightened *Semper*'s load to the minimum and then, with his engine racing against the current, he took Chris over the river. Festooned with rope and climbing equipment, the mountaineer stood up in the rocking boat. Joe brought his craft with throttle wide open against the cliff and then Chris leapt, found a hand- and toe-hold and started climbing at once. In a minute or so he was in the cave and lowered the rope, which Roger, who came across next, helped to secure as a fixed line. Richard was the last to go and soon all three climbers were inside the caves.

'The place is full of pottery and basket-work,' yelled Chris. Joe ferried the archaeological finds back to the camp, while Roger shot a small bat for the zoologists. It appeared that we had discovered some ancient refuge which had not been used for many centuries. The floor was deep in bat dung which gave off a nauseous smell, and the remains of an old leather rope provided a clue to how the former inhabitants had got in. Perhaps in the dry season there was a ledge beneath the caves.

Just before midday, the cave party returned and we spread out their discoveries for photographing. As we gazed at the potsherds, old bones, fire carbon and old leather rope, I heard a distant whooping cry. This was the usual way that one Amhara shepherd signals to the next, but it was repeated and sounded excited. I could not read the strange language, but I had heard our guide use it often enough to realize that the tone had much to do with the message.

'I think we will have a quick lunch and press on,' I said.

'What, and leave the caves only half-explored?' said several of the team with disappointment in their voices.

'Yes,' I said crossly, 'just grab a Mars bar and let's pack up and go.'

I had intended to continue the exploration in the afternoon. Quite why I suddenly changed my plan, I shall never know. The tone of the shepherd's cry would not have been sufficient by itself. Something made me uneasy. I have felt this once or twice before when danger threatened and there is no doubt that when you are living in the wilds, your wits become much sharper. But the matter was not all that urgent, and I knew it would take us at least thirty minutes to pack up and load the boats. However, I simply felt we must move.

I am not a particularly good photographer and rarely have time to use my camera anyway, but I was so taken by the beauty of the waterfall behind the camp that I decided to take a quick snapshot before we left. In the little canyon it was cool and pleasant and I spent a few moments deciding which would be the best angle for a photograph.

The sharp crack of the rifle and the shower of chippings from the rock face made me duck instinctively. I looked up. There, at the top of the bluff, a hunter stood clutching his rifle and watching me.

'Look out, be careful. You nearly hit me,' I shouted in anger and, ludicrously, also in English. The man opened the bolt of his rifle to reload and I suddenly realized that he was trying to hit me! My right hand flew down to my holster, but I had taken off my gun-belt a few moments before when going to commune with nature. Now it was lying on my pack in the camp.

My feet hardly touched the ground as I raced back down the gorge, leapt the stream-bed and rushed into the camp.

'Blashers running?' said the look on the faces of my friends, but before they could speak, I shouted, 'Hurry, we must get out quickly, just grab everything and get into the boats.'

Now we moved fast and I had just loaded my pack on to *Semper*, when a horn sounded several short, strident notes. A bullet smacked into the shingle a foot away and I looked up to see the cliff top on the far side of the river alive with some thirty armed tribesmen. They were only sixty yards away!

A wild fuselage of shots followed, ricochets whined off the rocks and spurts of water sprung up from the river. Our attackers gave blood-curdling war-whoops and angry shouts. Up on high ground beyond the cliff-top, I could see long lines of white-robed tribesmen coming to join their friends. Obviously the lone rifleman had given the game away too soon, perhaps my appearance with the camera had surprised him, but what on earth had prompted the attack? This was not the moment for analysis. We all ran for cover under the trees.

Army training in dealing with hostile civilian crowds brought to mind the words: minimum force. I seized the loud-hailer and dashed out on to the beach.

One man seemed to be the leader and addressing him, I boomed out, 'Tanastalin, tanastalin, we come in peace and are your friends.'

To my relief, the firing ceased and Geronimo, as he was instantly nicknamed, bowed low in the customary Ethiopian manner. I guessed that they had never heard a loud-hailer before and I hoped to gain time by keeping him talking. After all, they could not reach us. Having completed his bows, the man deliberately raised his rifle and fired at me from the waist. The bullet came uncomfortably close, others and also some sling-shot followed.

In another attempt at appeasement, I again told Geronimo in my

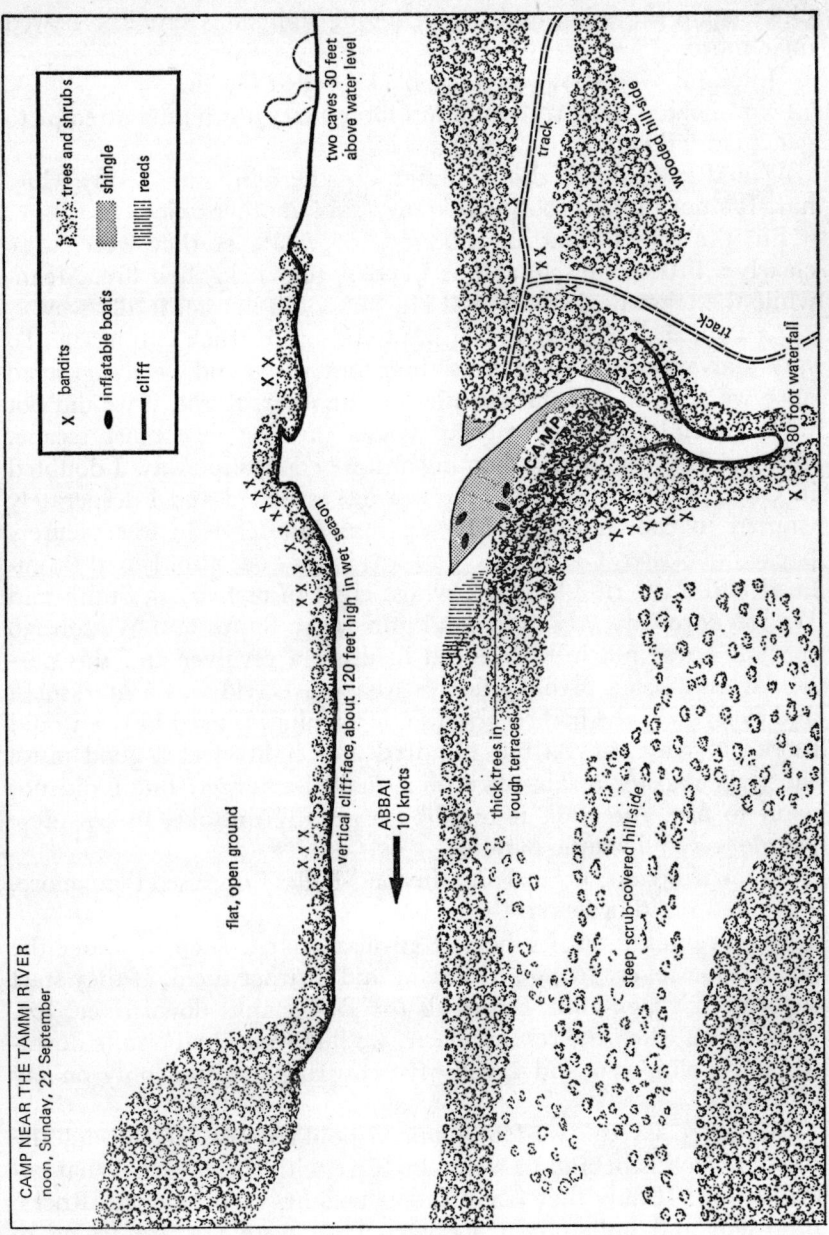

CAMP NEAR THE TAMMI RIVER
noon, Sunday, 22 September

x bandits
● inflatable boats
― cliff

trees and shrubs
shingle
reeds

two caves 30 feet
above water level

flat, open ground

vertical cliff-face, about 120 feet high in wet season

ABBAI
10 knots

thick trees in
rough terraces

CAMP

steep scrub-covered hill-side

wooded hill-side

track

track

80 foot waterfall

First bandit attack

broken Amharic that we came in peace and offered him a Mars bar!
Once again the firing and stone-slinging stopped. Geronimo bowed
once more.

'John, for God's sake let's fire back,' yelled Garth.

'No,' I said, 'must try minimum force first; just let me attempt to
get them talking.'

'You'll get yourself shot standing out there in your bloody white
hat. It's not bullet-proof, you know,' said another voice.

But the rebels, bandits, tribesmen or whatever they were, were
clearly a little confused, and as I spoke, they held their fire. Meanwhile the team packed up vital kit, but could not get it all away.

As I spoke I tried to switch my mind on to track two again. To
stay and argue would give us time, but we would be slaughtered
once we tried to run the gauntlet on the river. Right, if we did not
want to end up with squeaky voices (at best) we must escape.
Perhaps they would stop shooting and we could slip away. I doubted
it. Once you've opened fire, the war has escalated and I desperately
wanted to cool it down. My 9.3 mm Mauser rifle was securely
packed in *Semper*. Garth's shotgun was in his boat also. David Bromhead had a .22 rifle at hand, whilst eight of us had .45 Smith and
Wesson revolvers. My own hand gun was a Smith and Wesson .38
special. I was not inexperienced in using a revolver and this particular gun was a highly effective weapon. David was a marksman
and everybody else had received some training. If need be, we would
shoot our way out. At one hundred and eighty feet a good pistol
shot will register a fair score on a man-size target. But I did not
want to fire. After all, it must be a ghastly mistake, unless these
people were all simple bandits.

As the tribesmen argued and the loud-hailer impressed them more,
I shouted rapid orders to the team.

'We are going out by boat, Red-shanks first, keep in under the
far cliff for cover. Joe, go upstream and distract them. If they start
shooting, zigzag. John, escort all the Red-shanks down river. Joe,
pick me up when the rest are clear, we'll regroup half a mile downstream. Colin, you and I will give covering fire, but only on my
orders.'

Suddenly, several two-foot diameter boulders crashed through the
trees. The cliffs behind us were also alive with the enemy. What co-
ordination! If only they could shoot straight, we'd be dead. Rocks,
sling-shot and bullets rained down. They were not just trying to
frighten us and we were certainly surrounded. Already the Bejimir

tribesmen behind us were beginning to descend into the gorge. If we wanted to avoid a hand-to-hand fight, we must leave now.

'Listen,' I yelled, using the loud-hailer to overcome the noise of of the gun fire. 'Get ready.'

'We'll all be killed,' shouted Chris. 'We can't go out there.'

'Call for an air-strike, it's suicide,' were the remarks that I heard coming from the assembled men.

'I'm bloody well giving orders here,' I said. 'Shut up and do as you're told.' For many it was a baptism of fire and for all of us it was quite frightening.

The fire was now very heavy and it seemed incredible that the boats lying in the open had not been hit.

'Right, to the boats,' I cried.

Joe was out first. He showed no regard for his own safety and as the storm of bullets and stone raged about him, he calmly pushed his recce boat into deep water. Then, shouting and shaking his fist, he sped upstream to draw the enemy fire. I watched him for a second and thought, 'In the best traditions of Nelson, I only hope he survives.'

John Fletcher and Colin Chapman were in *Ubique* and ready to escort the Red-shanks on their way downstream. One Red-shank was launched and being paddled furiously for the relative safety of the far cliff. The surface of the water was dancing with plumes of spray from the missiles. At any one time, six or seven stones could be seen in the air and many struck the boats. It will be a miracle if we can come through this, I thought.

The second Red-shank was caught up in some reeds by the beach, and the crew was struggling to get it into the main stream. I was alone on the beach. Around me lay the scattered debris of our camp. My .38 special was in my hand and I looked up to the Bejimir side. As I did so, a bullet hit the beach between my legs. The firer stood on a rock slab twenty-five yards away in the Tammi gorge. I raised my revolver and fired whilst he was re-loading.

Slightly to my surprise, he doubled up, dropped his rifle and ran up the cliff path. I think I probably hit the butt of his weapon and this had saved his life. Behind the slab another man appeared brandishing a curved sword, but as he had no gun, I turned my attention to a group of men higher up, who carried long-barrelled rifles of an early vintage. One shot drove them to cover and hearing a clang of stone striking metal, I spun round to see a jerry-can of fuel standing on the shingle. Nearby lay the precious artefacts collected so laboriously from the caves. Joe was planing downstream at top speed, weaving in and out of a pattern of missiles and yelling at me. His revolver was clutched at the ready.

'Get aboard,' he shouted.

I seized the can of petrol and regretfully left the artefacts. Running flat out across the beach, I was up to my knees in the swirling water before *Semper* reached me. Half falling over the side, I collapsed into the boat. At once Joe accelerated across the river. The sky above me was full of rocks and sling-shot. A five-pound lump of stone struck the boat's inflatable tube and bounced off with a loud *pong*. Forty yards ahead I could see the Red-shank now coming under aimed fire. John Fletcher was pushing them downstream.

'Fire,' I cried and from *Ubique* came the roar of Colin's .45. I swivelled round and faced the Gojjam bank. Geronimo was there, standing in full view atop a buttress or rock; I saw his rifle kick. The bullet sent a shower of water over me and missed the boat by inches. Joe's tense face was watching ahead.

'Chris has been hit,' he said in a matter of fact way.

'Oh God, what a mess,' I thought.

Geronimo was trying another shot as I took aim at him. My bullet struck the rock six feet beneath him. His went on towards the Red-shanks. In the time it takes to squeeze the trigger, I fired again, the strike was three feet low. My last shot came almost at once. Geronimo reeled backwards and with his arms outstretched as if seeking support, he fell out of sight. I turned to face his followers, but they were now hiding behind the rocks. The odd long-range shot whistled after us and splashed into the river, but now we were beyond pistol range. During the battle Joe had calmly taken a Red-shank under tow, blood was running from a stone-wound in Chris's back and trickling down the side of the boat, but he was not badly hurt and already his camera was in his hand.

'Look left,' he cried.

Joe and I spun round to face the next enemy, click went Chris's camera. I suppose it may have looked authentic! It was 12.10 hours. The whole incident had taken only ten minutes.

For several miles we towed the Red-shanks down river. The gorge had given way to sloping hillsides, plantations of maize and a few tukuls. Great square blocks of basalt lay like islands in midstream. When I judged we had gone a safe distance, we halted to reorganize.

As I dressed Chris's wound, Joe set up the radio. Quickly I scribbled a message for base. 'Sitrep. Attack on camp by forty natives from both banks with rifles, rocks and slings. No serious casualties to us. Fire was returned in self-defence. No enemy casualties. Bonington minor casualty. Do not cause flap over this. Tell base all O K, but much kit lost. Do not release to press. Sunray.'

I hoped that this statement would keep the whole matter at a very low key and that was why I had not mentioned Geronimo, or any other enemy casualties that, in fact, I believed had occurred. The radio we were using was a Racal squadcall high frequency set fitted with a twelve-foot rod aerial. Such aerials are only designed for short distances. To our utter astonishment base, almost one hundred miles away, answered our first call, although Mount Chokai (13,000 feet) stood between us.

We cruised on throughout the afternoon. Whoops and shouts followed us down the banks. 'Here come the tax collectors,' they probably said. Eventually all was silent, but I knew that dozens of unseen eyes were watching us and sitting with the Mauser in my lap, I scanned the hills through binoculars.

Crocodiles were beginning to appear here and there on the banks, but they made no aggressive movement. I estimated we had covered twenty-five miles since the ambush at noon. Now I felt that we had probably out-stripped any pursuit. Darkness usually fell at around 18.30 hours, so it was as well to stop an hour or so before this. At 17.00 hours we were still some three miles north of the junction, when I saw another canyon ahead. The walls were much wider apart than in previous cases and I recognized a pinnacle of basalt leaning outwards from the Gojjam cliff in the far distance. I had noted this on my air reconnaissance and remembered that it marked a short stretch of small rapids and also the start of a longer stretch of vertical cliffs. If we got into any difficulties in those rapids, darkness would probably catch us in the gorge. We drifted on downstream and came upon a long, flat, shingle island. A patch of trees and scrub grew in the centre. There were a few driftwood logs that could be used for defences, firewood looked plentiful and no crocs could be seen. The current was quite fast and even the narrow channel on the right contained deep water. The river-banks around the island were largely devoid of cover and the nearest high ground was at least half a mile back. It seemed a reasonable defensive position and probably the best we should find for miles. It will take a determined bunch to attack us here, I thought.

We established camp under the trees in the centre of the island, pulling the boats up on a shingle spot on the east shore. In order to get the radio equipment near to the camp, Joe sailed *Semper* into the narrow channel on the Gojjam side and moored her to a tree.

We were sipping tea when we saw three boys swimming diagonally across the river from the Bejimir side. Any bitter feelings we had felt after the ambush had abated and we waved a friendly greeting to the newcomers, who treated crocodiles and the swift current with such contempt. They came out of the water and stood at the edge of the island. They were stark naked except for a small silver Coptic cross on a string around their necks. These people had probably known Christianity when our ancestors were painted blue, but unlike most natives we met, they seemed shy and hesitant and simply stared at us. Eventually our gestures and offers of small gifts tempted them to come into the camp and, once there, they lost all shyness. I doubt if they were older than fourteen. They spoke a dialect that none of us understood and even Colin, whose Amharinya was better than most, could not get through to them. They seemed quite amicable and we presented them with aspirins, plastic bags and Mars bars. Like all Ethiopian young men, they displayed considerable curiosity in our weapons and, when they swam home a few minutes later, I felt rather suspicious about this interest. Was it the normal respect for guns, which are a great status symbol in this wild land, or was there more to it? I was still pondering when Joe called me for supper. We had been forced to abandon some of our rations at the Tammi, but, although on a reduced scale, the meal was adequate.

As it grew dark, I held the usual daily briefing and outlined the plan for our defence and possible withdrawal, should we be attacked that night. We arranged to have two sentries on duty at all times and built a rough zoriba or fence around the camp. Colin and I were carrying ministar flare-launchers which we would keep loaded and close at hand. Each man was given his responsibilities and ammunition was reallocated.

'It's Sunday and after orders we will have our usual service,' I said. Richard selected a hymn from the Army prayer book, and just then it began to rain. The congregation, made up of all ten members of the group, huddled under my basha and we sang, 'Now thank we all our God, with Hearts and Hands and Voices . . .' The words seemed appropriate. After a couple of simple prayers, we ended with the blessing.

The night was very black and, apart from the patter of the rain and hiss and gurgle of the river, all was silent. I wrote up the log, penned half a letter to Judith and then lay fully dressed on my sleeping-bag. I undid the laces but kept my boots on. Positioning my torch nearby, I checked my revolver and laid it beneath the topee which served as a pillow. I then cleaned and oiled the big Mauser and loaded the magazine before placing it in its plastic tube. This I pushed inside the sleeping-bag. The final act was to dress my suppurating fingers and swallow a paludrine anti-malaria tablet. In the battle at the Tammi I had lost my walking-stick, but my knee was hardly giving any trouble now. It was just after 22.00 hours when I blew out the candle and sank into a deep sleep and, as my friends told me, snored like a pig!

In the distance I heard yells and shots. A faraway voice shouted 'Stand to, stand to,' but it was all a dream. Or so it seemed for a long time, which in fact could not have exceeded three seconds.

As I woke my hands groped for the ministar launcher; the shots and war-whoops were very close. Somewhere a hunting horn was sounding short blasts. Tearing my shirt-pocket open, I felt the pen-sized device and rolling out of the basha, I thrust it upward and fired. The red flare curved through the sky lighting up the island and the river. The shingle beach was alive with shiny black bodies advancing on the camp. One figure, carrying a short spear, was only fifteen yards from the fence. My hand was searching for my gun when I saw David, the second sentry, crouched by a tree. He brought up his ·45 and its flash and roar came together. In the last light of the dying flare, I saw the leading attacker totter backwards. Another flare rose into the sky almost at once, probably fired by Colin, and in its light I buckled on my belt and drew my revolver. We were all awake now, and as I put up a second ministar a volley crashed out from the camp.

'They're coming through the trees!' I heard someone shout.

'For heaven's sake, guard the boats,' yelled Chris.

My own arc of responsibility was the trees and the narrow channel. I strained my ears to detect any sound from this direction, but in the pitch black between flares, I could hear nothing definite. Suddenly a blundering figure came rushing through the scrub.

I raised my gun and was about to shoot John Fletcher, when I heard him say, 'Joe's down by *Semper*.'

It was not until this moment that I realized that the heaviest fire was coming from the river-bank on the Gojjam side. The bandits' covering party had been in position there all the time and was now trying to pick us off in the dark. I let go another flare, horizontally this time, at the next rifle flash and, to my delight, saw half a dozen

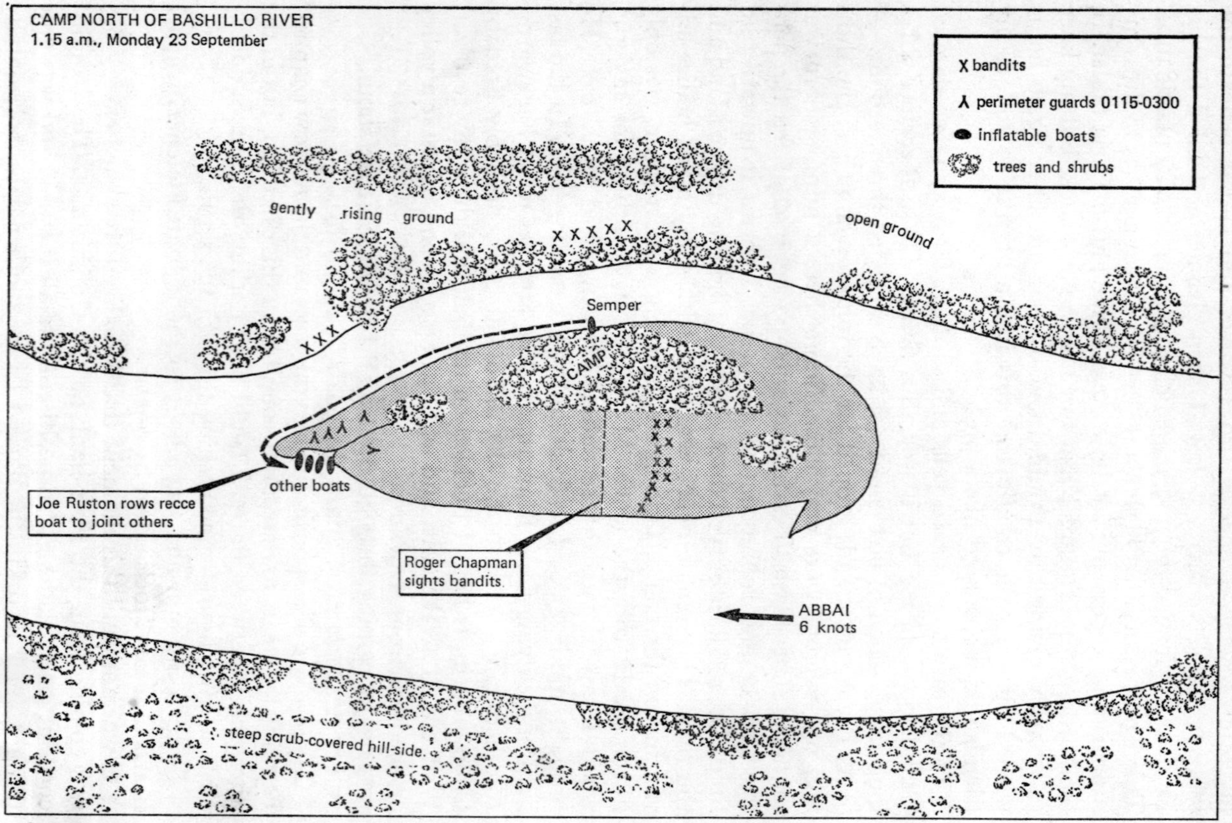

CAMP NORTH OF BASHILLO RIVER
1.15 a.m., Monday 23 September

X bandits
Y perimeter guards 0115-0300
● inflatable boats
trees and shrubs

open ground

gently rising ground

Semper

other boats

Roger Chapman sights bandits

Joe Ruston rows recce boat to joint others

ABBAI
6 knots

steep scrub-covered hill-side

Second bandit attack

white-robed figures scampering away in panic. Meanwhile the raiders were still on the north end of the island and trying to work their way through the scrub.

'I'm firing into the bushes,' I yelled, not wishing to risk the chance of an accident with one of our own men.

There was no reply and I advanced a few yards and waited. Low voices muttered about twenty yards ahead. More firing and whoops on my right showed that Roger and his party were busy by the boats. Then I saw a definite movement a few yards ahead; one or probably two men, I thought. Someone was calling out in the local tongue on the bank. The figures showed again and I blasted two quick shots, deliberately aiming low in the scrub. With much noise of breaking undergrowth and grunts, the bandits fled to the north.

'Beach is clear,' came the cry from the right.

'Garth,' I shouted.

'Yeah,' came back the faint Australian accent.

'Take David and recce forward up the island, see if there are any of them still here. We'll switch our fire to the covering party.'

Alastair Newman had joined me and, together with ministar and revolver, we took on the bandits on the mainland. The tactics were simply to watch for a gun flash, put up a flare in its direction and get off a couple of quick shots whilst the target was illuminated. Joe Ruston was already dismantling the headquarters and packing up the radio.

'The dipole's caught in the branches,' he muttered. 'I'll have to climb the bloody tree with the torch and sort it out.' As most of the shots from the enemy were passing over our heads and through the branches of this particular tree, it would be a hazardous undertaking, but the dipole aerial was essential as the radio was of little value without it.

He started to climb up the thorny trunk and, as he did so, I heard hoots of laughter from the bandits. I'll swear there was a clink of a bottle, and I realized that the gentle thudding I had heard earlier was a ramrod being driven down some ancient musket barrel. To confirm my impressions, there was a bright flash, a roar and a cloud of white smoke jetted out from the trees. A six-inch nail or some similar object crashed through the branches near Joe, who swore loudly.

A few minutes later, he jumped out of the tree. 'Got it,' he gasped. 'See you at the RV.' And clutching the radio, the aerial, his pack and machete, he staggered down to *Semper*.

Then, continuing to ignore his own safety, he pushed off into the channel and drifted silently downstream between the firing lines. Although there was no moon, the night seemed to be getting lighter as my eyes became accustomed to it. It was possible to distinguish large objects, especially on the water, and the bandits were only twenty yards away from Joe.

The fire-fight continued for another fifteen minutes and slowly all of us pulled back to the pre-arranged RV at the far end of the island. Roger had brought the boats down the shore and was joined by Joe in *Semper* from the other side. It was Roger who, as sentry, had gone to inspect the boats at 01.05 hours, had spotted the bandits and challenged them at the water's edge. They had opened fire at once. It was Roger's shouts of 'Stand to' that had woken me as he raced into the camp pursued by a dozen of the enemy.

Alastair and I pulled back to the defensive position last. There was a low shingle bank, but we were close to our boats and had a completely clear field of fire. Everyone was there. Garth reported the island clear of enemy, but said he could not find the body of the man David had shot. They must have dragged him off. Ammunition was quickly redistributed; we had three rounds left for each .45 and although we had more liberal quantities for the other weapons, we were not well off.

I checked each man's arc of fire and coming to Richard, I said, 'You cover from that bush to . . .'

'John,' he interrupted quietly. 'I feel there is a small point I should raise at this juncture.'

'What on earth is it?' I said tersely.

'I haven't got a gun,' he replied.

I found it difficult not to burst out laughing. Richard, as gentle and unassuming as ever, was clutching his penknife.

'Would you like your topee now?' he said.

In the opening stages of the fight I had given it to Richard to carry to the boats. Guarding it like an Imperial Eagle of Rome, he had carefully concealed it from view throughout the battle. Now he was eager to rid himself of this bulky target. I took it back and hid it beneath a groundsheet in *Semper*.

It was now 02.00 hours and I planned to hold out until just before dawn, then slip away when the light was sufficient for us to see the way through the cataract that lay approximately a mile down river.

The bandits' shooting was as bad as their tactics and field-craft were good, so I doubted if they would be able to hit us as we moved down river. I could probably discourage them from following too closely with my own rifle. But it meant holding them off for another three and a half hours at least. They were brave men and I suspected some of them were well primed with local alcohol. It is difficult to estimate the numbers involved, particularly as we were fighting at night. However, I believe a reasonable approximation would be forty to fifty enemy against ten of us.

There was only occasional firing from the bank, and this we returned with the rifle to conserve revolver ammunition. Once I thought I saw a figure swimming the channel between the island and the mainland. If indeed it was a man, my shot must certainly have worried him.

At 03.00 hours Richard reported a growing movement on the mainland opposite his post. I listened and could hear a lot of muttering and shuffling amongst the bushes. The bandits were probably massing for another attack, so I put up a flare which revealed nothing.

'If they make another determined attack we shall have to withdraw,' I said. 'Simply not enough ammunition.'

No-one questioned the plan, but all wondered how we could negotiate the rapids ahead in the dark. I gave instructions for the order of withdrawal and, to avoid giving our movement away to any enemy cut-off party who might be lurking downstream, I said that no engines were to be used except in dire emergency.

The silence was broken by the short, sharp notes of the hunting horn. Just as we had heard earlier. I put up another flare and, in its light, I could see a mass of white-robed figures assembled amongst the trees on the far bank.

'Right, man the boats,' I whispered loudly and firing several shots at the massed bandits, I clambered into *Semper*.

'Life jacket,' said Joe, thrusting one at me as he pushed us into deep water. 'By the way, I think we've been hit somewhere up front. We've got a frightful leak,' he said, and I felt the soft, squashy forward-tubes of the boat.

As we pulled away from the island, I rummaged about and found one of the foot-pumps. Fortunately, it was easy to connect to the valve and from then on I was able to sit and use one foot to keep the pump going. My hands were free to use the paddle.

We reached the far bank and at once the current forced us against some low trees.

'Push clear quickly,' came Roger's warning, 'or we'll be dragged under the branches.'

We had been on the water for some little time when whoops and horn-blasts announced that the bandits were attacking our evacuated position.

'We've got a good start,' I said to Joe, but he was too worried about his craft to notice the events behind us.

'Keep pumping, we're losing air fast,' he said.

To help keep together, each recce boat took a Red-shank in tow and it was in tandem that we reached the cataract. Ahead in the blackness we could hear its thunder, but could see nothing. As we raced towards it at some six knots, it was an eerie, unnerving experience. The terrifying noise got louder and louder. In daylight it is possible to choose the best route through white water, but now we had no idea whether we were coming upon a small waterfall, a huge rock in the mid-river or some shallow rapids that would tear our hulls open.

Straining my eyes ahead, all I could see was inky blackness. To our left *Ubique* and its Red-shank were now invisible. The water hit us without warning and we were hurled up and over a towering wave. Behind us the Red-shank was completely engulfed. A second wave swept over us and the rapidly deflating front tubes almost bent double.

I lost the foot-pump in the chaos and heard Joe yelling, 'Can't go on like this!'

'OK, let's use the engine to run into the bank,' I said, 'but we'll have to cut the Red-shank loose.'

'Can't make it,' called Joe to the boat behind. 'We're going ashore for repairs. Casting you off, pull in further down, good luck,' was his farewell to our friends.

At least they would have a better chance without us. The tow-line parted and at once they were swallowed up in the darkness and the raging river.

Our outboard started almost immediately and, demonstrating his superb seamanship, Joe took the sinking craft astern and out of the main stream. We crunched into a shingle bank and Joe killed the engine at once. For a few moments we sat still with drawn revolvers, trying to hear any enemy, but the noise of the cataract drowned everything. Suddenly from the darkness, two shapes appeared in the water. It was *Ubique* and her Red-shank. They landed ten yards away and we heard their horrific story of a capsize in mid-cataract. David and Richard had both gone overboard and were only saved by a miracle. Much kit had been lost, including a vital box of rations. We were now soaked to the skin and very cold.

'Where's Chris's boat?' said Colin.

As if to answer him, a light appeared flashing dimly downriver. The signal, in morse, read 'O . . . K'. So they were safe too!

Joe had discovered *Semper's* trouble: a leaking valve which was easily cured. Someone passed round a handful of boiled sweets, and we cracked one or two nervous jokes.

Making a quick reconnaissance, I discovered to my delight that we had landed on a featureless shingle island, separated from the mainland by a fast-flowing stream. However, we dare not show lights or speak loudly, as I expected the bandits would not be far away. Thankfully, cloud still covered the moon. We worked quietly in the dark to refit the boats, and it was about 04.15 hours when John Fletcher lost the nipple that held on the propeller of his boat's engine. It had slipped from his wet hand into the river. Without this, the propeller could not be secured and therefore the engine was useless. John tried everything his resourceful mind could dream up, but it appeared there was no solution. As a last resort, he mixed a paste of Araldite in a tobacco tin and glued the propeller on to the shaft.

'How long will it take to set, John?' I asked.

'About an hour and a half if I can keep it dry,' he replied.

'You reckon that we can sit here in daylight, do you?' I exclaimed.

'No, I realize we must push on, and if necessary I'll lash a plastic bag over the propeller when we go. We'll just have to hope that it will set – and paddle meanwhile,' he answered. Boat-fitters, like John, are worth their weight in gold on expeditions!

It was 05.30 hours when the sky began to lighten and I gave the order to cast off once again. We skirted round the tumbling cataract and picked up the missing Red-shank and its crew from downstream. The dawn was fantastic. The growing light revealed an incredible view. Towering cliffs, giant boulders and natural limestone arches were painted shades of brown, pink and yellow. The river was like a mirror, much wider and slower and only a gentle wave or two to disturb the surface. Nevertheless, I kept the Mauser handy and watched the cliffs. We passed the Bascillio Junction, but I reckoned John Wilsey must be at the Scita River, further south.

Along the banks we could make out the shapes of dormant crocodiles, and it was not until the sun began to reach the gorge that they started coming out to inspect us. We watched warily, occasionally hurling in a rock to deter them. They kept their distance, and at

07.00 hours Joe managed to raise base on the radio. Once again it was a miracle of communication, for he was only using the twelve-foot rod aerial.

I had just spoken to Nigel, my deputy leader, and now the base commander, when I saw Joe's mouth open. 'Oh, my God,' he said.

Looking up, I saw a leviathan of a crocodile literally galloping with its legs extended. It came towards us at a frightening speed over a shingle bank.

I yelled, 'Crocodile attacking!' over the radio and leapt for my gun.

The reptile plunged into the water and came speeding straight at us. A small bow wave was caused by its great head. The huge tail propelled it like a torpedo and I took aim with the Mauser at a point midway between his evil yellow eyes.

'Don't shoot,' shouted Colin. 'He'll stop short.'

If you're wrong, my friend, I shall kick you off the cloud when we meet in Heaven, I thought.

The huge creature closed to within eight feet of the boat, then dived and passed beneath us only to surface on the far side. He then cruised alongside us for about twenty-five yards, giving me a chance to estimate the size, which was even bigger than the boat. At a conservative guess I would have said fifteen feet in length!

Suddenly he had disappeared beneath the muddy water again and this time went for good. Base was trying desperately to contact us on the radio.

'Sorry for that interruption,' I said and gave them a brief outline of the battle at the island. 'Don't get the authorities all worked up yet,' I said. 'Give me a chance to get well clear before Haile Selassie's jets come thundering in to deal with the bandits.'

'They've got troops standing by to come in by helicopter to get you out,' said Nigel, 'and John Wilsey is twelve miles south of the Bascillio Junction.'

'Fine, but we need ammunition and food, in that order, so may we have a drop when we meet John?' I went on.

'Our stocks of rations are almost out up here,' retorted Nigel. 'What has happened to all of yours?'

'Oh, I gave them to the friendly people around here,' I said sarcastically.

We switched off the engine to save fuel and drifted for a while. More crocodiles came swimming out to investigate, but Colin was right, they always stopped short. However, I could see how any inexperienced person would assume they meant business and open fire long before they had got within eight feet of him.

It was 08.15 hours as we rounded a bend and saw the assault boat. A great cry of greeting went up and I stumbled ashore to shake John's hand. For several hours the crews swapped stories. Cataracts grew bigger, bandits multiplied and crocodiles became ten times as aggressive.

John himself had a great tale to tell. For seven days he had struggled upstream, his boat leaping rapids like a giant salmon. No-one had ever brought any form of powered craft so far up the Blue Nile before. It was a fine achievement and we were terribly glad to see them.

We washed, shaved, cleaned our guns, refuelled and ate a meagre breakfast. Food was very short. At mid-morning the Beaver roared into the gorge and dropped several bundles to us. They only had one parachute left and that was used for the petrol and ammunition. The rations came in by freedrop. Unluckily the pack hit a rock and burst open on landing. The contents were all they had left at base. This consisted of ten packets of Ritz biscuits, six packets of Ovaltine biscuits, some rice, sardines and cheese, plus a four-gallon plastic container of whisky!

'Well, at least we can lay on a cocktail party,' joked Ticky. The whisky container was leaking, so we had liberal gulps before setting off to study the last part of the river.

The remaining time passed quickly. We ate guinea-fowl, fish and even a crocodile tail. A new menace hit us: mosquitoes! The dry season was coming and already the trees were turning brown and the river beginning to drop.

It was 24 September when we sailed from our camp on the Uolaka Junction and began the final run to Shafartak. On the radio we heard that quite a reception awaited us, and it was hard to realize that we had got through and now, after nearly two months, it was all over.

At 16.20 hours the Beaver came skimming over the river and we knew we were very close to home. Ten minutes later we ran ashore and the champagne corks flew. The base group had set up a radio on the beach.

'Have you any message to send to UK?' asked Nigel.

'Yes,' I said, 'Just send – mission accomplished.'

7

DESERTS IN THE SEA

THE damp twig hissed and spluttered in the embers and a thin wisp of smoke curled upwards into the darkening African sky.

'Somehow we've got to keep this team together,' remarked Richard Snailham.

'Yes,' I said slowly, 'we've got a lot to build on.'

Both of us had been thinking the same thing for some time, as indeed had others. However, it was 1969 before any of us had time to put our thoughts down on paper and meet informally at my home in Camberley to discuss the formation of what we called the Scientific Exploration Society.

While we still remembered the explorers Dampier, Cook, Livingstone, Stanley, Speke, Scott and Shackleton – indeed their names had become household words – there is somehow a ring of the past about the word 'explorer' itself. Had the breed ended with Sir Vivian Fuchs and Wilfred Thesiger? Was there no possibility of discovery in the 1970s? The exploration of our planet was being said by some to be over, and that future work lay only in space. We did not believe this, but preferred to follow the view put forward by Professor Simmons in *African Discovery*:

The fifth phase is that of detailed scientific exploration, a necessary prelude to the full political and economic development of a country. We are still in this stage today.

A good deal of ground, we decided, in Africa, Asia and South America had been overflown and mapped, but never properly visited. There seemed to be a wealth of scope for the fifth and perhaps final phase of terrestrial exploration – a thorough scientific investigation. So far there had been only haphazard support for this work, from international agencies, governments and learned institutions. For over ten years our circle of servicemen and civilians in Britain had been joining together to undertake overseas expeditions that had been increasingly far-flung and ambitious. On these projects scientists and soldiers had worked, often in exacting circumstances, in many difficult regions. Their results had been excellent, new species had been revealed, to the delight of zoologists, and the little-known past of primitive societies had been further opened up by archaeological discoveries. What was more, the demand for such expeditions was growing.

We likened ourselves to the East India merchants, who, each year, purchased a ship, launched a spice-buying expedition, sold the goods, sold the ship and then next year, started all over again. At Sandhurst we had a store of boats, engines and camping equipment and firearms. The weapons, held quite legally on a firearms certificate, like all the stores were used by one expedition after another. The real difficulty was to say who exactly owned them! In effect, we were already 'keeping the ship'.

Our numerous useful contacts established with commerce, industry, the press, scientific bodies and universities needed linking to some permanent body. Now we were aiming to keep our pool of experts and material in being, in the hope that new ventures could be more easily mounted.

We also recognized the lack of liaison between the scientific and educational establishments, the armed services and industry. It might be possible to bridge this gap. We hoped that our mutually advantageous relationship with industry would flourish and the publicity provided for really successful items of equipment would encourage manufacturers to continue backing us.

In order to convince people that we, the soldiers, were not all rude and licentious, we proposed to offer more vacancies to civilians, including possibly young executives from the firms that supported us and one or two pre-university youngsters.

With the closure of Britain's overseas bases, the cost of joint civilian and service exploration had rocketed, and if we were to continue exploring, we must pool and make the best use of available resources. To achieve this, John Adair, one of our founder members, proposed that an information centre should be established to advise everyone interested in adventure-training, expeditioneering and character-building. We all agreed that it was most desirable for, although there were many exploration societies, there was no common information bureau. Many had hoped that the Royal Geographical Society, centrally placed, with its excellent library, map rooms and fund of knowledge, might take the lead and provide the nation and the world with this valuable service. Unfortunately, this august body showed no inclination to become deeply involved in such a project, which would undoubtedly have been a heavy burden on their funds, already well stretched.

Dean Acheson had stung us in 1962 by saying 'Great Britain has lost an empire and has not yet found a role.' We felt that we wanted to play a part in strengthening what looked like being Britain's new role – no longer direct and imperial, but co-operative and complementary. We thought that, in the long term, our society could help to improve relations with peoples overseas by giving various forms of assistance, by seeking knowledge and disseminating it at home and abroad. To do this we must have an international membership and, as our group already included many people from foreign and Commonwealth countries, this posed no problem.

Direct aid to developing countries was given, of course, by governments and charitable organizations with considerable resources. Our society's aims were broader, and apart from the scientific exploration explicit in the title, included many intangible ideals. Some of these, perhaps, overlapped from the days of empire, when a spirit of adventure and a healthy contempt for difficulties and dangers were part of the required equipment of an explorer like David Livingstone in his quest for knowledge and the promotion of a better understanding between peoples.

As the whisky level dropped in the bottle, those of us who sat around my dining-room table that night felt we had a common bond. We were by no means puritan in outlook, and we enjoyed life to the full, but we were all a little tired of daily reports of student unrest, drug-taking, the permissive society, civil strife and war. I think, in all honesty, we hoped to promote something worthwhile, peaceful and, hopefully, adventurous, that would be of real service to mankind.

We published our proposal, and at once over fifty of our chums willingly parted with a ten-shilling subscription. The Scientific Exploration Society, or simply SES as we all knew it, was founded. At the first meeting, I was elected chairman and Richard became the honorary secretary.

Naturally some old established organizations regarded us with suspicion. But for every doubter and every critic, there were many supporters. Scientists, servicemen, Members of Parliament, businessmen, newspaper reporters and undergraduates liked the idea and were sympathetic to our aims.

We expanded our membership carefully, ensuring that everyone who joined was willing to do something positive to help the society achieve its objects. Within three years our number included a member of the Royal Family, an ambassador, members of both Houses of Parliament, a field-marshal, an admiral, half a dozen generals, senior scientists and physicians as well as soldiers of non-commissioned rank. Explorers from other lands joined us and we established valuable liaisons with exploration groups at home and overseas. During these early days, we were indebted to *The Daily Telegraph*, Anglia Television and a host of kind people who did everything possible to assist and encourage us.

A base was essential, and for several years it was a huge yellow caravan in my garden. However, in 1971 one of our members, Jack Ainslie, very kindly lent us Home Farm in the quiet Wiltshire village of Mildenhall. Jim and Joan Masters moved in as wardens and established the society's headquarters, from which they administered our growing interests. This all took time, but meanwhile the expeditions were launched.

It was perhaps fitting that the first major venture to be organized by SES was once more to Ethiopia.

After the conquest of the Blue Nile, we were summoned to the Emperor's Imperial Palace. With so many members of the expedition we had the usual problem of marching in and out, bowing and dodging the lions, but happily the occasion went well. After talking to the Emperor about our exploits on his river for some fifteen minutes, he suddenly looked at me with his keen, sparkling eyes and said, 'Now you have made history, but what about your next expedition?'

'What would your Majesty wish us to do?' I enquired.

'Have you heard of my Dahlak Islands?' he said with amusement in his eye.

I was caught slightly on the hop and had to confess, although I had heard mention of them, I didn't know exactly where they were. At that moment one of the court officials intervened and, as the audience was drawing to a close, the Emperor said 'Why not go there? I know Hapte Selassie is interested in them for tourism.'

I promised him that I would look into the matter immediately.

Thus it was that I conferred with Ethiopia's head of tourism, His Excellency Hapte Selassie and my old friend John Blower. I learned that set in the Red Sea off the Eritrean coast of Ethiopia there was

The Dahlak Islands

Inset (top left):
ARABIA
ADEN
AFRICA
Dahlak Islands

RED SEA

Map labels:
• PERLA has engine trouble
KUBARI ISLAND

250,000 cigarettes found
Lagoon of Thirst

Tribe of the Blind
NORAH ISLAND

RED SEA

Village of the Sheikh
DAHLAK ISLAND
Lagoon of Hope
DAHLAK-KEBIR 'City of the Dead'
SHUMMA ISLAND

NOCRA ISLAND
Expedition main base
Wreck of the URANIA
DISSEI ISLAND

DOHUL ISLAND
old Italian guns found

→ to Massawa

miles
4 0 4 8

a group of low-lying coral islands, scattered in a haphazard pattern over an area about the size of Devon and Cornwall. There were approximately one hundred and thirty islands, but only six were said to be inhabited. Barren and almost waterless, they supported only a scanty population of fishing folk, most likely more Arab than African, who eked out a pretty miserable existence under the blazing sun. From the maps and charts, such as they were, it appeared that there were no harbours, other than natural ones, although we were told that the people based what economy they had upon the sea.

Set against this harsh lack of modern amenities, however, the islands, with their white beaches and turquoise waters, were thought to offer a possible tourist attraction. Hapte knew a little about the major islands and told me that the average winter temperature by day was about eighty degrees Fahrenheit. In the summer no one knew quite how high it would go, but clearly the tourist season would need to be limited to the winter. He explained that the islands were said to have a great variety of wildlife, including birds and gazelle. There might even be other larger creatures there and, as few people have visited the islands and no serious scientific exploration had been carried out, it was anyone's guess what we might find.

On my return to Britain, I made further investigations and came to the conclusion that, although there would be a wide variety of bird-life, the greatest wonders were likely to be in the shallow seas and amongst the coral reefs and gardens which surrounded most of the islands. Here, I believed, there would be countless specimens of marine life occupying the warm waters. There was just a chance that we might find that rare and gentle creature, the massive dugong, whose almost human appearance had given rise to the legend of the mermaid.

If we would come and examine the islands to see if they were suitable for tourism, Hapte promised that he would provide most of the financial backing necessary for the expedition. Already I felt my old love of exploring beneath the sea coming back and thus, with the backing of our newly formed society, we launched the Dahlak Quest.

As always, there were funds to raise, members to recruit, information to read up and equipment to procure. Fortunately I was then at the Staff College in Camberley and, although my military work took up a fair amount of time, I was centrally placed to liaise with all our potential sponsors.

The Daily Telegraph Magazine kindly offered to help the project and send with us an amusing and topical writer, Anthony Haden-Guest, and a very fine photographer named Stuart Heydinger. Our team consisted of members of SES who had served together before. Nigel Sale, now a civilian, was once again to be deputy leader. Garth Brocksopp took leave from the Royal Irish Rangers and acted as quartermaster and signals officer. Kay was to go out in advance to pave the way and, as usual, would be the General Manager and PRO. Richard would do the historical and sociological work and Jim Masters took his usual appointment as chief engineer. Philip Shepherd managed to get some leave from the War Office and came as our surveyor, whilst Staff Sergeant Hank Mansley RE became the expert on water resources. Johnny Johnson was to take film and study the bird-life. The underwater activities would be filmed by a very experienced diver and underwater photographer named Slim Mac-donnell. There were of course other newcomers, including Captain John Cuthill of the Royal Army Education Corps, who was known for his expertise in boats and was also, from university days, a geo-logist. A Camberley architect, Gerald Batt, was with us to study the native buildings and also design anything that we would recommend to the Ethiopian Tourist Organization. A scientific group included experts from Britain, Ethiopia and the United States who would cover biology, entomology, conchology and a study of algae.

While all this was going on, David Bromhead and Jim Masters went out to do a recce.

One bitterly cold afternoon in mid-December we packed our stores and despatched them in advance by air. A few days later the expedition assembled at London Airport and trying to keep our-selves warm in our tropical clothing, set out for a very different climate.

It was still early in the morning when we landed at Asmara, capital of the turbulent Ethiopian province of Eritrea. The whole district was now attracting world attention, due to its problems with the Eritrean Liberation Force. Therefore it was perhaps understandable that the customs were not terribly happy about our guns and ammunition. Worse still, the main expedition freight, sent out well in advance, had not arrived. Fortunately we had with us sufficient equipment to start, but we could not continue with our survey for long without the essentials that should now be here awaiting us. The Ethiopian officials smiled, but shrugged their shoulders helplessly and clearly the problem was not of their causing. I managed to reach a compromise with the customs over the arms. They allowed us to take the shot-guns and small calibre rifles. Then turning to Nigel, I said,

'Come on, let's get on with it before something else goes wrong.' Nigel, having come out in advance, had arranged for a small Cessna monoplane to be waiting at the airfield so that we could set out immediately on an air reconnaissance of the islands.

Leaving the other members to take breakfast at a local hotel, we walked out over the heat-softened tarmac and climbed aboard. Immediately after take-off we dropped over the edge of the plateau on which the provincial capital stands, and a short time later Massawa, the sprawling coastal town that was to be our rear base, passed beneath us. Heading east over the blue green sea, we soon saw the start of the archipelago. Through the haze, the low, flat, shimmering islands appeared. They were just as described: dun-coloured pancakes in the sea. Near the coast one or two were quite hilly and topographically resembled the mainland, but elsewhere the feature which struck me was the overall flatness of the Dahlak Islands. Coming down to a few hundred feet we saw large numbers of gazelle and birds on Dahlak Kebir, the largest of the islands. Soon we were flying over the site of our expedition headquarters on Nocra. As our shadow touched the shore, several figures emerged from the buildings that I knew to be the old prison on this former 'Devil's Island'. Flying in a tight circle, we turned around the island and I could make out our advance party, with some of the boats and equipment, waving to us from the ruined jetty. I could also see a fishing vessel of about fifty tons anchored in the channel and I guessed that this must be the boat hired for us by the Ethiopian Tourist Organization.

The islands bore only a vague resemblance to their shape on the chart, but, as this had been made in 1883, this did not surprise me. I noticed particularly one or two large inlets that reached right into the centre of the big island, and in these I saw numbers of strange creatures. At first I thought they might be dugong but, on closer inspection, they turned out to be camels standing in the shallow water, probably to keep cool.

That night we dined beneath the whirring fans in a small hotel on the sea-front. With the exception of Jim Masters, who had already gone out on to the islands, the whole expedition was now here. The scientists, noticeable by their beards, had come up from Addis Ababa, and Sue Fyson, who had arrived from South Africa to be my secretary, was already taking notes. Kay had everything superbly organized, and thus it was that with the minimum of fuss we were able to sail on the following day. The vessel had been chartered for the journey and, by lunch time, was laden with quantities of hastily purchased stores and rations with which we hoped to make up the deficiencies caused by the missing air freight. With us was Sheikh Seraj, ruler of the Dahlak Islands for the past thirty-five years. A small, rather delicate man, he wore a pale green turban, flowing robes and a T-shirt. My Arabic was very rusty, and my Italian extremely poor, so our conversation at this first meeting was somewhat limited. However, he did say aptly, 'The Dahlaks are deserts in the sea.' At this point, the gang-plank came up and we chugged slowly out of Massawa harbour.

At five knots I calculated it would take us seven hours to reach Nocra, which would mean that we should get there just before dusk. The members lay about the decks talking and smoking, the sea was mirror-calm and occasional flying fish flitted across the surface around us. Soon the mainland had receded into the haze and the monotonous thump of the diesel lulled me to sleep.

I had been dozing for a while when John Cuthill roused me. 'Sorry to bother you, John,' he said, 'but I am a little concerned about the navigation.' As he was the expedition navigator it was his duty to be.

'What's wrong?' I asked.

'Well,' he said, 'I have been watching that low island to the south and the other that is barely perceptible to the east for almost an hour and they don't seem to be changing position.'

Shaking the sleep from my eyes, I almost said 'so what', but then realized that he was telling me that we were not progressing. Indeed we were probably being swept back by some current or tide. Getting to my feet, I noticed that the weather had deteriorated and that now we were riding a heaving grey swell. The wind was getting up and at that moment Garth came round and said, 'Hi, you fellows, come and look at this.'

Clambering over the prostrate bodies of our comrades, we made our way astern, where Garth pointed to the rising and falling waves, as he did so I caught sight of a large fish with a strangely shaped head sliding down one of the waves in our wake. There was little doubt that it was a hammerhead shark.

Ali, the ship's captain, smiled politely when I suggested that he was off course, but once again my Arabic failed me. So I sought the assistance of Tigist, our Ethiopian liaison officer. Tigist was already showing signs of sea-sickness and his efforts with our Arab captain achieved no more success than mine.

'Why not ask the sheikh?' I suggested, but the sheikh, I was told, was praying and sure enough I could see him bent upon his knees on the floor of the small cabin behind the bridge.

The sky was now decidedly black and a heavy wave broke violently over our bows. Everyone forward of the bridge was soaked to the skin.

John Cuthill was now trying to calculate our position, and those of us who were not being ill grouped about the bridge offering him suggestions. The boat was rolling alarmingly, and the engine had begun to make slightly ominous rattling noises. Ali would rush down into the hold occasionally and scream hysterically at the engineer, a mythical figure whom we never saw, but guessed must live somewhere down in the bilges.

I cast my eyes about our stores and wondered whether we should inflate one of the rubber boats. That would hold at least four of us if the need came, but how ironic if the whole expedition were to start with a shipwreck. However, at that moment, I was more concerned in case we should simply founder and go down without trace. The wind was now force six and life had become distinctly uncomfortable. Surely, I argued, the sheikh, who knew these waters intimately, was the man to guide us. So I decided to interrupt his prayers, which had gone on for a very long time anyway. Sliding back the cabin door, I was about to speak when I realized that the poor man was not invoking the Prophet, but being ill into a bucket.

For no apparent reason we suddenly appeared to be making slow progress again, although the weather continued to be as bad as ever. It was about last light when I saw the next hazard. Ahead, in the growing gloom, I could make out a line of breakers on what appeared to be a long low reef. Undoubtedly, we would end up on this stretch of scissor-bladed coral unless Ali took us astern very shortly. Protesting loudly, I pointed the reef out to the deputy master, who had now taken over. Peering at me through his cataract-infested eye he nodded and gave me a toothless grin.

The breakers were only a few hundred yards away and beyond them I could see the black outline of some jagged rocks. We appeared to be heading straight for destruction. I had reached a point when my patience and nerves could stand no more, and was seriously considering taking over the helm by force, when the door of the cabin opened and Sheikh Seraj stepped on to the bridge. I pointed over our pitching bow at the reef. Squinting into the driving spray, he looked forward and then said several quick words to the helmsman who altered course barely a degree.

Then turning to me he said simply 'Dahlak.'

Richard shouted to me from the bows. I could just hear his words above the wind. 'There a channel, there's a channel.'

Sure enough, as darkness fell, we entered the narrow passage that led from the open sea to the Lagoon of Hope. Minutes later we altered course to the north and saw the lights of the prison on Nocra Island.

By the time our anchor was down and secure, the wind had risen to an even greater force. On the shore, Jim and his advance party had rigged up lights to guide us and we began the difficult business of unloading people and possessions in a pitching sea. Fortunately, spirits were high and the disembarkation was complete by midnight. At about that time the storm ceased as abruptly as it had started and the moon rose to reveal the stark outline of our new home. The sheikh had disappeared, but in the distance we heard the beating of drums welcoming him home. Jim had swept the prison warder's quarters and, exhausted, we collapsed on to our camp beds.

The union jack was already flying over our base as we assembled for a hastily-cooked breakfast. Before starting the exploration, we held a briefing at which I outlined the programme, and gave instructions for emergency drills and action to be taken in the event of any hostility. The Eritrean Liberation Army might well use the islands in its gun-running activities and I was not taking any chances.

'The charts are not very accurate,' I explained, and went on to tell everyone that coral grows at the rate of approximately half an inch a year and as the maps were made eighty-seven years before the inaccuracies were only to be expected.

On our island were other buildings, some still inhabited by local fishermen. A small police post of coffee-coloured rock was situated on the highest ground looking towards the main island across a field of stone cairns. This was the prison cemetery and, from the numbers of graves, it was not difficult to calculate how many of the inmates had never returned home. Outside the prison warder's quarters had been a jetty, now in disrepair, and once there had stood a statue, supposedly of Mussolini, but now only one boot remained. Nearby was a large fasces carved out of the pale brown coral. We propped it up against our front door.

The expedition mother-ship, *Perla* ('she smells, but she floats', was Jim's description), looked even less seaworthy than the local hired vessel that had brought us over from the mainland the previous night. *Perla*'s crew of taciturn Eritreans regarded us with bewildered amusement, but pointed out that they had trouble with the engine. I did not fancy a long sea voyage in the ill-charted waters with a doubtful craft and decided therefore to begin work by making a general overland survey of the main island, using our Lambretta motor scooters and also by exploring some of the more sheltered local waters with our Avon inflatable boats, aptly named *Solomon* and *Sheba*.

To start the overland exploration, we crossed the sound from Nocra to the main island and were sorting out our equipment when, to our horror, a large crowd of clearly hostile natives appeared on a track that led down a long gentle slope towards the water. We could see them at the distance of about a kilometre running towards us, making a fearful noise shrieking and screaming as they came. I prepared to return hastily to the boats when something else caught my eye. In front of the horde was, believe it or not, a motor-car and, as it drew close, I could make out Sheikh Seraj at the wheel. From his expression, he was having difficulty in controlling the vehicle and it was obvious that he had no brakes. However, he managed to stop by skilfully piloting the motor car into a large pile of small rocks.

Climbing out, with great dignity, he raised his hand and saluted me. 'Salam alicum,' he said.

'Alicum we salam,' I replied solemnly.

The archipelago's only motor-car was a Balilla truck of about quarter-ton capacity, probably made in 1935, and doubtless abandoned by the Italian Army. It now had no brakes, the minimum of instrumentation and the tyres were stuffed with straw. The engine only functioned on two cylinders and the steering was of doubtful efficiency. Nevertheless, it was the sheikh's pride and joy.

He had come down to convey me to his village for a discussion on the expedition and the islands, he said. I clambered into the back of the truck and, pushed by a large number of his people, we set out towards his village. The palace was an enclosure of low stone buildings and sitting beneath an awning, we sipped tumblers of sweet tea and coffee. Communicating in a mixture of Arabic, Italian, English and Amharic we learned that there were two or three tracks suitable for the sheikh's motor-car, but that our scooters could go almost anywhere. Otherwise, travel would have to be around the coast by boat. He went on to explain that the people grew no crops, but kept large numbers of goats, sheep, donkeys and camels, whose voracious appetite obviously helped to account for the sparseness of vegetation. He also mentioned that the dugong, locally known as the aroussa, could still be found in the waters around the shallow reefs.

We had already heard rumours that a tribe of blind people lived in one of the islands to the north, but the sheikh told us that blindness was not confined to this one island, but was found all over the archipelago. Unfortunately, not having a doctor with us, there was little we could do to alleviate or even investigate the high incidence of this affliction.

Seeking to find some small gift for the sheikh's wives and children, I produced a number of items of costume jewellery and a few imitation pearls. The old man fingered the pearls thoughtfully, and then rubbed one against a tooth. He handed it back to me, and reaching into the folds of his robes produced a small leather bag of fat and very genuine pearls which his divers found around the islands!

That evening we discussed the results of our first day. Johnny Johnson enthused about the prolific bird-life of the area. Already he had seen reef heron, Caspian tern, tropic bird, osprey and many others amongst the rocks of this arid domain. The osprey were particularly numerous, and indeed we could see these handsome predators wheeling and screaming above their nests all day long. With little difficulty, it was possible to approach to within a few feet of a sitting bird before it would fly off, leaving its squawking chicks to be filmed.

Jim and Hank had already begun blasting. At about seven feet down the soil had suddenly become damp and fresh water had begun to trickle in. The origin of this still mystified us, but there was a theory that either some form of filtration occurred in the coral island turning the salt water into fresh or that the rain water, when it fell, soaked through the coral and then lay as a meniscus on top of the salt water already soaked into the sponge-like tissue of the island. Had we sufficiently powerful pumps with us, we might have been able to prove which theory was correct, but as it was, we still awaited the stores from Britain.

Drinking warm Melotti beer, we worked on long after dark writing up our notes and preparing equipment for the next day's work.

A huge box of specially printed Dahlak stamps accompanied us and now Richard and Kay were busy fixing these to colourful envelopes for use in our own internal postal system. The labels were of no use outside the islands, but doubtless would be a future source of interest to the philatelists who seemed to follow the progress of expeditions with enthusiasm.

Meanwhile, our diving team examined the Lagoon of Hope[1] both

1. Name added to map by the expedition.

above and below the surface. This stretch of water is well protected on all sides, so is spared the worst of the strong Khamsin wind that blows for several days at a time from the south-east. Along the edge of the lagoon there were numerous small coves and, particularly on the north shore, attractive sandy beaches. Many of these beaches housed colonies of land crabs, fascinating little creatures scuttling along at the edge of the tide. We also found a land-locked salt lake and discovered that the area was surprisingly rich in wildlife, both on the land, in the air and under the water. We also saw the gazelle, which from David Bromhead's earlier recce, we believed to be soem-merrangs. Apart from the prolific bird-life, there were dolphins to be seen on the surface, and a great deal more beneath the waves. The silent underwater world was as rich as the arid islands were barren.

Anthony Haden-Guest, correspondent for *The Daily Telegraph Magazine* encountered an unusually hostile shark on his first dive. Later he wrote:

and now this (my first) shark is still gone to ground. We hang in a pellucid warmth, and an air-breather's panic in an ominous element temporarily subsides. A tri-D composes itself, the Life of the Reef, and please capitalize, because it does resemble one of those *Geographical Magazine* spreads, or a manicured aquarium, luminous as an aqueous Disneyland but through a blue-green filter, and more blurry with motion . . . drifts of paper-white sand, and coral inhaling/exhaling, Constance Spry arrangements of sea-cucumbers, shiny-black urchins with foot-long spines, and giant clams – deckle edges opening on cobalt interiors – and anemones waggling their toupees and weeds. And the fish . . . fluorescent parrot fish, knobbly bluish Napoleons, and stripey fish, and flecked and mottled, and angelfish, silky yellow-barred rhomboids, and a solitary scorpion fish, trailing plumes, elegantly venomous, a self-propelling Ascot hat . . . and, beneath, the felt malevolent presence of the shark. My flippers are a size too small, and my face-mask is leaking, and there is an odd rattling in my breathing-tube. The plankton floats around me, and stings. I waggle the prod, and the shark comes out, with an overload of effect, because my tooth-cap comes out simultaneously . . . The shark is not fast, but, well, purposeful. MacDonald gets it – a five-footer, its skin disgustingly coarse, and it heaves around the Avon inflatable *Sheba*, man-trap jaws working hazard-ously for minutes in death, as ugly as one could imagine, with missile nose and fins, and teeth. And my own tooth-cap is now part of the furniture of the coral reef.

Although sharks were plentiful only this one had to be despatched. Nevertheless, it was hard to dispel the uneasy feeling in the pit of my stomach when the vague outlines of the predators appeared at the limit of visibility. Even the smaller ones had an evil look, and their eyes seemed to follow me everywhere. I preferred the great grey basking shark that I had met in Cornwall.

The sun was nearing the horizon as, seated in *Solomon*, we sped home across the lagoon. The mirror-like surface was alive with flying fish and dorsal fins. Suddenly the water beside us heaved and I saw a great black carpet moving parallel with us a few inches beneath the surface. The carpet had wings which flapped gently. A tip broke the surface with a splash, the underside was pure white. We were in convoy with a school of giant rays. 'Manta,' said Slim, already pulling on mask and flippers. 'Stop the boat.'

Yellow submarine camera in hand he slid into the sea with amazing grace, for Slim, like myself was no midget.

Donning masks, we peered cautiously into the depths and, to our amazement, watched Slim join in the sunset ballet of the giants. There were four manta, all about twelve foot wing-span. Their graceful movements seemed inspired by music, and I found myself humming *The Blue Danube* as they waltzed and pirouetted around us. However, under-water conditions for filming were poor. The sun had almost gone and the lagoon was filled with a mist of drifting plankton. Perhaps it was this that the manta were feeding on. Slim grumbled that the light had gone and we sped on our way once more. However, later in the expedition, he did manage to take a remarkedly good sequence of these huge fish at play and this featured in a television programme about the islands.

The Lagoon of Hope contained much of interest to us. At the southern end lay the rusting wreck of the *Urania*, once an Italian luxury cruise liner, that had been scuttled by Mussolini's navy in 1941. Gliding down between the weed-festooned metal-work we saw the ship's swimming pool, still tiled, but now inverted and the playground for shoals of exotic fish. Sue managed to get some stained glass from the ballroom windows and Slim shot a mammoth grouper, which at four hundred and fifty pounds must have been a Red Sea record. Nearby, it was said, a U-boat lay on the bottom, but we did not find it.

Perla was not the most reliable of craft, and it was with many misgivings that we set out on our first voyage of exploration to the north of the archipelago. I wanted to investigate the mysterious rumours we had heard concerning the tribe of blind people said to live on Norah Island. The sea was flat in the shelter of the sound as we set out. The diesel thumped away and choking fumes rose from the hold where Mamoud, the engineer, toiled in the sweltering heat. Ali, the captain, smiled confidently. 'Today, the motor she very good,' he grinned, and to prove it raised the speed to six knots. However, Mamoud was soon complaining bitterly, the fumes became intolerable about five knots, so our speed slackened to the usual slow crawl.

The girls produced a tasty lunch which included some of Slim's fish and a few priceless tomatoes. John Cuthill navigated, Johnny watched the bird-life, and Sue wrote to David who sadly, having done the reccee, was unable to join us for the expedition. Nigel, his fair skin already beginning to blister, applied liberal quantities of Nivea Creme and spun for barracuda. He was not without success, to the consternation of the sleeping expedition members who suffered occasional rude awakenings when a silvery killer was hauled thrashing over the stern.

Jim Masters scouted ahead in *Sheba*, fitted with the echo sounder. 'You can't get between those islands,' he warned me by the pocket radio. Ali did not believe him. Had not he and his father and his father before him always sailed through this passage? My attempts at explaining the annual growth of coral were to no avail, nor was he convinced that Jim had an electronic gadget that could measure the depth without the aid of lead and line. Sure enough when the inevitable crunch came Ali merely shurgged his shoulders and said it was the will of Allah.

Perla only drew four feet so, by making everyone stand in the sea and push, we managed to get her afloat after an unnecessary hour's delay.

I was not in the best of moods when we reached Norah Island and, on discovering that we had an unforeseen long walk ashore through shallows, likely to contain resting rays and a few sea snakes, my patience with Ali, fountain of all knowledge on matters nautical, was exhausted. We loaded *Soloman* with out kit and pulled it through the shallows towards Sahelia, the Village of the Blind.

Standing on the glaring white shore the single-storey houses were mostly built of sticks covered by matting. A few buildings were of stone. As we landed two pathetic figures felt their way towards us with canes.

'Salam alicum,' they called, stopping to listen for an answer.

'Alicum we salam,' I replied, and shook the hand that the blind man offered.

His bony fingers gripped mine with amazing strength and I suppose he was summing me up by what he could feel. Satisfied, he bade us follow him to the village, where, seated outside the rest-house, we enjoyed the customary ceremony of tea drinking. The little glasses were produced and filled from a long-spouted kettle with hot, dark sweet tea and later coffee.

'Oh! do look at that poor child,' said Sue.

We all turned to see a coffee-brown curly-haired toddler squatting in the deep shadow of the house. A mass of flies hung to the youngster's eyes, nostrils and lips and yet he showed no sign of distress nor did he even attempt to drive them away.

'He's blind, like the others,' said Jim and, bending down, he tenderly brushed away the flies and waved his hand in front of the child's eyes. There was a slight flicker from the lids, but, in general, they looked dead.

Sheikh Serag shook his head. 'Mallo, Mallo,' he said.

None of us had any real medical knowledge and Jim, our first-aid orderly, could not see any obvious reason for the widespread blindness that afflicted these people. Stuart took some good close-ups of the eyes and I questioned the sheikh. Later we were to see more evidence of the blindness, and it was apparent that a high proportion of these simple people were affected to some degree. It certainly looked like trachoma, but why was it so widespread?

We accepted a kid goat that the tribe could ill afford, only because it would have given great offence to refuse. We gave them chocolate, biscuits, aspirins and plastic bags, but as we chugged away into the dipping sun I was already wondering if we could give these people a really worthwhile gift – their sight.

For several days we cruised the turquoise sea amongst the flat islets, stopping from time to time to disembark boat-loads of scientists who would storm ashore like assaulting troops to seek out the archipelago's secrets. Overhead, ospreys wheeled and screamed. Along the beach land crabs scuttled for cover, and in the shallow water of the reefs our marine biologist and Molly, the conchologist, collected their nautical specimens.

Alas, activity was brought to a halt by one of *Perla*'s more serious breakdowns and we were forced to limp home to Nocra. Having failed to reach the north-east sector of the Dahlaks by sea, I decided we must attempt it overland.

Using the sheikh's ancient buggy and the two motor-scooters we planned to cross the intervening fifteen miles of desert to the Lagoon of Thirst and there launch a two-man rubber-dinghy. In this Garth, our rugged infantryman, and our American entomologist, Dr. Woodbridge Foster, would explore the shores of the lagoon, while the rest of us collected botanical specimens and enquired after the dugong.

The day was clear and bright with the usual cloudless sky as we bumped over the desert. Gazelle and wild camel stared in amazement at the strange convoy and then fled in dismay at the sound of our horn. A motor-scooter is an ideal vehicle for firm, flat, smooth desert, but in soft sand or among rocks it became the bane of our lives. We sped past a ruined town and saw in the shimmering heat haze a lone building. It was beside the track and looked a likely place to stop and take a drink.

'What on earth is it?' said Richard Barnes my lightweight pillion passenger (and chief pusher).

'A cricket pavilion,' I replied. 'Surely you know the MCC stop over here on their way to Australia.'

And that was exactly what it looked like – a square, pale green wooden pavilion with three largish rooms and a verandah.

'Even got a score-board,' exclaimed Philip Shepherd, pointing at a weather-beaten notice board.

'Medico,' said the sheikh, but medico for whom, I wondered. However, the sheikh was already at the wheel of his beloved Balilla, so we left another mystery of the Dahlaks behind us.

By mid-morning we stood on the lagoon shore looking at a low island that, according to our map, should have contained a ridge of black hills. 'Obviously eroded away,' said Garth – for the island was just as flat as elsewhere.

In no time a handful of local fishermen had gathered to greet the sheikh and see the roumi (strangers) that he had brought. As always there were the blind and one man with the stump of an arm, the result of an encounter with a shark whilst pearl-diving. The jaw bones of hundreds of the predators littered the beach, and the smell of fish was almost overpowering.

As we pumped up the boat, a man stepped forward and showed me a handful of huge worn molars.

'Aroussa,' he grunted. The grinders were certainly the teeth of a large vegetarian. I accepted the useful addition to our collection and gave the man a shining cigarette lighter; thus encouraged he rushed off and returned with a thick, yellowed hide that he said also belonged to an aroussa. He explained that these gentle creatures sometimes became trapped in his nets and, being mammals, they drowned. He assured us that he did not hunt them – had not his ruler the sheikh specifically forbidden the hunting of the aroussa.

Their habitat was amongst the weed banks on the coast, he told me, and there was still dugong to be seen. Then, to our delight, the sheikh delivered a speech on the need for wildlife conservation.

Leaving Garth and Woody to the lonely quest, and the sheikh to be about his business, the two motor-scooter crews set off on a botanical hunt. Philip's machine was running erratically, and if he stopped the engine it was rather difficult to restart.

'I'll go on slowly,' he shouted. 'You can easily catch me up.'

'Right ho,' I replied, 'I'll just gather some plants and follow on.'

Some ten minutes later we set off in pursuit. The milometer showed that we had gone eight miles when I stopped.

'Funny, can't see any sign of Philip,' I said to Richard who, thinking the same thing, was already examining the tyre-marks on the desert floor.

'This is the way we came, but there are no tracks returning, he must have turned off,' said Richard.

'Or broken down,' I replied, 'and we've got the one tool kit.'

What a damn silly thing, here I was in the middle of a mini desert, on an island in the Red Sea with no drinking water for at least twelve miles – and, worse, Philip had the only spare tyre we possessed. If we had a puncture, a highly likely event, we were stuck, and if he had one he could not change the wheel, because we had the tool kit. So consumed had I been with my search for the plants and the dugong that I had broken all the basic rules of desert travel.

'We must back-track and pray we don't get a puncture,' I told Richard.

For almost an hour we motored slowly, dodging sharp rocks and watching for tyre-marks. Eventually we reached the oasis without seeing any sign of Philip. I refilled our water-bottles and we set out again looking with infinite care at the tracks.

'Look, there!' Richard pointed and I saw a faint set of tyre-marks leading left. The tracks were partly obscured by camel spoor and thus we had not noticed them before.

Philip and Gerald were squatting by the Lambretta in the shade of a thorny tree.

'Got a plug spanner,' Philip said, with remarkable good humour.

Above them, on the branch, two vultures stretched their scrawny necks forward to watch the proceedings.

'Damn,' swore Philip as the plug broke into two pieces. The vultures hopped forward with delight. Clearly they thought the end was nearer, but Gerald fixed the plug with sellotape and string and we were on our way again.

The tide was in when we reached the coastal track, The shallow creek crossings that had been no more than puddles on the way out were now nearly two feet deep, as we discovered too late when we hit one at speed, and ended up sitting in the water with a drowned motor-scooter.

Next day Garth and Woody returned with the sheikh.

'No dugong, not even an amopheles mosquito,' complained the aggrieved scientist.

'Found a few fags though,' remarked Garth.

'Fags,' said half a dozen smokers at once. 'How many?'

'Oh, about 250,000,' said Garth, nonchalantly sipping his long-awaited beer.

'Where?' screamed the nicotine addicts.

It transpired that our gallant pair had stumbled on a smugglers' hoard of Rothmans filter tips in a cave.

'What did you do with them?' everyone asked.

'Neither of us smoked,' said Garth,' so we just left them there – now if it had been whisky.'

'Or Melotti beer,' said Kay, winking at Hank whose broken collar bone was now encased in plaster of Paris, following a little difficulty with navigation on Christmas Eve which had resulted in him falling off one of the prison walls.

In fact Christmas would have passed unnoticed had Kay not produced, in her usual way from nowhere, a plastic tree, paper chains and a few tinned puddings.

As time went on our casualty list mounted. The marine biologist not surprisingly contracted acute septicaemia from his dealings with spikey and venomous specimens. Woody and Molly also suffered in the cause of science. Sue succumbed to what we thought must be an air embolism; a painful and dangerous condition, caused by air being squeezed into various unsuitable parts of the body when diving. She coyly declined the offer of the kiss of life from a dozen volunteers, and was rushed off to convalesce by a brace of Imperial Ethiopian naval gunboats, who arrived hot-foot in response to our emergency radio call.

Later the young French doctor at the naval base radioed us to say that he reckoned she was simply suffering from 'malnutrition' and he was keeping her under observation in bed for a few days. The members muttered darkly.

On every expedition Jim has a lucky escape, and this was no

exception. He was ferrying people and kit from *Perla* to the shore on one of our nautical forays. Everyone was ashore and Jim alone in *Sheba*, was bringing in a last load of stores. A sou'westerly wind had blown up and the sea outside the reef was already choppy. As he reached the line of coral heads some two hundred yards offshore, an unusually large roller curled up and struck the boat from behind. The craft flipped on end, depositing Jim, who, on this routine run, had forgotten his lifejacket, into the water. The motor went on running and to his annoyance he saw the boat heading away. As he started after it, a wave lifted him up and over the reef, but he was still in deep water. Fifty yards away a black dorsal fin cut the surface momentarily. Like myself in the desert, Jim cursed his basic neglect. But the tiller must have been knocked over, for the boat was circling.

Jim swam frantically to get ahead of it, but before he could grab a line the boat was on him and he had to kick himself downward from the hull to avoid the thrashing propeller. Three times he tried and three times he was run down. At the last attempt a sharp pain in his leg told that the propeller had hit him. Blood attracts sharks and now he was too exhausted to make the two hundred yards to the shore. He just had to catch that boat.

On the shore his friends watched helplessly as the drama continued. There was no other boat to come to his aid. The craft came surging towards him again: Jim dodged the bow and hurled himself with all his strength at the trailing stern line. His fingers felt the rope and he seized it, immediately being pulled along in the wake. By the time he got one arm over the gunwhale and turned the throttle down he was a shattered man, without an ounce of energy left.

The islands had many strange sights. Richard Snailham found a vast necropolis by the ruined city of Dahlak Kebir. It contained numerous grave slabs of blue-grey stone, not found in the islands and with highly decorative Cufic inscriptions. We also found underground cisterns, tunnelled into the rock – a reminder of greater days in the islands history, when Dahlak Kebir was their capital. Now, only a handful of blind inhabitants eked out a living amongst the caved-in dwellings, ever watched by the vultures and black kites perched upon the ruinous mosques.

On Dohul, Philip, our surveyor, but also a gunner colonel, was delighted to discover five Italian coastal guns still standing undamaged in their emplacements. Ammunition was scattered about and, although the optics and breech-blocks had gone, the weapons retained an air of menace as they looked out over the Massawa channel.

I had to leave the expedition early to take up my new job in Whitehall, but the team went on to complete the work under Nigel. Jim and Hank continued to blast for water, Molly conchologized, Johnny pursued his feathered friends and Slim explored his silent world. Although the survey produced no major new discovery, our collections were certainly appreciated by the Natural History Department of the British Museum and the various other scientific bodies concerned. In spite of our illnesses we could confirm that the islands presented no biological hazards of any serious nature – marine, terrestrial or airborne – which might inhibit tourists. Gerald produced a splendid design for the prison to be converted into an hotel, and Slim made up a first-class colour film.

Egyptian radio made references to sinister goings on in the Dahlaks; obviously, they hinted, connected with Israeli aggression.

Our trophies went on display in the windows of *The Daily Telegraph*, and a gentleman with an oriental accent rang to make me an offer for the tusk of the great dugong, which he said was one of the finest aphrodisiacs in the world. Feeling it might prove a valuable hedge against deflation, I declined.

However one thing still bothered me, the fate of the blind.

Back in Britain, we learned with sadness that our friend and supporter Mr. Alec Gale, founder of the Wiltshire honey firm, had died whilst we were abroad. Mr. Gale was almost totally blind and yet his enthusiasm for exploration was considerable. Therefore it seemed most fitting that an expedition to investigate the problem of this blindness should be mounted as a memorial to him. His family and friends thought it an excellent idea and in no time had raised ample funds to finance the project.

Freddy Rodger, explorer and expert on tropical eye disease, had recently joined SES and was the obvious choice as leader of the small team. John Cuthill, lately our navigator, went with Freddy, and in November 1971 the Alec Gale Memorial Expedition reached Nocra. It is not for me to tell the story of their adventure, but journeying through the desert islands by boat and donkey they made a thorough investigation of the malady. They witnessed extraordinary weather including a sudden tropical cloud-burst, which produced a plague of small frogs, who were in turn eaten up by the storks. The great birds gorged themselves until they could no longer stand, then lay vomiting and regurgitating in the mud. Next day, as the sun returned, mud frogs and storks disappeared as suddenly as they had come.

The team returned in triumph. Freddie decided that the blindness was largely caused by the intense ultra-violet radiation, and, what was more important, he believed that in many cases a cure might be possible. He suggested that we bring the Dahlak dresser Al Amin, Sheikh Seraj's young nephew, to Britain, train him to treat the eyes of his people, and then send him back with another medical expedition to start work on the afflicted. It seemed only a few weeks since we had taken tea with the courageous people of Sahelia. There is much suffering in Africa, and several knowledgable people suggested that our efforts and the money could be better spent in a dozen other places. Nevertheless we could identify ourselves with this project; we could see the progress; it was our thing – and I, for one, felt a deep satisfaction from helping these simple unselfish people who, possessing few worldly goods, had shown us kindness as great as anyone could expect in our own world.

8

A SMALL EXPLORATION
PROBLEM

THE telephone rang for the hundredth time that morning. . . . Grabbing it, I said, 'Just one minute, please,' signed the two letters that my clerk was holding in front of me, nodded my acceptance of the offer of a third cup of coffee by Mrs. Lewington and elbowed a file marked, 'Immediate' towards my colleague. Scowling at the aged, chipped, black telephone with barely concealed malice, I wondered which lost cause this call would ask me to support. As an officer in an army staff duties branch of the Ministry of Defence, I found myself regarded as an eternal provider of men, machines and material.

I swallowed a mouthful of the steaming coffee from my flower-patterned mug, and, trying hard to sound eager to assist, said, 'John Blashford-Snell, I am sorry to have kept you waiting.'

The voice at the other end sounded polite and hesitant. 'Some friends and I have a small exploration problem on which we should value your advice. Could you lunch with us next Thursday?'

I flicked open my desk diary and saw I had a very dreary meeting to attend that morning. A good lunch would be more than welcome. 'Thank you very much,' I said, 'where shall we meet?'

'The Hispanic Council in Belgrave Square,' came the reply.

I had heard of the Hispanic Council: Anglo-Latin-American relations, trade, cultural and economic links. I had become very interested in South America whilst acting as rear-party officer for the Roraima Expedition, which explored the site of Conan Doyle's *Lost World* that summer. The mystery of Colonel Fawcett's disappearance also intrigued me, but I wondered why anyone should want to consult me on exploration in South America. I had never been there.

'Have you ever thought about driving a car from Alaska to Cape Horn?' said Colonel Julian du Parc Braham, eyeing me through his monocle.

'No, but I do not imagine there would be much of a problem, simply a question of time and petrol.'

'Then you do not know about the Darien Gap,' he said sharply. I didn't!

Over a very good lunch, the British Darien Action Committee told me their problem. I learned that the Pan-American highway system, seventeen thousand miles long from the snows of Alaska to the deserts of Southern Chile is a bloodstream with many arteries, feeding twenty-three nations with trade, tourism and the exchange of ideas. But it was not complete. In the middle, at the Isthmus of Darien where the Atlantic almost meets the Pacific, there was a tiny block, a thrombosis that stopped the flow of the lifeblood between North and South America – a mere two hundred and fifty miles of hills, jungle and swamp that had so far beaten the highway engineers of both continents. This was 'El Tapon' – The 'Stopper' or the Darien Gap.

Tim Nicholson, the committee's secretary, explained that a Bill recently passed by the United States Congress would provide two-thirds of the one hundred and fifty million dollars needed to build a road across the barrier. President Nixon, commending the Bill to the House of Representatives had said, 'Completion of the Pan-American Highway is a goal I have long advocated and supported.'

But words were one thing, action another. The area was receiving publicity through being the site for alternative projected routes for a new Panama Canal, but the road was a poor relation. A spark was needed to fire men's imagination and translate words into the deeds so desperately needed by the nations concerned.

This spark, the Colonel said, had been lit by the Darien Action Committee of the United States, Panama and Colombia, by their establishment of the British Darien Action Committee. Now it was promoting and seeking support for a pioneering British expedition which planned to try something never before completed because of the natural hazards; to drive specially-equipped vehicles all the way from the Arctic Circle to southern Chile, traversing the Darien jungle and swamp for the first time. Other hazards and obstacles it would meet included almost perpendicular razor-back ridges, bridgeless rivers, wild beasts, reptiles and insects in profusion. The expedition, it was claimed, would bring a dream a step nearer completion by providing the publicity and 'spark' needed to get money for the road-builders.

The committee explained that it was their plan to send a party of six in two Land-Rovers to tackle the journey in the coming December, and they wanted my advice on the feasibility of the plan. There seemed to be no real difficulty in getting from Alaska to Panama and from Colombia to Tierra del Fuego. The only problem was the Darien Gap. Apparently several expeditions had reached the Panama-Colombian frontier, only to run out of time and be caught by the rains which came in April. The most difficult part of the obstacle was the Atrato Swamp, almost the size of Wales, which nearly severs South from Central America.

At first sight it seemed to me that, to be successful, an expedition from the north must get its vehicles to the frontier in time to cross the swamp before the rains. The team must then have a proven method of crossing the morass and know a feasible route. I wondered if it would not be better to tackle the swamp first, by going from Tierra del Fuego to Alaska, but, by questioning the members of the committee, I realized that they lacked any real information about the swamp and their knowledge of the Darien jungle was itself pretty sketchy.

They estimated the cost would be £6,000. My advice was that before they risked such a sum, they should make a thorough reconnaissance of the Gap, especially the Atrato Swamp at the same time of year in which they proposed to tackle the obstacle. This meant postponing the expedition for twelve months.

A week later, Tim Nicholson telephoned to ask if I knew a suitable person to do the reconnaissance for them. 'I'll find one,' I promised and began to look through the list of SES members for a determined, self-sufficient person with a keen eye for observation and the stamina of an ox. Brendan O'Brien at twenty was a wild, but well-travelled Irishman. A keen amateur naturalist, qualified civilian parachutist and a good photographer, he was physically very strong. His amusing, easy manner and winning smile helped him to get on with people, who rarely took him seriously. Brendan accepted the post without hesitation and, after some rushed training in Spanish and field engineering, set off for Darien in January 1971.

While our stalwart friend was hacking through the jungle, I did a little research into the type of vehicles and equipment that might be used in the Gap, assuming that, as a result of Brendan's reconnaissance, the committee decided that the project was feasible. The expedition's leader was Lieutenant Denis Silverwood of the Royal Navy, and at this stage I was an honorary advisor to the committee. I was already deeply involved with a proposal for an extremely interesting venture in the Blue Mountains of Jamaica, and Richard Snailham had drawn my attention to some little-known areas of the Congo River. A friend, working in Nepal, was urging me to lead a scientific team to the Himalayas, and I felt that I must get back to the Dahlak Islands to keep our promise to the blind. At the same time the SES was keen to investigate the Gore Forest in Ethiopia. The Darien Gap did not offer any particular fascination and, privately, I thought the whole scheme madness.

It was while studying the Maroons of Jamaica, in connection with the Blue Mountain Expedition, that I discovered they were connected with the Cimaroons, who had helped Sir Francis Drake to raid the Spanish from hideouts in the Darien jungle. Following this lead, I read David Howarth's excellent book, *The Golden Isthmus*. By the time I had finished it, my curiosity was aroused. Why had the earlier vehicle expeditions in Darien failed? What was it about this three hundred mile stretch that really destroyed men and vehicles? Could not a well-planned task force of the type I had led on the Blue Nile succeed? Tim Nicholson telephoned me again.

'Silverwood's been posted to a new job,' he said with apprehension in his voice. 'We've got to find another leader. Would you be interested?'

I said I would, provided that the Army agreed.

From what I already knew, I realized this was going to be a hard fight and I should need a good team and the best equipment. Recruiting began at once. Rosemary Allhusen, a charming and highly efficient young lady, with enough self-sufficiency and determination to put half a dozen men to shame, volunteered to be my personal Assistant. Rosemary or Rosh as everyone called her, had been on a previous expedition with a mutual friend, Ran Fiennes.[1] She had a real love of adventure, and experience of handling horses that was to be of considerable value in Darien. I have always preferred to work with men, but slightly to my surprise, I found that Rosh and I worked well together. Even so, I must have driven her mad at times and I'll never know how she put up with me.

In April Brendan returned from Darien looking thin and haggard. For two hours I listened to his story and examined his photographs. In the end he said, 'Well, there it is. I think you can do it, but don't ask me to come with you.' With that he rushed off to the Hospital for Tropical Diseases, leaving me to reflect on the magnitude of the task. For several days two voices argued inside me.

1. Captain Sir Ranulph Twistleton-Wykeham-Fiennes, Bart.

One said, 'It will be bloody horrible; snakes, insects, heat, rain, jungle, swamp and what's more – very costly. The General Motors expedition, with all their careful planning, well-tried vehicles and generous funding, could not make it. How on earth do you think you can do it? Back out now with dignity.'

The other voice argued, 'Difficult yes, uncomfortable certainly, but nothing's impossible. A flexible plan, good logistics, sound equipment and a carefully chosen team could do it. What a challenge.'

Sifting the mass of information, I now had to make several assumptions before I could devise my plan. The weather pattern dictated that we should move from north to south in the dry season, a purely relative term, which could be assumed to run from mid-December to mid-April. Roughly a hundred days, if I gave the ground a little while to dry out. To fit this timetable, the vehicles should leave Alaska in early December and they would probably reach Tierra del Fuego in May.

The permission and support of the Governments of Panama and Colombia would be essential. The help of the United States Forces in the canal zone could be extremely valuable and furthermore, political clearance was required to cross frontiers. Lastly, it would cost at least £25,000 in cash, in addition to the generous support in kind from the British services and other sponsors.

So, I told this to the organizers, now renamed the British Trans-Americas Expedition Committee, and added that it would take about six months overall and my team would be around sixty persons, including scientists. I insisted that the expedition must have a scientific programme. It was of little real value just to get the vehicles through, we must explore the region as thoroughly as possible. So we planned to undertake important investigations of a zoological, botanical and geological nature in what was, by any standards, a remote and inaccessible area. This task would be an urgent one, in view of the ecological disruption which might follow on the construction of the highway. I also believed it was important to study the local people before their lives were changed forever.

My studies of various types of all-terrain vehicles showed that whilst an amphibious tracked vehicle would be best for the Darien Gap, it would not be able to maintain the high speed on metalled roads necessary for the easier parts of the journey. It simply had to be a reasonably fast, light-weight, economical and robust wheeled vehicle. An old friend, Major Charlie Hale of the 17th/21st Lancers was very interested, and we spent much time talking to Ministry of

Defence experts and examining reports on a wide variety of vehicles that might fit the bill.

'What you need is an up-engined Land-Rover,' said Charlie, one night as we rumbled home on the 6.30 p.m. train.

He was quite right. In fact, in response to a letter from Colonel Julian, Lord Stokes, the progressive chief of British Leyland had already offered to provide some vehicles. So I had asked Captain Gavin Thompson, a cavalry officer with rallying experience in the Americas, to head our vehicle section and he now advised that the newly-produced Range Rover might be an answer to the problem. The Rover Company was confident that their more powerful brother to the famous Land-Rover would indeed be the best vehicle and they seemed enthusiastic about the opportunity to have it take part in such an expedition, which, if successful, would be valuable publicity for the new car.

The only worry that I had was that it might be unwise to take this brand-new, more sophisticated model on such a trip, especially as it was almost twice the weight of a Land-Rover.

Gavin, whose knowledge of vehicles I respected, was impressed by its power and pointed out that this more than compensated for its 5,250 pounds weight. Jim Masters and Ticky Wright, sappers of the Blue Nile team, had joined the new venture.

'Well, if it won't swim, we'll have to make it float,' they muttered and phoned our friend, Ken Catt at the Avon Rubber Company to discuss making an inflatable raft that could carry the load and, when not in use, could be stowed on a Range Rover. Jim thought it a hell of a weight to get over the narrow ravines, and sought advice from the RE bridge experts on the construction of special alloy ladders that could be carried on roof-racks, and then laid over the gaps. Meanwhile, Rovers began to test a Range Rover with various types of tyres and other fittings that might make it suitable for the expedition.

We need something to carry the cordage, tools, explosive, jacks and equipment for the engineers,' said Jim at one of our many meetings. 'Must keep the weight on the vehicles to the minimum.'

'I was hoping to get mules for this,' I replied, 'but I hear you can't get them for love nor money in Panama and because of foot and mouth, they won't permit them to be brought in from elsewhere. The Embassy say that only pack-horses are available and they don't carry more than one hundred and twenty pounds each.'

So off we went to another expert. This time it was Colonel Alfred

Above: Sheikh Seraj's Balilla truck, vintage 1935

Below: Blind villagers of Sahelia, Norah Island

Above: Before Darien: raft trials. *L to r:* Cpl Ross, J. B-S, WO2 Ticky Wright (on roof), Lt Phil Church

Below: Before Darien: pistol training with the girls. *L to r:* Carolyne, Suzie, Tony Stansfeld, George Baker, Kay, Rosh and Peter Marett

Above: A struggle to save a Range Rover

Below: On the Tuira River. Sgt de Leon holding pole

At our base in El Real

The bridging ladders got us out of many difficulties. Ernie Durey at the wheel

Lock in one of the engineer equipment branches of the Ministry of Defence. The Colonel produced a brochure on a tracked, motorized wheel-barrow and said, 'I can't tell you much about it and we've never tried it, but it might be an answer. It's called a Hill-Billy.' So in no time, we had trials of equipment going on all over Britain. Our 'experts' examined the Range Rovers, Hill-Billys, rafts, power-saws, outboard-motors, radios and food.

The rations were, as usual, Kay Thompson's department. During her fleeting visits to Britain, Kay filled every hour with sixty minutes of hard work, smoothed out problems as they occurred, and generally took up the reins as general manager and public relations officer. She and Rosh got on terribly well and were the nucleus of my staff in London. With all the committee doing full-time jobs, much of the work fell on the girls' shoulders, but, amazingly, they never seemed to lose heart.

They were also assisted by Voice and Vision Limited, a public relations company which was very kindly helping us with the publicity. Organized by Voice and Vision, the initial press conference at the Royal Automobile Club in Pall Mall was a great success, and there followed a steady stream of really good articles in many national papers at home and abroad. Television and radio also took up the story, but alas, having educated Britain to the horrors of the Darien Gap, we found that people believed the project was doomed to failure, and were not inclined to give us the support we now needed badly. Newspapers, television companies and publishers shied away as I had never seen them do before.

'Look John,' said an old chum in the media business, 'I've put this project of yours to everyone I know – they all say the same – you've bitten off more than you can chew this time. If it's half as bad as the press reports, it's obviously impossible. Anyway, no-one in Britain cares very much about a road through Darien.'

But on the other side of the Atlantic, people did care.

Ultramar Ltd generously offered to supply us with free fuel, the Explorers' Club in New York helped us to recruit some scientists and the Governments of Colombia and Panama suddenly began to take a considerable interest in the project. The Latin America desk of the Foreign and Commonwealth Office was tireless in its efforts to assist, as were the British Embassies throughout the Americas.

From the United States came a letter of good wishes from President Nixon and from the US canal zone came welcome offers of support. I felt we were really getting somewhere at last, and when the Canadian Broadcasting Corporation bought the television rights, we reached our minimum fund-raising target. Funds and grants came in from British sources as well. While some learned societies regarded the whole affair as a commercial publicity stunt, certain to fail, it was noticeable that a number of enlightened organizations put their faith in us and backed the expedition to the hilt. Prominent amongst our supporters was the British Museum (Natural History). I have always found the executives of the museum very keen to take opportunities to further exploration with natural history objectives. Perhaps it is because, with less commercial potential than other sciences, natural history has been neglected in the past. There is a very friendly atmosphere about the museum and, prior to expeditions, I have enjoyed many a chat over a cup of coffee amongst the bugs, beetles, books and bats. The informal, organized chaos of the scientists' rooms is often more attractive to the young explorer and naturalist of today, than the austere victorian halls of other great institutes. Members of the museum staff, Dr. Philip Burton (ornithologist) and Mick Baachus (entomologist) were to form a scientific section with Jerry Carter, a young geologist, Robin Hanbury-Tenison, sociologist, and Dr. Al Gentry, a botanist working in Panama.

Colonel Peter Reid, a senior officer with an interest in natural history would look after this sections' administrative requirements. Another soldier who was also a keen ornithologist was the army's Engineer-in-Chief, Major General Caldwell, The general was extremely keen on exploration and had joined the BTAE committee at the outset. As the senior officer on the committee, he did a splendid job in helping us to get services assistance and full-scale support from the Royal Engineers.

Captain Ernie Durey, a well-fed, energetic forty-year-old sapper, with much experience of crossing obstacles, joined our team on the general's recommendation.

So the expedition assembled; sappers, infantrymen, cavalrymen, pilots, and an army doctor and his SRN wife. A dentist, a vet, scientists and secretaries, Americans, British, Latin Americans and a Gurkha. In all, fifty-nine men and five girls to join another forty or so persons in Darien. In October 1971 we announced the details of the plan.

Our aim was simply to take two Range Rovers from Alaska to Cape Horn (or as near to it as it is possible to drive), making a scientific study of the Darien Gap *en route*.

In early December, a six-man driving-team would set out from

Anchorage in Alaska, aiming to reach Panama City in early January. There they would be joined by the main body of the expedition. Our column would enter the jungle with David Bromhead's recce team scouting ahead, finding a route for Jim Master's sappers to clear for Gavin's vehicles. My headquarters would bring up the rear with the supplies carried on Keith's horses. Outside the Gap, Major Kelvin Kent, the deputy leader, would organize our re-supply by air and river. Depots were to be established in the Gap or on the coast, and a main base would be set up in Panama.

The Avon inflatable raft would be used to get the vehicles across the rivers and through the liquid portion of the Atrato Swamp. I intended to air-lift recce parties ahead of the expedition, so that they might have adequate time to examine the ground, especially the great swamp. The Colombian navy promised a gun-boat to act as a floating base on the Atrato River and both the Panamanian and Colombian armies would send soldiers to escort us in their territory.

The scientists would accompany the expedition's main body or set themselves up independently in the area, whichever suited them best. I hoped to reach the far side of the swamp by mid-April, when I believed the rains would start. We should all go to Bogota, and having sent the Range Rovers on to Tierra del Fuego, the rest of us would return to UK.

Put like this now, it sounds very simple. Basically it was, but above all else, it was the most flexible plan I could devise. In spite of Brendan's recce and all the information we had gathered, I still felt that there was far too much that I did not know about the Gap. Planning the attack on Darien was like preparing to assault a strong enemy position in war. Staff college training advised a commander to outnumber the opposition three to one. I knew that in this case the odds were very much reversed and the only way we could win was to concentrate our force at one point and maintain it for at least three months.

By December all was ready. The advance liaison officer, Captain Paul Arengo-Jones had already arrived in Panama to make initial arrangements and await the end of the rains. Meanwhile, feverish activity had been going on at Rovers until the last minute, and it was a crisp winter's morning when the cars were loaded into the RAF Hercules bound for Anchorage.

Back at the Ministry of Defence, my job had another month to run. My colleague, Colonel John Isaac, did a great deal to take the load off my shoulders, but it was not an easy time. I felt I must keep up my army work to the best of my ability, in spite of the ever-increasing calls on my time for press briefings, visits to equipment trials, discussions with sponsors and meetings with our scientists. Alas, my chum Charlie Hale, who had helped me earlier, was dying of cancer and I tried to spend as much time as I could visiting him.

Two years in Whitehall is not the best way to keep fit. Dieting, long walks and a little circuit training had only a nominal effect on my stamina.

In mid-December came the awful news that one of the cars had been involved in a bad crash on Alaska's ice-bound Alcan highway and the vehicle party was involved in all sorts of complications that would certainly prevent them reaching Panama before 10 January.

Paul signalled ill-news from Panama – the rain was still falling hard with no sign of a break.

Christmas was beset with worries, and I realised that I had become so consumed by the forthcoming campaign that I was now a real bore to my family.

At the farewell party the Minister for Defence said the expedition was the most ambitious ever undertaken by the British army. It made me feel terribly responsible. It was a cold, wet dawn when I climbed shivering into the cavernous belly of the Hercules. I felt very tired, extremely unfit and more like a week's holiday than three months in one of the most unhealthy regions in the world.

9

OPERATION DARIEN

'. . . when with eagle eyes
He star'd at the Pacific – and all his men
Look'd at each other with a wild surmise –
Silent, upon a peak in Darien.'

On First Looking into Chapman's Homer—John Keats

THE turquoise blue sea showed momentarily through the clouds, then as the Hercules altered course for Tocumen airport, I saw a range of low green hills protruding through the cotton wool. At first sight the jungle of Panama looked innocuous. Facing inwards again, I fastened my seat belt, gazed across the mound of equipment and awaited the landing.

The belly of the giant freighter was largely filled by the dismembered Beaver light plane. Its wings folded alongside, it rocked gently on its restraining chains, like some giant insect that had been captured and tethered. Around were dozens of boxes and crates, some labelled 'hazardous – with care', others 'fragile, this way up', and all bearing the words *Operation Darien*.

The weariness that had dogged me for the past weeks had gone. I now felt revitalized, alert and ready to go. Perhaps it was the welcome sleep while crossing the Atlantic, or the long-awaited sight o the jungle. Whatever, quite suddenly everything became very clear.

At last the great tail door swung down admitting a blast of humid tropical heat, which drew rivulets of sweat from every pore. Paul was there, Kelvin and his wife Jenny too, plus, thank heavens, the two Range Rovers.

'Everything's under control, John,' said Arrangement-Jones, as Paul was already nicknamed. 'The Ambassador's car will take you to the residence where you are staying tonight.' I thanked the crew of the Hercules, which, to the astonishment of our Panamanian friends, was already giving birth to the Beaver.

His Excellency, Mr. Dugald Malcolm, was an honorary president of the expedition, and as a one-time regular soldier, the Ambassador was able to understand both the diplomatic and military viewpoints involved with the project. Sipping our whisky in his air-conditioned study, I realized how very fortunate we were in having such an ally and supporter at the start line.

'Do you feel like a party?' he said cheerily.

'Certainly,' I replied, and found myself whisked off to the home of some friendly local residents.

Everyone wanted to know of our plans and volunteered a few candid opinions about the Darien Gap. I had a strange feeling that people were treating us with a certain respect, rather as one might regard somebody who had once had a nervous breakdown and would shortly end up in an asylum!

Some say the first few days when an expedition arrives are the worst. However, thanks to Kelvin, Paul and the British Embassy, all went remarkably smoothly. The Guardia Nacionale (Panama's Army, Navy and Air Force) was very co-operative and eager to assist. The expected problems of customs and immigration were waved aside. The US Forces in the canal zone bent over backwards to help and provided us with a base house, some transport, vital jungle boots, hammocks and a one-day course at their Tropical Survival School.

Further flights of passengers and freight came in on time and the task force quickly took shape. There were only two problems. The pack-ponies, so necessary as load-carriers, were proving difficult to obtain, and most serious of all – it was still raining hard!

Captain Peter Marett, our intelligence officer, searched Panama for detailed information on the Gap and the weather. Nothing new emerged, but our preparations continued.

On 13 January we gave a full-scale press conference. The British Ambassador took the chair and interpreted for us. This was as well because my Spanish was sadly lacking. The reporters fired their questions thick and fast.

'How will the rains affect you?'

'How will you cross the ravines?'

'Do you know a way through the Atrato Swamp?'

'What special work will the scientists undertake?'

'Do you believe the Darien road is a practical proposition?'

This last query came up in one form or another time and time again. It was the vital question. Outside the lightning flickered and the rain fell in sheets. I hoped my replies sounded confident. The conference ended with eats and drinks while the correspondents switched their attention to our ladies. Somehow the attractive, smartly dressed girls, fresh from swinging London did not look like the conventional idea of hearty women explorers. Did we but know it, they were every bit as intelligent, mentally rugged and tough as their Victorian forebears.

Our first forward base camp was established in an army training camp on the edge of the actual Gap. Near here at the wild west town of Canitas the Pan-American highway ended as a dirt track. In the long barrack rooms we hung our mosquito nets on the bunk beds and crawled on to the straw-fillled mattresses.

Dawn at the 'Centro Instruction Militar' (CIM) seemed to come very early. I was awoken from a deep sleep by the most hideous din. My watch showed 04.30 hours, yet blaring from the camp public-address system was a continuous arrangement of Panamanian martial music. Did our allies realize what they were doing? I thought not, and heaving myself from the mattress, rushed over to the guard room. Fortunately I grabbed my topee, for I suddenly found myself involved in a military ceremony. The guard, immaculately dressed in starched fatigues presented arms, as their national colours were slowly raised to the accompaniment of the piped music. Dressed in a colourful sarong (given to me by Sheik Seraj of the Dahlaks) wearing Malaysian rubber flip-flops and my white helmet, I was at least able to stand to attention and salute.

The guard dismissed, the orderly officer, a young lieutenant, marched over and with a smart salute said, 'Buenos Dias, Major.' With halting Spanish and convincing gesticulations, I explained that his music was driving me mad. The officer looked embarrassed and gave a sharp order. The din ceased immediately. Ah! peace, perfect peace. I thanked him in French and staggered back to bed.

'That was probably their national anthem and they'll shoot you later,' growled Morgan-Jones from behind a pile of saddles and veterinary kit.

There was not a moment to spare during those hectic days. The sappers prepared the tools of their trade, the doctor made arrangements for the inevitable casualty evacuations, the scientists liaised with their opposite numbers in Panama and organized the safe custody of specimens, while Kay sorted out the tons of rations and

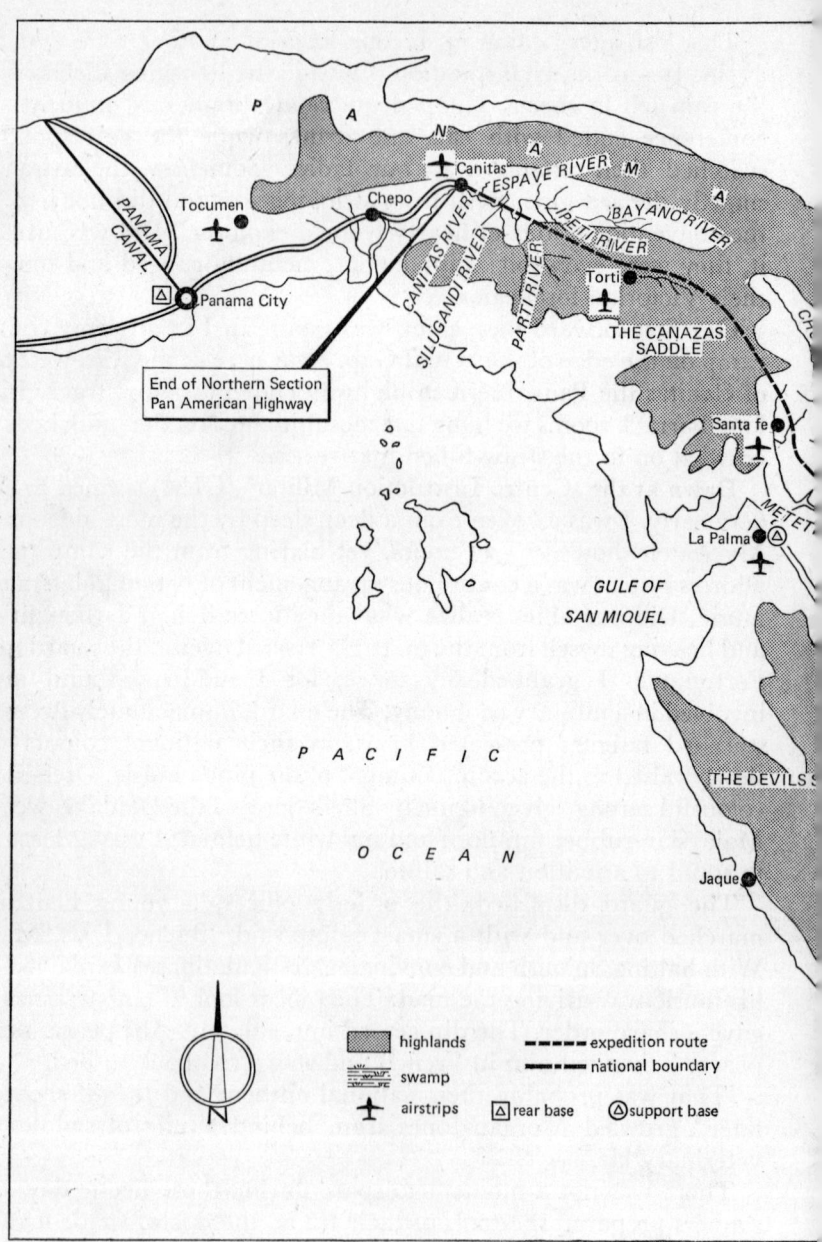

The Darien Gap

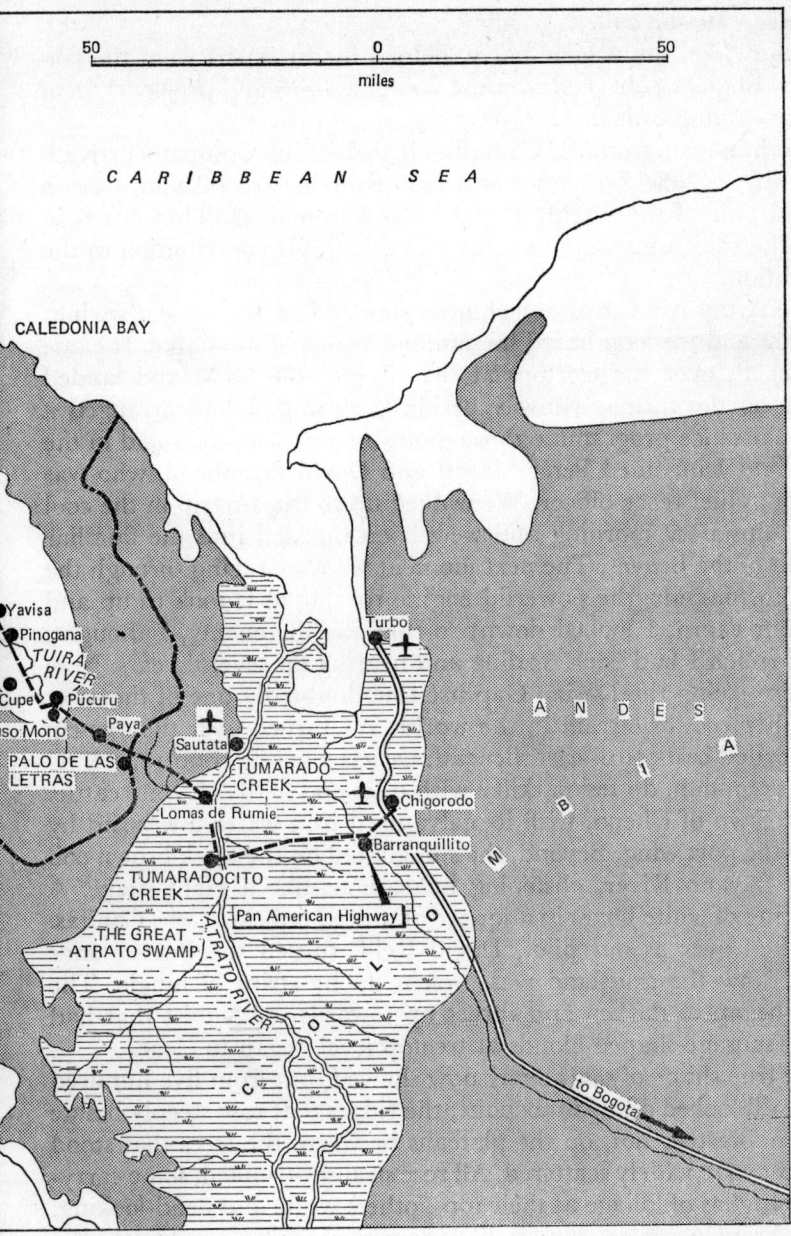

CARIBBEAN SEA

CALEDONIA BAY

Yavisa
Pinogana
TUIRA RIVER
Cupe Pucuru
so Mono Paya
Sautata
PALO DE LAS LETRAS
TUMARADO CREEK
Lomas de Rumie
TUMARADOCITO CREEK
THE GREAT ATRATO SWAMP

Turbo

Chigorodo
Barranquillito

Pan American Highway

ATRATO RIVER

A N D E S

C O L O M B I A

to Bogota

50   0   50
miles

special treats she called 'goodies'.

Meanwhile, the vehicle party, helped by an expert from the factory in England, checked over the Range Rovers and prepared them for the coming ordeal.

The film team from the Canadian Broadcasting Company arrived. Al Bibby, a New Zealander and Eric Rankin, a Scotsman, were a rugged pair of thoroughly professional film-makers. They fitted in from the start, and were to make a considerable contribution to the expedition.

The Army Air Corps detachment shortly had the Beaver's wings back on and we soon heard the familiar drone of its engine. It came floating in over the treetops at the edge of the CIM and landed neatly on the tarmac runway beside the camp. I had arranged a reconnaissance programme throughout the next two days and in the first flight I included Peter Marett and David Bromhead, who was now our chief recce officer. We walked up to the airstrip in the cool of the summery morning and were soon buckled into the familiar cockpit of the Beaver. The next moment we were racing through the cold morning air, the powerful engine roaring as it took us up and over our camp. I looked down; so this was the enemy, I thought, about which I had been reading and hearing for several years. Now we were facing the Darien Gap itself, undoubtedly one of the most difficult pieces of terrain in the world. We turned over the airstrip and headed east-south-east. Beneath us was a gentle country, rolling green savannah, dotted parklike with trees and herds of white cattle.

The town of Chepo, with its galvanized iron water-tower slid by under the port wing. Beyond, the sun glinted on the thick brown coil of the Bayano River, glistening beneath us like a giant snake. A scattering of white boxes in a square of turned red earth was Canitas. We tilted over as our pilot, David Reid, turned the Beaver once again. Now the grassland was broken up by strips of jungle. The green began to darken and thrust up towards us. A mist that had lain in sausage-shaped clouds at treetop level began to clear.

The true shape of our enemy now showed, but from five hundred feet it still looked oddly innocuous; the ridges that rose steeply beside us were forested, but, on the plateaus between, the trees that stood out most were widely scattered. All rose straight-trunked, some carrying umbrellas of foliage at their tops, others white and dead-looking. Their branches were spread like fingers reaching up to us. We dropped down to have a closer look. Glancing at the altimeter, I saw it read four hundred feet, yet we seemed almost to be brushing the tallest trees. I re-examined the green carpet around their bases; what we had been looking at was merely the primary jungle; the real problem seemed to lie below it. The most prominent trees must have been up to one hundred and fifty feet high. They rose out of undergrowth so thick that even from a modest height it looked solid, nowhere could I see the forest floor. This secondary jungle flourished where the tallest trees were sparse and let the sun in. Although it seemed like shrubbery, what we could see were the tops of lesser trees.

The Bayano alone broke up the mass. David throttled back and put the Beaver's nose down. We skimmed between the trees a hundred feet or so above the water, over one of the long, narrow outboard-powered canoes that serve as river transport in Darien. Faces turned up and arms waved. The Beaver's nose lifted and with a shattering roar from the engine we were carried over a loop in the river. The neat rectangular palm-leaf roofs of an Indian village clustered on the bank. Strangely, not a soul was in sight. We climbed to fifteen hundred feet and headed for the northernmost of the two mountain ranges that flank the Darien Gap. They, and the valley between, were laid out tidily and precisely as on the map; the relationship was strangely surprising considering the old maps we were using. The Beaver found a winding valley and we followed it at treetop height, weaving in and out between the timber-clad slopes, switchbacking over the ridges that blocked our path. We made a tight turn to take a photographic run; I found myself clutching the polaroid camera tightly to avoid it being sucked out of the open window. In the back, Peter quickly processed the film as I handed back the camera after each shot, making copious notes at the same time, using the tape recorder and watching the countryside flash past. Our eyes searched the ground for any sign of a track. There was none. The hills did not appear from the air to be too steep, but once you got low you could realize that they were not going to be an easy task to conquer.

The problem was to recognize the smaller features such as rivers, which twisted and turned under the green canopy. There were very few villages shown on the map, although we saw the occasional house dotted along the river banks. One of my main tasks in the reconnaissance was to discover the best place to cross the Bayano. We flew up and down the river line until our fuel was almost exhausted. Several points looked possible, but all would require rafting for the current was by no means slack. Once or twice I saw a track, apparently deep in sticky mud, leading to the river, but there seemed no obvious connection between the tracks on the river and the main track that led out of Canitas.

At last, I selected what I believed to be the best site. This was where an apparently good track came down to what seemed to me to be an aerial ropeway near the proposed dam-site. Another similar track led up on the far side to the high ground on the Pacific coast. To be honest, I could not trace the track all the way back to the main trail and it seemed to me that both trails disappeared in some dense jungle-covered hills that lay between the main track and the Bayano River. However, this looked like the only possibility, and I had decided to go for what I called the East Crossing, on the morrow.

So the Gap was no disappointment; it was certainly to be a challenge. As we landed, I could not help wondering how on earth Balboa in his suit of armour had staggered across this green hell to discover the Pacific. However, I could easily understand how Sir Francis Drake and his lightly-clad raiders had used the jungle to approach the Spanish treasure trail, and thereby enrich the coffers of Queen Elizabeth I.

The rivers looked quite fast, I should say something like four knots, and this was going to mean that river re-supply would be difficult, for our inflatable boats would not move as well against the current as the sleek Indian canoes. Undoubtedly it would be difficult for the Army Air Corps to find us once we were beneath the canopy. Thankfully, our preparations had been good and we had a plentiful supply of pyrotechnics and signalling balloons.

I was ready to launch David Bromhead's recce section into the Gap next day. That night I held my final briefing. Peter and I went through the information and the plan as thoroughly as we could. In particular, we stressed the need to keep loads to the minimum. Keith had only been able to find twenty-eight fit ponies, not the forty we calculated were needed. Above all, the Range Rovers load must be kept down, especially now that the rains were late and the ground would be even softer than usual.

I ended, as I always do before an expedition, by exhorting the members to work as a team. No individual would conquer Darien, it would only be achieved by our combined efforts. In every group of society there must always be someone to grumble at, someone to blame for all that goes wrong. In the army it is the headquarters, in the country it is the government, at school it is often the headmaster. I feel it is important for the morale that such a whipping boy should exist, for if he does not, when the strain comes, the organization will fragment and blame each other. On the other hand, those loyal to the leader will regard criticisms of him as an attack on themselves. It was with all this in mind that I now openly urged the members to grumble at me and not amongst themselves. Many of them scoffed at this suggestion, but they had not seen what real stress would do to tired men.

It did not rain on 16 nor 17 January. Kelvin and I went forward with David and his three-man team and crossed the Canitas River in mid-afternoon. 'This is an historic moment,' I wrote in my log that night, 'for we have now crossed the start line and are on our way.'

I planned to give David forty-eight hours, and then follow on with the main body. Thus, next day, we all moved up to Canitas and camped by the school house. Our seventeen-strong escort of the Guardia Nacionale joined us, weighed down with supplies and no horses. This problem I could overcome, but my temper flared when the vehicle section arrived late, heavily overloaded and without their snorkel devices that would enable the cars to motor through rivers with water covering the exhaust. They were sent back to Panama City to sort themselves out.

That night it rained hard, and at dawn it was still raining. Crawling stiffly from the pile of cement bags in the village school, I walked to the Canitas River and tipped a mess tin of muddy water over my head; brrrr, it was cold, but the soap lathered easily and soon I had scraped the growth from my chin. My mouth felt like the bottom of a bird cage – what on earth had I toasted the Guardia with the previous night? I let the toothpaste soak in for a full minute and felt better. Ernie Durey was already singing a refrain we were to hear for months to come, 'Happiness, happiness, the greatest gift that I possess'. Keith was bawling at everyone to get the horses watered. Lance-Corporal Steve Holmes, my signaller, was already bent over his radio set, twirling the dials. Rising from his neat wood fire, Sergeant Limbu offered me a steaming dish of baked beans and Kay pressed half a freshly peeled orange into my hand.

The loading of the horses was a comedy worth filming. Loads went on and loads fell off, but as there was no sign of the vehicles, we were not in any particular hurry. By midday, we had got the reluctant pack-animals in some semblance of order, when word came that the cars would not be ready that day. There could be no question of unloading the horses again and as the first five miles were relatively

easy going, through rolling open country, I decided to advance and
allow the cars to catch up next day. As we crossed the river the sun
appeared and spirits rose. Our first dangerous snake, a deadly fer de
lance, was slaughtered as it lay coiled in mid-track. The snakes of
South America are often the subject of wild and greatly exaggerated
stories. However, the fer de lance and its larger relative, the bushmaster, are truly venomous reptiles of the pit viper family, who are
guided to their target by their victim's body heat. The massive
anaconda, said to reach lengths of thirty feet or more, and be capable
of swallowing a deer whole, is relatively harmless to men, for like the
English grass snake it is a non-poisonous constrictor. Far more
dangerous is the brightly coloured and slow-moving coral snake,
which is often only a couple of feet long.

Jim and his sappers were already moving ahead with their heavily-
laden Hill Billys, but as they hit the first mud-patch, they discovered
a major problem. The tough little machines that had stood up so
well to trials in Britain could not overcome the sticky black mud.
Oozing up through their tracks, it was being baked rock hard by the
rising temperature and thus every few hundred yards the section had
to stop and chip it out. It was soon a case of the engineers supporting
the machine instead of the reverse. They had also learned that dead
trees contained ants whose vicious bite drove one section to take
refuge in a slimy pool.

That night the sappers slept by their Hill Billys, the rest of us in a
grove by a small river. Horses broke loose, the radios did not perform well and David reported that he had reached our first major
obstacle, the Bayano River. It was running fast and high. But the
rain had stopped.

Next day the Range Rovers arrived at 09.00 hours and we
marched on across the oven-hot grassland towards the great, green
wall where the Darien jungle would swallow us up for three months.
Just as the first mud patch had caused difficulties with the Hill Billys,
so it caused havoc with the Range Rovers. Whilst using the invaluable Tirfor jack to extract one of the massive blue beasts, a root
became entangled with a tyre valve, tearing it out. Thus five miles
from the start, one of our champion vehicles was crippled. I did not
like the look of the tyres, too little aggressive tread and the valves
definitely projected too far. Yet these were the best that our tyre
experts could recommend. I wondered, would not something like a
tractor tyre be more suitable? It seemed to me that, like the Hill
Billy, our trials in Britain had been on more liquid mud, which

drained easily from tracks and tread, but the Darien variety was sticky clay.

I motored on with Trooper Michael Webb in the other Range Rover, until that, too, became inextricably bogged. That night I wrote in my log:

We reached a point near to the Silugandi river, having used the aluminium bridging ladders on several occasions to cross ravines. It was hard work and all the expedition felt the heat and consequent thirst as they moved through the open pastureland today. Near the river, the mud was very deep and had not been improved by the passage of the horses, which had overtaken the vehicles when the tyre deflated. Here the jungle began, and the canopy of trees prevented the sun from reaching the mud and drying it up. Thus, leaving Trooper Webb with the vehicle, I marched on alone to catch up with the horses. They had reached the Espave river and had set up camp in a small clearing above the water. The scientific section, who had come up by river from Canitas, were established nearby. It was too late to do much about the vehicles and the engineers, as well as everyone else, are exhausted. It has been a hot march for approximately ten miles but nevertheless, people are in good spirits. Today as I came to the wall of jungle, I paused to look back at the sunlit savanna before entering this strange new world with its giant trees and buttress roots. Ahead of me was a tunnel of greenery, arched over by tangled growth and hung with trailing vines. The light was reduced to faint patches of yellow on the leaf-strewn floor, from which grew a garden of small plants. Ahead danced some large and beautiful butterflies with irridescent blue wings. Once in the tunnel, I began to meet the numerous small creeks and stream beds over which we struggle on the slippery rock slabs, or through the glutinous, oozing mud.

After dark, Sergeant Limbu and I went forward through the jungle to find David and Jim, whom we knew to be camped on this side of the Bayano river. It took a forty-five minute march, squelching through the thick mud and almost treading on a huge bird-eating spider (which we caught for the scientists) to reach the recce section's camp. As always, they were well organized and tucked deep in the jungle to the side of the trail. We discussed the crossing of the river which is now running very high at three and a half to four mph. I am satisfied, however, that we should be able to cross within the next two days and so I returned to our camp on the Espave. Limbu's night navigation in the jungle was uncanny and very accurate.

It took two more days of back-breaking effort to get the cars to the Bayano, during which time, to our utter embarrassment, we were passed by a hooting, siren-sounding gang of four-wheel drive enthusiasts from a canal zone club. Their impolite remarks about our tyres and heavy weight, although unkind, were true. But our problem was that the Range Rovers had to do 17,000 miles and carry spares and equipment for months of gruelling conditions. The four-wheeler's lightly laden Jeeps and Toyotos had only to keep going for the day.

Gavin and his crew looked depressed and I did what I could to cheer them up with recce reports that told of better conditions across the river.

One piece of news that brought joy to many hearts was the decision to abandon a Hill Billy that had broken down beyond repair. At the Bayano we loaded all the kit not considered really essential and sent it back to Canitas by boat. But this still meant additional loads for the ponies. Already a sounder of ferocious wild pigs called peccary had swept through Ernie's camp, wrecking it and stampeding the horses, one of which we did not see again. So now only twenty-seven remained and, to Keith's consternation, many of the mares were found to be in the early stages of pregnancy. Keith could not have known this, but now it made extra work for his section as the mares aborted.

We had seen a single white-lipped peccary at the Tropic Survival School. No larger than a small labrador, the aggressive beast had hurled itself against the wire of its pen time and again in an effort to reach us. Although an armed man could defend himself against one or two, there was little hope against a hundred. The Indians seemed to fear them more than the jaguars that they called 'tigers'. Already we had seen the local 'crocodile' or cayman, and Dustin Clarke, our Guardia interpreter and hunter, had shot a three feet specimen. I asked Tim to take the carcass over to the scientists' camp and he set off reluctantly to deliver his burden.

'Pop it down there,' said Philip Burton, 'I'll look at it later.' Tim was most alarmed next day to hear that when Philip had gone to inspect the reptile, it had walked away!

The Guardia relied upon the jungle to produce their food and we too sampled iguana lizard, which was like rubbery chicken; turkeys, which were excellent, and monkey; which was rank and distressing to cook.

On 23 January the Bayano dropped two feet and, as the expedition had all arrived at the obstacle, I decided to cross without further delay. The swirling brown water was still flowing rapidly between the rocky banks on top of which stood dozens of inquisitive brown-skinned Choco Indians. The horses went over first, tethered head to tail in groups of four or five, controlled by a stalwart Negro, whom we paid well for his expert help.

Ticky had the Avon raft built in record time, and Gavin drove on as if he had been doing it all his life. The river was too shallow for the outboards to be used, so Ernie and his merry men waded alongside in life-jackets and pushed. When they reached deep water, the sappers hung on the life-lines and Ticky used his motors to steer them to the bank. Both vehicles, the remaining Hill Billy and all our equipment went over without a hitch. A general holiday atmosphere prevailed, the sappers felt cocky, the drivers had renewed confidence and Keith was pleased that he still had twenty-seven horses.

As the tropical night closed in around us, I held the first of our many Sunday evening services. Keith formed the sappers into a choir (by promising them free beer, I later learned) and a volunteer read the lesson. Thirty voices gave a convincing rendering of 'Guide me O thou great redeemer', and I felt we all had something to be a little proud of. The first big obstacle was behind us. Already the cry was 'On to Bogota!' But that was a long way off and first we had to conquer two hellishly steep jungle ridges that we had nicknamed the Heartbreak Hills.

Rising hundreds of feet above the Bayano valley floor, the hills were surmounted by a logging trail with a slope of one in three, which had men, women and horses gasping for breath. At the top, we waited anxiously to see how the Range Rovers would perform. To our delight the cars took the first hill in fine style, with their normally silent engines giving out a throaty roar. They almost made the summit of the second but, due to a greasy patch of rock, had to use their capstans to winch the final thirty yards. At last the great cars had demonstrated the immense power of their three-litre engines. The capstans were an obvious success too. In three hours we had done 3·5 kilometres, easily the best speed to date. In our plan I had calculated that we must average three miles a day to get across before the rains. We were carrying supplies for five days and the Beaver would re-supply us by parachute. All our calculations would work out provided that we could keep moving.

I thought things had been going too well, for quite suddenly there was a yell, 'Watch it!' from one of the sappers. Gavin slammed his foot down and the car hurtled forward. It was just in time, for the track had collapsed and the Range Rover narrowly missed falling sixty feet into a gorge. Now the steep-sided ravines necessitated the use of the alloy ladders more frequently. Crossing these obstacles, the horses stumbled and shed their loads, some rolled over in the sticky mud, others sank to their bellies. Witnessing our agony, the insects began to attack and we met the black hornets for which Darien is famed. Nevertheless, by 16.00 hours we had covered eight kilometres and made our camp beside a small river. Slinging our hammocks from the trees, we placed a waterproof cape above to form a shelter and in between was arranged the vital mosquito net. All the guy ropes were thoroughly dusted with insect repellent. I found going to bed a tedious business. First, one unpacked a night set of dry clothes from a plastic bag, and then, balancing precariously on another such bag, peeled off the stinking wet day clothes, wrung out the worst of the moisture and popped them into a bag which would form a pillow. Then, using a torch and mirror, I inspected my body for ticks, thorns and septic cuts. Having removed the ticks with a cigarette, got the thorns out with a needle and tweezers, I applied liberal quantities of antiseptic cream to the sores, before climbing into my night-clothes and ensuring that every item of equipment was suspended by an insect-proofed cord above ground level. Now came the all important hop into the hammock. Great care was essential if one was not simply to plummet out the other side. Next, I pulled the flimsy sleeping-bag over myself, and positioned my pillow so that my day clothes, although soaking wet, would at least be warm in the morning. Finally, I gave the inside of my net a liberal spraying of anti-insect aerosol, which usually put me to sleep as well! The jungle around us was damp, and in the early hours we were chilled to the bone by the falling temperature. That night I began to notice the effect of the strange environment on my friends and in my log wrote:

I have noted that on previous expeditions people looked forward to mail from home. I think, on this one, it is heightened by the claustrophobic effect of the jungle around us, which not only cuts one off from civilization and everyone one knows, but also from the sun and light outside. Daily we advance through a tunnel of dense vegetation.

Our problems multiplied and I think 25 and 26 January are days I would not want to repeat. My log reads:

Tuesday, January 25, 1972. No rain

Last night was damp and cold, and we broke camp about ninety minutes after dawn. Through the jungle we moved in a long straggling column. Our prison, for that is what it is, is illuminated by a dull green light, which at times gives an almost translucent appearance to this eerie world. Giant trees rise up like huge pillars reaching for the sun which beats down on the canopy some hundred and fifty feet above. Lianas and vines hang down in a tangled mass to catch projecting horse-loads and to trip the unwary. On the ground, there is a mat of leaves which is constantly resupplied from above. There seems to be no change in the season of the jungle and I have noticed that there are very few, if any, yellowing leaves as one might see in more temperate climates. Underneath this mat there is a layer of humus from which grows thick undergrowth. Visibility is rarely more than twenty yards and all the time, day and night, the jungle resounds to the drip, drip, drip of the condensing humidity and the occasional crash of a giant tree falling. When it rains it usually falls in torrents, turning the track into quagmire. The thick black mud, ravines, gulleys, dense vegetation, fast-flowing rivers, patches of poisonous palms and stinging plants have combined against us. Now I can see why the ill-fated Scots colony perished in 1699.

Already some people are finding that their sweat-soaked clothes are rotting. As forecast, some leather equipment is going mouldy, although my personal belt kit, which I soaked in Neatsfoot oil seems to be standing the strain well, but I have found mould inside my Topee. On the other hand the US army jungle boots are excellent and far superior to the Far Eastern variety that we use in the British army. The Hill Billy's track is continuously clogging up with mud which then sets hard in the heat. It requires cleaning out for at least thirty minutes every two hundred yards. We have lightened its load to the minimum but I doubt that the one remaining machine can go on much longer.

The Range Rover swamp tyres simply will not cope with mud; there is no traction. We may try the old road type, but I am told that the tread is the same, so, in desperation I have ordered some special chains from USA to put on the wheels. Until they arrive, we may have to resort to using ropes. Naturally the vehicle crew is depressed by the poor performance of their cars in these difficult conditions.

We heard the Beaver pass overhead once or twice, but he cannot see us beneath this dense canopy. Ministars are vital and I curse the day they were put off the aircraft from UK. However, I hope to get them in on the next airdrop, as our gallant rear party, led by Major Bill Eggleston in London, is on to the problem.

The engineers have been working at a fantastic rate and already their clothes are becoming ragged; they have lost much weight and are looking very tired, but, thank God, their sense of humour goes on.

Wednesday, January 26, 1972. No rain

David Bromhead told me on this morning's radio schedule that the mud ahead is the worst he has seen so far.

The going today was slow. Phil Church is getting steadily weaker and the MO says he has pneumonia or pleurisy, probably caused by the damaged ribs. He rides in the second vehicle, and we are trying to carry him forward to the next clearing as gently as possible. I will get a helicopter in there to pick him up. To get round the mud, we had to cut a track through the virgin jungle in the end.

In doing so, we really came across the insect life of Darien. The mosquitoes, gnats and flies became a constant plague; there were inch-long black ants whose bites hurt like hell for hours, and also some stinging caterpillars. The heat and humidity was oppressive and we worked dripping with sweat the whole time. Clusters of aggressive and vindictive hornets, living in hollow trees and nests, swarmed out to meet anyone who disturbed them. I have never seen insects so vicious. Within seconds, a well-ordered column could turn into chaos under attack from hornets. The sappers are carrying smoke bombs as a defence against them! Apart from this we have seen some inch-wide centipedes and black scorpions which have stung one or two people. Spiders, some as large as dinner plates, probably of the bird-eating variety, are also common.

When brushing against the foliage we pick up ticks which, almost unnoticed, bury their teeth into our flesh with such tenacity that we often require them to be removed by the MO. If the beast's head remains in the skin after it is plucked from you, it becomes a source of constant irritation and sometimes infection. On the other hand snakes, although numerous, are usually shy and we have come across few aggressive varieties.

In cutting a new track we learned another lesson, that the trees must be cut right down to ground level, for as soon as the Range Rovers started on the new trail, they tore out a tyre valve on one of the projecting stumps. In order to try to get more traction, we fitted ropes around the wheels but this time they twisted behind the wheel and dragged off a complete brake calibre. Fortunately, the crew was able to replace this, but it is another idea that simply will not work. It has been very slow all day in deep, deep mud, with the sappers using ladders and winching most of the time. The vehicles got to within half a mile of the campsite before the exhausted crews and engineers stopped for the night.

We are camped on the Parti river I think (the map is indifferent). This afternoon a FAP (Panamanian Air Force) helicopter came in. He brought in supplies for his men and also kindly toook Phil back to base. The Hill Billy, which arrived in the late afternoon, became finally bogged down in deep mud and its magneto packed up. The Beaver dropped a spare, but, due to a strange coincidence, Cliff Taylor, the pilot, discovered a man in a green uniform wearing a white hat waving some red cellophane approximately ten miles from us. Understandably he thought it was me and dropped magneto, some bread and, alas, a supply of pyrotechnics to this strange and, as yet, unidentified figure deep in the jungle.

The men are very exhausted, but Rosh and Carolyn go on in good humour, despite the muck and insects which must annoy them every bit as much as they do us.

I have decided to stay here tomorrow to recuperate and receive another airdrop; certainly we are in a bad shape at the moment, and a day's rest will do us good. It will also enable us to wash our clothes and get the sun to our bodies, as in the clearing it beats down with relentless heat.

In ten days we had been reduced to an exhausted, filthy and rotting group of quick-tempered mud-babies. The jungle was simply consuming us mentally and physically. Now we emerged into a clearing; our pallid skin was sun-burned in an hour. But the day's rest made all the difference and we received vital re-supply by parachute of goodies, tyres, beer and mail. The tyres were the old road-type, but I felt that anything would be better than the Swamp variety.

I added a fillip to the improving morale by ordering the abandonment of the last Hill Billy. But if spirits were high, I knew that they would sink again once we moved on, for David had warned me of terrible going ahead, and already three of our engineers were in poor health.

We attempted to advance again next day, but mechanical problems with the vehicles delayed us, and I decided to spend the time in a detailed reconnaissance, giving my colleagues another day's rest. I tried riding Cromwell, my powerful bay horse in order to move more quickly, but it was safer and quicker to walk. The track was knee-deep in mud and the ground on either side was strewn with the massive roots of the giant trees. Tangled undergrowth and thorn bushes were interspersed with ravines and stream-beds. Nature had devised the most impenetrable barrier to vehicles that I had ever seen.

'It's rather like cutting a way through two hundred and fifty miles of giant rhododendron bushes,' said Peter, as we paused to sharpen our machetes.

'Well, we can't get through that mud,' I said. 'We must cut a new track parallel to the old one.'

'That will take years,' gasped Tim, when I told him of my plan.

'Well, we'll all be very fit at the end,' I remarked and, at dawn next day, we started to cut a new track through Darien.

On 30 January we reached a large clearing by a small river I believed to be the Piriati. Lush grass abounded and our horses could fill their bellies. In the jungle they were fed on air-dropped corn-cobs and giant leaves from the trees.

On 31 January, I recorded an unusual incident in my log:

During the night the guard (at that time Rosh) heard the frightful roaring noise of what was believed to be a large cat, possibly a jaguar, near at hand. The horses had been agitated in the night, but this was caused by the presence of some wild Indian horses in the same clearing. There was obviously a stallion amongst them and this quite upset our old boy, 'Randy'. We caught one or two glimpses of the horses in the moonlight – they were handsome beasts, mostly greys with long, flowing black manes, not at all shy and thus difficult to drive away. The health of our horses is a constant source of worry and Keith's team spare no effort to keep them going. They are being pestered by the vampire bats, and like us all, by the insects. Without Keith Morgan-Jones I believe that many of them would be dead by now.

My affection for Cromwell was not enhanced by his impatient habit of jumping gulleys whilst I was still half way across with the result that I usually got pushed face down in the mud. He had really exceeded himself a few days before by doing his usual trick, forcing me into the slime with his hoof. At the same time he smashed the spirit flask in my rucksack, so that I emerged covered in mud and soaked in whisky. Nevertheless, the horses were dear to many of us, and a few days later when Rosanante, a poor mare who had grown steadily weaker since aborting, had to be shot, I felt as if we had lost a friend.

Indeed, willing or unwilling, we were all rapidly becoming enslaved by the Gap. I began to envy those who had been evacuated by air. Tim had gone and the job of writing the press reports fell to me. Perhaps it was as well, because, although as tired as the rest, I was probably the only person who understood the whole situation. I tried hard to brief everyone fully, and yet put the best face on a rapidly deteriorating situation. To the press, I stressed the problems, while maintaining an air of cautious optimism and avoided stating the actual distance the cars were making. Instead I talked of the recce section's advances and the scientists' successes. But we badly needed a leap forward; already people were asking what point the Range Rovers had reached.

To make matters worse, the cars began to suffer even more mechanical problems, and it was not until midnight of 5 February, with everyone heaving, pushing and winching that we got the stricken vehicles to the camp by the Piriati. Here, next morning, their crews set to work to locate the trouble that had caused them to lose all drive on all wheels. After an hour we knew the worst. The differentials had disintegrated! This really was a major blow. We had some spare differentials, but too heavy to be parachuted, and helicopters were £100 per hour unless we could scrounge a free lift from the

FAP or USAF. It seemed that we had struck a major weakness in the vehicle, and I therefore gave instructions that base house should contact Rovers in England.

I hoped they could solve this latest problem, because until they did, the vehicles were stranded. We simply did not have the money to air-freight heavy spares from UK, which would take weeks anyway. We had done thirty miles in seventeen days and still had over two hundred miles to go. According to our information, the worst going lay ahead on the Devil's Switchback, with which, by comparison the journey so far had been a gentle training run.

Already we had four sick at base house and another six getting slowly worse in the jungle. The Beaver, limited to three hundred flying hours had flown almost one hundred. The grazing at the Piriati was now exhausted, one horse was lost and one dead. Both Hill Billys had been abandoned. The first batch of our rations that had come out by air were about to run out, and due to a shipping delay the second consignment was still on the high seas.

It was Sunday and seemed an appropriate moment to hold a service, at which I read the prayer of Sir Francis Drake:

O Lord God, when thou givest to thy servants to endeavour any great matter, grant us to know that it is not the beginning, but the continuing of the same unto the end, until it be thoroughly finished, which yieldeth the true glory: through him who for the finishing of thy work laid down his life, our Redeemer Jesus Christ. Amen.

I hoped it would help us. Drake had died in Darien!

10

AGAINST ALL ODDS

I<small>T</small> was after midnight when I finished my calculations and the re-arrangement of our plans. Peter was still squinting through his theo-dolite in an attempt to fix our position.

'Where are we?' I enquired.

'Somewhere in the Pacific,' he grumbled, scratching his head.

Not feeling tired I filled in another page of my log, before turning in.

While we sit and look at the broken-down vehicles, morale will go down very quickly, and therefore I propose that Headquarters advance towards Torti and eventually to Santa Fe. One engineer section is to advance ahead of us and clear the track as much as possible so that, when the Range Rovers do get going again, the way will have been made relatively easy for them. At the Orders group tonight I gave instructions for us to move out in the morning.

Throughout the next day we plodded forward in the dense jungle. The trail got steadily worse. The horses, in spite of their long rest, were surprisingly weak and many went down in the deep mud. We soon passed Ernie and his sappers hacking away at the endless green vegetation. Ernie, for once, was silent, looking pale and feverish. I noticed that others, too, were showing signs of strain and one man, whose physical fitness I had always admired, collapsed when we stopped at a river-crossing. Was it the sudden exertion after days of enforced idleness or was it a general lowering of morale due to the crisis?

Marching along, I found it helped to pass the time by discussing everything with Cromwell. He had a knowing look and sometimes I even thought he understood me. 'Better watch it,' I cautioned myself, seeing the ever-impassive Limbu coming up, 'or they'll be saying that JBS's cracking up – talking to his horse now.'

But then my other voice said, 'Why the hell not, you always talk to animals, so why not now, anyway our animals like being talked to,' and I smiled as I remembered many an animated conversation with a plump yellow Labrador on the likely whereabouts of the next cock pheasant. I felt it was far better to confide my fears and worries to my horse. To my colleagues I must display confidence and good cheer. For if I seemed dispirited morale would probably sink even lower.

At the Ipeti River the monotonous scenery gave way to a picturesque view of Indian huts, sweet corn, a few bright flowers and a clear slow-flowing waterway. But a heavy rainstorm turned the track into a quagmire. For days we had struggled through the most dreadful conditions, and all the time we seemed to be getting steadily weaker. Somehow I must inject fresh energy into the expedition, and what we needed most was more labour. This I found by using members of Kelvin's support organization, who had been held in reserve. They landed by Beaver at a convenient jungle airstrip which we had discovered, quite by chance, at a small village called Torti. Here they hired local labour and began to cut a track towards the Ipeti. At the same time I decided to try to hire some of the wiry little Cuna Indians from a nearby village. Broadly speaking, there were two tribes of Indians in Darien, the Choco and the Cuna.

The Choco were a stocky people with sharp features, and the men had short pudding-basin style haircuts. Both men and women were naked to the waist. They were usually found in the valleys where they often lived as isolated family groups and, in general, were more friendly than their suspicious rivals, the Cuna.

Strangely, although they appeared less primitive, the Cuna kept themselves apart from everyone else in Darien. Their women wore a unique form of dress, consisting of an elaborately patterned blouse called a 'Molla', whereas the men were frequently attired in a western-style shirt and jeans. Slightly built and finer featured than the Choco, the Cuna generally lived in large tidy villages on the higher ground.

It was to the Cuna village of Ipeti that I must now turn for extra manpower and I recorded an account of the meeting in my log.

Travelling silently upstream in the dark, propelled expertly by two young braves, we were greeted by others at the entrance to the village and taken up to the council chamber. As we entered the low, smoky building, we could make out many glimmering candles or lamps set on little tables, beside which sat the women of the village, embroidering and smoking from rather conventional looking pipes; olive skinned children, almost naked, scampered about the floor. Up towards the roof, sitting on top of the tiered seats, rather as you might see in a government chamber, sat the few men of the village who were not out earning their living in some distant part. In the centre of the room was a long bench rather like a garden seat, which faced two hammocks set at right angles to it. On these hammocks swung the wrinkled old chief and his deputy. Our own interpreters, rather like the defence counsel in a magistrates court, sat on the right and we felt very much like prisoners in the dock. With me were, Peter and Sergeant Limbu.

Very, very slowly the questions began after the customary greeting. It was so slow because everything we said had first to be translated from English into Spanish and from Spanish to Cuna. The chief would then put any major decisions to the entire village and a vote was taken. Eventually we learned that we had been able to hire the requisite number of men, approximately twenty, at the reasonable price of $1.50 per man per day. They asked us how we would communicate with the people who could speak no English or Spanish. I must confess I was stumped for a moment, and then said, 'Ah, but I have a Gurkha!'.

'How prudent', said the Chief, not really understanding what a Gurkha was. Sergeant Limbu just smiled.

The Chief then asked us many questions about our work and also asked me to design an airstrip for him, which I did on the back of an envelope. He was particularly keen that his people should become educated, for he saw this as a means of advancement. He was naturally worried about the Bayano Dam which had been built near Canitas, and what would happen to his hunting grounds and, indeed, to his village if the resultant lake spread up the Ipeti River. Finally he asked us about England, and his last question was rather touching. He said, 'Are there Indians in your country, and do they have schools?' I replied that there were Indians and that they all went to school. He said, nodding his wizened old head, 'Ah, it must be a good country.' I noticed, in particular, the concern for education and the apparent lack of it which worried the Indians; they told us many of their political problems, and how indeed they had voted for a man who had promised them all sorts of things, including a school, but nothing had happened. I told them that such injustice occurred in our country also. These people, although proud, have a great many grievances but one hopes that the government of Panama will try to look after them as progress of the road and dam opens up the Darien Gap.'

After dark the jungle, when viewed from the river, becomes a towering wall of blackness, broken only by fireflies. At night the creatures of this luxuriant world come forth to hunt and feed and, as we moved inexpertly against the current, the noise of the beasts reached an awesome crescendo. Frogs croaked, monkeys screamed and chattered and birds flapped loudly in the tall trees. At the river level my torch revealed pairs of red eyes glowing from the bank as small caymans waited expectantly in the shallows. With two of our Guardia on the pole we returned to camp. It was not a successful trip as our allies had little experience of boats and only avoided sinking on several occasions by a hair's breadth.

Next day I placed Sergeant Limbu in command of a Cuna working party, and leaving Lance-Corporal Joe Booth to give them sapper advice, the column struggled on to Torti. The mud was the worst yet, horses sank in, loads came off, hornets attacked and tempers flared. Three miles from Torti, Rosh advised me that the horses were getting very weak and so I halted the column in a small clearing, in the centre of which stood a deserted hut. The owner was said to have been murdered!

There was a base already set up at Torti, so, leaving Cromwell to rest in the clearing, I shouldered my pack and marched on to plan the next phase.

The five hundred yard airstrip was the nearest point to the stricken vehicles, where I could air-land the heavy axle assemblies by Beaver. To get them to the Piriati would need a daunting porterage operation. The only real answer was to helicopter the spares direct to the cars. Kelvin would have to use all his ingenuity to achieve this. I had complete confidence in my deputy, but it was as well to be prepared with a new plan if the helicopters could not be obtained. So I sketched out yet another contingency plan in my notebook which was already filled with a mass of illegible hieroglyphics.

Torti had ample grazing, good water and a reasonable amount of local food. Beyond this point we should be climbing out of the Bayano valley, leaving behind the sea of black mud. The way ahead was by contrast dry and almost waterless. David had reported several formidable obstacles, many fallen trees and an unusually large number of aggressive peccary. He said the insects were also bad and that the snakes seemed more plentiful. Even the Indians avoided this region and it was not easy to find guides.

Now we needed water, dynamite, more engineer tools and power-saws to cut the trail through to a cattle ranch on the Gulf of San Miguel – called Santa Fe.

Torti was a good place to pause and reconsider. It also enabled me to fly out a few people at a time to rest and recuperate at Paul Arengo-Jones' forward supply base, at the Panamanian version of a Cornish fishing village we knew as La Palma. Whilst waiting for

the Range-Rover crisis to be solved, I could make an air reconnaissance of the way ahead and the Atrato region in particular.
Thus, on 12 February, five of us festooned with cameras squeezed
into the Beaver and roared off the red earth strip at La Palma. I
described what we saw in my log that night.

We climbed towards the frontier, trying hard to spot Palo de las Letras,
but, as it is only a small plinth, I was not surprised when we could not
locate it. Suddenly we saw the land beyond. The jungle came to an abrupt
end, and in front of us, as far as the eye could see, there stretched a vast
flat waterlogged plain. The colour was a bright green and the monotony
was broken up by great pools of flat, calm water which reflected the azure
sky. Running across our front, the wide and muddy Atrato River formed
the western edge of the swamp. In the haze, on the far horizon, we could
see the towering peaks of the Andes. The whole view was awe-inspiring and
I am sure we all said inside ourselves, 'How can we ever cross that?' It was
laid out as on the map and I noticed that the road at Barranquillito
reached out into the swamp just as Brendan O'Brien had told me. The
track from Lomas de Rumie on our side of the Atrato certainly goes up
towards Palo, and, although I was able to follow it from the air for some
fifteen kilometres, it then disappeared.

'Well, what did you think of that?' I asked Sergeant Major
George Baker the sapper representative from the recce section when
we got back.

'It's a hell of an obstacle, a really bad place,' he said, trying not
to sound too pessimistic.

Before returning to Santa Fe, I scribbled a provisional plan for
dealing with the swamp in my notebook. There were a lot of
question-marks in the margin. However, while I returned to take
the column along the Santa Fe trail, the necessary recces could be
put in hand, and Jeremy Groves, a fresh-faced efficient cavalry
officer was already in Bogota for this purpose.

'I am afraid you must all lighten your loads again,' I said as we
prepared to march out of Torti. 'Remember we've got to carry
water now.' Keith had been dealing with the humans as well as
horses since we left the doctor at the Ipeti. Now he dished out a few
medicaments all round and reduced his load to the bare minimum
of veterinary equipment. 'I've only one thing left,' he said fiercely.

'What's that Keith?' asked an explorer with an ingrowing toenail.
'My bloody 45,' came the terse reply. His patients vanished.

The Santa Fe trail led through jungle, not as dense as we had experienced in the valley. David's beautifully drawn sketch-maps gave

me an excellent guide to the route, but showed few sources of water. To overcome this, I planned to carry all the water we could, and use the filter pumps to draw a small supply from any muddy pools we might find. This would provide sufficient for the personnel, but for the horses I needed a hundred gallons a day. Therefore, Paul had a number of oil drums scrubbed clean and prepared for parachuting water to us.

We did what we could to clear the track as we advanced, and spent a long hot evening digging down the banks of a particularly large ravine in preparation for the day when the Range-Rovers would come. The horses were frustratingly slow and the insects ravenous. Ticks were specially troublesome and I picked fifty of the bloated little horrors from my body one evening. As fast as you got them off, others fell on you from the trees.

The Indian guides deserted on the first day, after Randy, our evil-tempered stallion had bitten one of them. I felt this was simply an excuse, because Randy bit everyone, and it wasn't a very bad bite. However, they did not like the area and, being frightened stiff of the peccary, would not continue in spite of offers of a generous cash bonus and an air lift back to Torti at the end. The peccary were certainly there, and a sounder of about a hundred forced our Guardia escort to take to the trees.

There were other hazards too, as we discovered when cutting through a grove of broad-leaved plants which left our arms a mass of irritating and swollen stings. Keith had to shoot one horse exhibiting the dreaded symptoms of highly infectious equine encephalitis. Another poor beast was put down when it became too weak to go on, even without a load.

The Beaver dropped in water and supplies, using special jungle parachutes which suspended the loads on long nylon lines to get them through the tree canopy. On the third day we did over eighteen miles, getting extra liquid by slashing vines and drinking the clear, cool, woody flavoured water. Wild pineapple, in small onion-like pods were thirst quenching, but too many left the tongue burning.

The radio was not working at its best, and I found it quite maddening to hear of problems occurring elsewhere in the expedition without being able to intervene. Corporal Holmes, my long-suffering signaller (nicknamed by Keith, Private Parts), put up with my occasional ill-humour amazingly well. The expedition was now spread out from Ipeti to Santa Fe, and if my guess was right would soon be even more dispersed. Until the Range-Rovers were moving satisfactorily again, I decided I must have more mobility and better communications. I needed to be able to move rapidly up and down the route so that I could control the battle and our meagre resources more efficiently.

People were anxious to know what was happening and indifferent briefings by radio were not the answer. I wanted to be able to visit the widely scattered groups and use Polaroid photographs and a map covered in self-adhesive symbols to put them in the picture. This might keep morale at a reasonable level until our fortunes changed, and in moving by air or water to trouble spots I had discovered that the rivers of Darien are the real roads.

It was early morning when Tony Stansfeld and I, marching at the front of the column, heard an unusual sound – a heavy diesel! Five minutes later we rounded a bend in the green 'tunnel', and came face to face with a gigantic yellow bulldozer.

'Oh you great big gorgeous creature,' I said, slapping its steel tracks. The operator, a funny little old man with dirty blond hair, spoke Spanish with a guttural accent. Using the special expedition dictionary that Rosh had produced, I discovered that the bulldozer was opening a new logging trail into the Chuchunaque valley and for some of its length would be using our route. I was musing on our good luck when I noticed the operator looking at me in an odd way.

'Americano?' he enquired.

I told him I was a British army officer and he paled slightly. So for fun I said, 'You are from Germany?'

He muttered something about 'Many years ago', and jumping into his seat went clanking off down the trail.

Suddenly, as it always did, the jungle ended and the sunlight hit us as we stepped out into the open rolling plains of Santa Fe. It was like entering another world, and to our amusement we were striding up the first hill in lush pastureland when Charles Keyes, who had flown in ahead of us, ambled into sight. We thought he might utter something historic, but spying a smoker in our midst, he said, 'I say, could you possibly lend me a cigarette?'

Setting up a temporary base near the airstrip at Santa Fe, I moved to La Palma to establish a new command and control organization to cope with the crisis. I had already decided to continue cutting a track, and thus David Bromhead was now trying to find the best way to Yavisa. Following his path was Ernie and his sapper section, recently air-lifted from Torti to Santa Fe, resupplied, rested and revitalized.

All we had to do was get the cars moving. The Rover company were flying out their Range Rover expert, Jeff Miller, with a pile of spare parts and I had no reason to doubt that he could solve the problem. But, a nagging voice said inside me, 'What if it really is a major fault that cannot be solved in the jungle?'

To make the best of a bad job, I could salvage some of the expedition's honour by getting another vehicle to carry on from the point where the Range Rovers had broken down. The Toyota representative in Panama had already let it be known that his company would be delighted to provide us with a vehicle – free. My patriotism and a sense of responsibility to Rovers would not permit me to accept this, even if the committee were to agree, but Kelvin had discovered a battered second-hand Land-Rover.

If we could obtain this vehicle, and somehow get it into the jungle, it would, in the last resort, fill the role originally intended for the Range Rovers. If, as I hoped and prayed, Jeff could solve the differential problem then the lightweight Land-Rover could be used as a pathfinder vehicle, carrying an engineer section's equipment and tools to clear the path for the Range Rovers to follow. I could see no possible objection to this plan and, in addition, believed it would bring about a spirit of competition which would draw the best out of our depressed groups. Kelvin, Jim, Ernie, James Beattie, Gavin and David were all men who would respond to a challenge. While I did not want to create a foolhardy race, having lost almost a month's driving time, we needed to press on with all speed. Furthermore, a vehicle with the track-clearing sappers would act as a gauge to tell them what a vehicle could or could not negotiate. This might answer the drivers' complaints that the trail was sometimes too steep, too narrow or had been left with tree stumps too high.

There were only two small problems. With what to buy the Land-Rover and how to get it into the Darien Gap? The first was easily solved. The money reserved for Phase 3 (Bogota to Tierra del Fuego), would not be needed if we did not cross the Gap so I authorized Kelvin to use it. I felt confident that more could be raised later, if necessary.

Stripped down to its bare essentials, the Land-Rover could be air-lifted by a very large helicopter from Panama City to about as far as Santa Fe. Of course, the Range Rovers might never reach Santa Fe, but that was a chance we had to take. Alternatively, we could bring it in by sea.

I radioed Kelvin to buy the Land-Rover and borrow a giant helicopter. Then I appointed James Beattie, our wiry Scots dentist who acted as the administrative officer, to be officer in charge of the new pathfinder group.

Now I could turn my attention to another problem. The worst terrain in the Gap was known to be in the area of the Panama–Colombian frontier. We called its slippery undulating jungle-clad hills, ridges and ravines, the Devil's Switchback. It had been the undoing of every vehicle expedition so far. The vegetation was at its densest, the hills at their steepest and the information about it minimal.

Broadly speaking there were two possible routes, east or west of the Tuira River. On his recce Brendan was not terribly happy about either, although he felt that with plenty of time we could make it by the western route. Now we had no time to spare.

My early air recces revealed little, except that the western side did look marginally easier.

I was turning the problem over in my mind when we dropped out of low cloud on Darien's Caribbean coast and circled for fifteen minutes looking down at Caledonia Bay, site of the ill-fated Scots colony of 1699. 'Poor devils,' I thought, 'let's hope we don't end up as another Darien Disaster.'[1]

Flying back to the base at La Palma, I wondered what other problems could confront us, and I did not have to wait long to find out. Stepping from the Beaver, I heard the terrible news that five of our Colombian allies, who made up most of our recce party in the Atrato, had been drowned in an accident off the small seaport of Turbo. Only Jeremy Groves and a Colombian marine major had survived. I later learned that the tragedy occurred when a small boat belonging to the Colombian Navy's gunboat (that was to support the expedition) had been swamped in a rough sea. Displaying both common sense and courage, Jeremy had done everything possible to try to save one of the drowning officers, but it was to no avail, and indeed Jeremy was very lucky to be alive.

There seemed no end to our troubles. On the way to Yavisa, David reported that his guides were lost, and dozens of confusing tracks were causing him to walk literally hundreds of extra miles in an effort to find a way through. In the team I noticed that one or two of the less experienced were beginning to show signs of nervous stress and fatigue. I found my own patience being exhausted by some of the petty matters that people allowed to grow out of all proportion

1. John Prebble, *Darien Disaster* (Secker and Warburg, 1968).

as compared with our overall aim. Even so I had to try to listen to everyone's pet theories and complaints. I very much regretted not having a second-in-command actually with me in the field. Now would have been a time that such a person could have acted as an invaluable filter.

Meanwhile, back at the Ipeti River Jim Masters and his group patiently awaited the new axle assemblies. We spoke twice a day by radio, and I kept them abreast of the situation as best I could. They had a reasonable camp-site with a crystal-clear river in which to swim and, knowing Jim well, I was not unduly worried about their morale. I was somewhat surprised, therefore, when confronted one evening with a terrible tale of stress and strain in the Ipeti Camp.

'The men believe you've deserted them and no one cares about the Range Rovers any more!' was the accusation made by one of the officers who had come back to La Palma. I determined to look into the matter as quickly as possible, and a few days later I flew to Torti with Jeremy Pass, our SKC cameraman and marched to the Ipeti Camp some nine miles away. Without the noise of the cars the jungle seemed strangely still and peaceful. Where the track passed through clearings numerous butterflies of all colours and shapes danced ahead of us. Great green and blue dragonflies hovered beneath the wide leaves, and underfoot dozens of tiny frogs hopped around amongst the armies of ants that scurried about their business. We reached the river after lunch and found the stranded men looking remarkably happy and healthy. I now realized that the real stress and strain was at base and not in the jungle. That night I wrote in my log:

All the wild tales I heard about men being desperate and going mad in the jungle were obviously nonsense, although I understand that they have had a frustrating time. However, I was able to brief them on the full situation and they cheered up even more when they could see clearly that things were not as black as they had imagined. It is unfortunate that in situations like this men can do little but sit and listen to the radio conversations. We have only one net, which is not always the best thing, especially in a difficult situation as now, when it is vital for me to occasionally have a confidential conversation with base. Having seen this problem, I shall now have to use code phrases to ensure security of contingency plan preparations. I feel that most sensible persons will realise that the command element do not wish to hatch conspiracies by requiring this facility, but it is a particular problem with all communication being by radio on one frequency.

I must say it is good to be back with the sappers. They have a great sense of humour and we yarned long into the night and sang an amusing song, which their idleness has given them a chance to compose, called 'The Range Rover'. Apparently they were having competitions in song-writing to keep themselves occupied whilst awaiting the spares from England.

Tuesday, 29 February 1972

I stayed with the vehicle party until 10.00 hours and then heard the delightful sound of a FAP helicopter coming in; with it came Kelvin and Gavin, also an attractive ebony skinned Guardia lady captain called Margot Hutchinson! Her first remark to me was, 'Are the natives friendly?' She spoke perfect English and had been in London recently. Apparently she is in the Civil Affairs Department of the Guardia and her husband is a lawyer. She was beautifully dressed in a well-tailored suit of jungle-green, every bit as smart as her male counterparts who spend much time on their turn-out, and she obviously had a deep interest in both her job and the people around her.'

My trip back to base aboard the FAP helicopter was less alarming than a previous flight aboard a Panamanian Civil Aircraft when I had noted an interesting incident in my log:

It was a hair-raising trip in a small Cessna, because it was mostly held together with wire and adhesive tape. It took us an hour to get the single engine started and, as we were flying over the Pacific, the air speed indicator fell out of the dashboard. It was not working anyway, but I noticed, with concern, that the space behind it was filled with a postcard of the Virgin Mary!

In Panama City Kelvin's organization was in topgear. Jeff Miller had arrived, boxes of spares were coming in and, after a quick in-spection by Jeff, we purchased the Land-Rover. Kelvin had already persuaded our long-suffering USAF supporters to lend us a giant helicopter, and preparations went ahead to airlift the little green vehicle to Santa Fe. Meanwhile I had reconsulted everyone I knew who had ever visited the Devil's Switchback. They all said the same thing, 'The only route is west of the Tuira'. Even so I had doubts and decided to launch three reconnaissance teams to examine both sides of the valley.

Throughout all this drama one section of the expedition went quietly from success to success. Colonel Peter Reid, our scientific team leader, had now returned to Britain, and so it was the tall, fair-haired Irish Guards Ensign, John Windham, who, assisted by the able Sergeant Farrell, was now looking after our scientists' needs.

While those interested in the fauna, flora and rocks, pursued their quarry, Robin Hanbury-Tenison, recently arrived from Britain, sought out the Indians and examined their problems. Robin, champion of primitive peoples, already knew more about the jungles of South America than any of us. His charm and eloquence, combined with an easy, self-assured attitude had a settling effect on the tense nerves of some of our colleagues. With the minimum of fuss, he had gathered a few stores and set off into the forest to make contact with his beloved Indians. From time to time, this elusive and almost mythical figure, whom many of the expedition never saw, would emerge and quietly restock his rucksack with film and small gifts. Those who met him during these fleeting visits to civilization heard the case against the road skilfully put and realized that there was another side to the argument.

But for most of us the jungle was a cruel enemy contesting every step. The long column of some forty men and women with twenty-four horses winding through the hot, humid valley were closing up on Yavisa, and Pathfinder, as we had named the Land-Rover, had reached Ernie's sappers and was making splendid progress. Behind them Jeff had got the stricken Range Rovers repaired and to our joy on 3 March the great cars had crossed the Ipeti. Alas, our happiness was shortlived. In my log I summarized the problems:

Apparently, on the 4 March, two miles had been travelled when one of the new differentials broke up. It was immediately replaced with a spare of the old pattern. Driven on by desperation, the party pushed towards Torti and the airstrip, where at least they would be accessible to the Beaver. Favours could not be asked endlessly of the FAP and the USAF, and private helicopters have proved ruinously expensive. By 5 March, another differential was starting to make ominous noises. And at the end of the day a total of three had gone or were going! The cars had just managed to drag themselves to Torti before coming to a standstill, and today Jeff flew back to Panama to talk to Rovers by telephone.

The next day we met at the forward base and my log recorded our discussion.

Jeff and Gavin saw me today at La Palma. They were despondent about the chances of the Range Rover. Jeff suggests that it may help if we reduce the load by fifteen per cent for he says that they are indeed that much overloaded. We should also use the capstan on every slope. The ladders on the roof, which weigh about one hundred pounds each, may also be causing the trouble, for a high load sets up severe torque on the back axle as the vehicle goes up a slope. Even so, I am sure we shall have a difficult time getting them to Santa Fe, as well as having a shortage of drinking water. I briefed Gavin very carefully on this and he must take precautions because, if the vehicles breakdown, in a waterless area, they will be in real trouble. Jeff is clearly sparing no effort to beat the bogey. I told them that, if the Range Rovers can get to Lomas de Rumie by 12 April, I think we have still got a sporting chance of getting them through the swamp.

Meanwhile the Pathfinder stormed ahead and spirits rose. If only the Range Rovers would move, I knew that with their superior power they could soon close the gap.

As the horses and my depleted Headquarters approached Yavisa, I set up a new base at El Real, the riverside town once sacked by Keith's piratical ancestor, Sir Henry Morgan. Although morale was high, our casualty list was growing. Rosh had suffered an allergic reaction to a hornet sting and had been evacuated in a dramatic dash down the Chuchunaque. John Richardson, the medical officer, had been unwell for weeks and was now under investigation in Panama City. Meanwhile Susie, his energetic wife and our nurse, was acting as doctor and doing a great job. Elsewhere Keith's St. John's Ambulance training was being put to good use. But I was running very short of manpower.

The horses too had suffered casualties and it was with a pang of remorse I noted in my log the loss of Cromwell whom I had loaned to the sappers.

The Pathfinder is now five miles south of the Meteti and going well. Ernie has now joined it. Unfortunately he has lost Cromwell, who was nearly driven mad by the blood-suckers and vampires. Corporal Yuen dressed him in a length of parachute silk, in the form of a nightdress as a protection after dark. One night he escaped and rampaged through several Indian villages, a pink apparition, causing great consternation, especially when he passed through a drinking orgy.

The complete change of character in the animal had made him unmanageable and reluctantly he was left with the Indians whom he had so terrified.

Loco, the mad albino mare loaned to the Guardia, was reported as having died of snake bite, although she turned up miraculously in an Indian village a few weeks later! While the advance continued, Ticky positioned his raft at Yavisa to await the Pathfinder. Keith's fit horses swam the Chuchunaque and the Tuira to reach El Real, while the weakest were moved by Ticky's raft, slightly modified and aptly renamed 'Noah's Ark'. Horses, Ticky decided, were not his favourite passengers, after one had delivered a load of fresh manure into his lap.

Meanwhile I had again visited Colombia, this time landing at a small airstrip in the Atrato valley to confer with Jeremy Groves and a newly-appointed team of Colombians who had replaced those so tragically lost at sea.

Beyond the swamp the deep green pattern of undulating cauliflower-covered hills faded into the blue haze. 'Do you think you'll ever get this far,' said David Reid as he flew us home.

As preparations continued in Colombia, Jeff and the vehicle team worked on to solve the Range Rover's problems. Returning from a two-day river reconnaissance of the Tuira with Kay, I was overjoyed to hear that the bogey at last seemed to have been overcome and the cars were thundering on towards Santa Fe. Now the race was on, but it was also a race to beat the rains which would start in early April. It was now 10 March.

At El Real there was another problem to cause delay. The area we were moving through was in places heavily cultivated. To make a track into Yavisa and over to Pinogana we should need to cut down numerous banana plants. The local authorities accepted this only on condition that we paid for the damage. Our rapidly diminishing funds simply would not run to an additional bill of over a thousand dollars. The only solution was to use the raft to float the cars from Yavisa to Pinogana, thus avoiding the plantations. An overland distance of only about two miles, by river it was a difficult voyage through twenty-two miles of tidal waters, liberally sown with giant logs. I hoped that the sturdy craft designed for relatively short crossings would cope in its new role. In fact I need not have worried. With Ticky and his crew the raft was to accomplish feats beyond their wildest dreams in the weeks that lay ahead.

On 12 March the Pathfinder reached Yavisa and HE Mr. Dugald Macolm, our strong supporter, flew down from Panama with a party of friends to see us. The Range Rovers were making excellent progress, the weather was fine and the ambassador's party brought an ample picnic which they generously shared with us. Spirits soared, but that night disaster struck again.

This time it was the faithful Beaver which had broken down. Part of the tail wheel suspension had collapsed as it landed at Tocumen. Probably the result of many heavy impacts with the rocky strip at La Palma. Once again spares must be sent from Britain and now, with out columns stretched from Santa Fe to the Atrato, we had lost our vital air support. Not only would we be without the ready means of parachute re-supply but we could not make all-important air reconnaissance. We were too far from Panama City for all but the largest USAF helicopters and too distant from Colombia for help from across the border, even if that could be approved by the Panamanian government.

In Panama City Kelvin rose to the occasion and obtained funds from the British Ministry of Defence to hire a civilian Beaver for real emergencies. Meanwhile, at El Real I drew up a plan for re-supply by boat, horse and porter and wrote in my log:

Without the Beaver I must establish a chain of depots along the river as far as the frontier. By hiring three piraguas I can collect stores from La Palma and bring them to El Real, there they will be re-allocated and taken upstream in slightly smaller piraguas to depots at Pinogana, Boca de Cupe and then overland, by horse, to Pucuru or up the river by even smaller piraguas. If the river does not fall much more I can even send stores all the way to Paya by boat. The major problems I have with establishing these depots include lack of radios, personnel to act as storekeepers, money to hire piraguas and, of course, we only have four twenty horse-power outboard motors, two of which are in use on the raft. The cost of hiring outboards is prohibitive. Petrol is very difficult to obtain up here, and my main supplies are at La Palma where Kelvin has brought forward all the remaining stores from Panama, using one of the Guardia gun boats. In fact Palo might as well be Mount Everest, and I might be halfway back towards Khatmandu! However I do have the river.

Now extra manpower was even more necessary and I seized every opportunity to get able-bodied workers. We hired as many Panamanians to cut the track as our meagre funds could afford. I borrowed half a dozen illegal Colombian immigrants from the prison at El Real, having agreed to take them over the border and release them there. Meanwhile I would feed them in exchange for work. A wandering young Englishman joined our ranks for interest and food when I found him at a small riverside town. *The Daily Telegraph* had been printing regular articles on our progress, and now they sent in a smiling photographer, Paul Armiger, to join us for a month. The next to arrive was an American hobo who was avoiding, so he said, the tax department and the CIA. He had followed us on foot from Canitas, having heard that the English were building a highway through Darien!

So the force was built up, and when the recce teams stumbled in from the Devil's Switchback, I knew I would need every man and more.

The western route was the densest jungle Peter had seen and was clearly out of the question. However, to the east, David and Tony Stansfeld's patrols had discovered a track that led from Pucuru to Paya to Palo de Las Letras. Both David and Peter's teams had also found wrecked Chevrolet vehicles deep in the jungle; sad reminders of the ill-fated General Motors Expedition. The only problem now remained to find a route from Pinogana to Boca de Cupe and on to Pucuru.

The Pathfinder was now ready to move and, seeking to save time, I dispensed with the recce of the route to Boca. This was a bad mistake. Within a day of leaving Pinogana, they were hopelessly lost and rightly cursed me for not sending a recce party ahead. However, I had no one to spare for further recces and so the Pathfinder group had to live up to its name.

Meanwhile, I was anxious to find a way to link up the smuggler's footpath that led to Palo, with the dirt road I had seen leading into the hills from Lomas de Rumie. So David set off once more. In the swamp Sapper Captain Richard Summerton and a small team were already operating from the Colombian gunboat and getting valuable information on the various routes in the green morass.

The local people at Boca said there was a way through to Pucuru and, had Tony Stansfeld been able to walk, I should have sent him to check it. However, like most of us, Tony's feet were in a dreadful condition due to the effects of 'jungle foot'. He was only able to hobble with a stick and it would be days before he could march again.

The Beaver was still grounded, and thus air recce was out of the question. David had been unable to find a path through to Pucuru and it looked as if we should have to cut a new trail all the way. Accordingly, I engaged more cutters and then, armed with haversacks of dynamite, set out to blast a way through to the Pathfinder group, who were struggling in from Pinogana. When they reached Boca they could take all the cutters and hack their way up what we now called the Pucuru Heights.

It was 19 March, a significant date – it began to rain again. The day was hot and sticky. More so than usual. We walked through plantations and rocky ground and, using the explosive, blasted through stubborn hardwood tree stumps and eventually came upon a small river. The banks were about twelve feet high and vertical so, much to the delight of our cameramen, Staff Sergeant Brian Blackford and I blasted through the bank. Thereafter we went through groves of banana until we began to rise up a steep slope into heavily wooded country. Our cutters were excellent and worked ahead at high speed. We found numerous hardwood trees across the track and continued our demolitions. In this high temperature the smell of vapourizing nitro-glycerine from the explosive was strong. After a short while I noticed that Blackford was not looking at all well and, while we were tackling a ravine crossing in the jungle, he suddenly became very sick. The problem was undoubtedly what is known to sappers as plastic explosive sickness. It is caused by the vapour being inhaled which lowers the blood pressure to such a point that it causes a severe headache. Usually the answer is to give the patient some form of mild stimulant such as tea or even a glass of beer. Any drug such as aspirin, which will further depress the blood pressure, is not likely to succeed. Alas, on this occasion my spirit flask was empty and all we could do was to advise Blackford to lie down and take it easy for a while.

A little later my own head started to ache and I realized that it was affecting me in the same way. The heat and humidity were stifling, the insects simply would not leave us alone. At 15.00 hours when our cutters reckoned that they had done enough for the day, an unfamiliar noise disturbed the jungle. All around us the leaves began to tremble as heavy raindrops struck them. At the same time it started to thunder and a tremendous tropical storm broke. There was no question of shelter. I washed my hands in the rain and managed to get off most of the explosive residue. We had just reached another deep ravine, which was already beginning to trickle with the new flow of water when, suddenly through the undergrowth on the far side emerged the resolute figure of Corporal Mick Hough, whom we knew to be with the Pathfinder group. Shortly afterwards Ernie appeared and told us that for some hours they had heard the roar of our demolitions and this had done a great deal to raise their morale. Eventually more of the Pathfinders arrived, and in the distance we could hear the singing of the power saws and the revving of the vehicle's engine. And so they came through, over the demolitions, past the river-beds, through the difficult going and the plantations. They stopped for the night just outside the town and slept soundly as only utterly exhausted men can sleep.

That evening was mostly spent arranging the rafting for the morrow, but it was difficult to work in the town because of the constant noise from the cantina's juke-box. However, we did manage to hear on the radio that the Range Rovers would be in Yavisa that night. This was a tremendous effort and great credit was due to Phil

Church and his five sappers who had forced them through. The three-man vehicle party of the 17th/21st Lancers also deserved high praise for their efforts. I also heard the Beaver should be in the air on 22 March. Meanwhile, we were still using the horses to carry forward stores to Pucuru.

At Boca I turned to Charlie Thompson, a friendly ex-Jamaican Negro who spoke English.

'Is this *the* rains, Charlie?' I asked.

'Rains, man,' Charlie shook his grizzled old head down which the water cascaded and smiled. 'No, sir – this is jus' hoomidity!'

But he also told me that the main rains were preceded by a few days of the small rains. Then, some two to three weeks later, the proper rains would start. I looked at the map and wondered how much good luck we could count on.

DEFEAT INTO VICTORY

'Only he who attempts the ridiculous can achieve the impossible'
– Will Henry, *Chicago Tribune*, New York News Syndicate
[Inscribed on the wall of the office of Colonel Hans Ruthe in the Canal Zone]

ERNIE'S undauntable sappers roared into Boca with their noisy, battered, beloved buggy, drank the cantina dry of beer and, before a large crowd, crossed the river on the Avon raft in fine style. They were clearly enjoying the attention. Charlie Thompson sat watching from the steps that led down to the river. 'You know what the people call you men?' he said, stroking his stubbly chin.

'Loco Inglese?' I enquired.

'Some do say that,' he grinned, 'but others say you Los Quebracha.'

'What does that mean, Charlie?'

'The Quebracha is a hard wood tree – I thinks it's hardest of them all, name means "Axebreaker".'

'Don't tell Ernie.' I said, 'he might think it an insult for engineers to be called that.'

'Ah seen men come and men go on this river a long time,' wheezed the old sage, 'and ah got a feeling that you'll get through.'

For the next few days I busied myself with the problems of the growing number of casualties. One of whom was Jim Masters.

'He ought to be evacuated,' insisted Suzie.

'You must keep him going,' I argued.

'Have you seen his arm? It's a terrible abscess.' She scolded me, then added, 'All right I'll see what I can do – but no promises.'

But Suzie was a good doctor and, two days later, I blessed her when the next crisis occurred.

Having got about half-way to Pucuru, the Pathfinder group had suddenly come upon an obstacle they could not beat. Already they

had winched their car up near vertical slopes – slopes so steep that
the front wheels were lifted clear of the ground by the pull. Even
Ernie was despondent, for now, climbing to the top of a hideous
slope, he found the way was blocked by a ravine so big that he
simply stood on the edge and gazed at it in horror. Recces to the left
and right produced no alternatives.

The expedition heard the worst news yet calmly. 'You'll find a
way round – you must, John,' urged Kay. Having given people a job
to do I am always reluctant to interfere, but now some of the group
leaders were utterly worn out, and I felt it was time to take command of this particular operation myself. 'Get me that civilian
Beaver,' I told Kelvin on the radio, and next day we looked at the
problem.

My log records:

We flew for several hours around this confusing area. Using the Polaroid
camera, we photographed the difficult terrain which we now know to be
in front of the Pathfinder group. There appears to be one particularly
steep ridge running right across their proposed route, from the Pucuru
river to the mountains in the east. All round us the forest was burning
where Indians are taking advantage of the last few days of the dry season
to burn the dead wood and undergrowth in the clearings. There seems to
be a possible route on the Pucuru river bed, although I am not certain
about this. On examining the air photographs more clearly, I am a little
doubtful. The hills are certainly very bad and there is no apparent solution to our predicament. It is easy to be wise after the event, but obviously
our hurried reconnaisance in this area has caused problems. Another
possibility is in the Capeti region to the north-east, but this is a long way
round.

Thus I went forward to see the problem on the ground and, taking
Jim with me, we marched up from the river. The tired filthy men sat
around their beast of burden whilst James, Jim, Ernie and I discussed the route. James who had worked non-stop for weeks was very
depressed and considered that we were done for. Ernie was determined to go on, if I could find him a route. With us was Sergeant de
Leon of the local Guardia, who like a village policeman knew the
area and everything about it. Suddenly he said, 'There is a place
called Cruso Mono, not far from here, it is where the Indians drag
logs down to the river.'

'If a heavy log could come down a vehicle might be winched up,' I
thought.

'How can we get there?' I asked.

'By river,' said de Leon, 'The place is very narrow – that is what the name means – the Monkey Crossing.'

Next day at dawn we set out to examine the place and my log records:

Moving upstream in Canito's piragua, we took one and a quarter hours to do a straight distance of only two miles. After passing the Pucuru turning we found there were fifteen rapids before we came to Cruso Mono. There are many shallow areas of the river where vehicles could motor easily and a few deep poles where a raft will be needed. It is really a question of hopping from one sandbank to another across the river. We also tried to investigate the Pucuru river, but it was so shallow that we could get no more than ninety yards up from the mouth.

It is my impression that we could, with luck, get one or two cars forward by this method of rafting and driving, but whether the raft will take the constant battering in the rapids and on the rocks I simply do not know. Certainly it is quite a gamble, but it may be the only choice.

Above the crossing the river-bank rose like a wall for hundreds of feet. It was covered with trees and shrubs, and a narrow track led to the water's edge. Sergeant de Leon explained that a path ran from the top of a bank to the village of Pucuru and said he would get a local man to show it to me on the morrow.

Meanwhile, I decided to see if we could negotiate the river with the Pathfinder and the raft. So Ticky and Ernie's team started out for Cruso Mono next morning. As they struggled through the rapids and rattled over the shingle banks, I went ahead with a small party to examine the supposed path. It was long after dark when I recorded the details of that recce.

At Cruso Mono there are flat rock ledges ending in deep water at the side of the river. It'll be simple to use the raft and land vehicles on the ledges. We set off up the first steep hill, some four hundred feet, at a slope of forty degrees which had a step-like structure. Then came a long flat ridge which the guide, Fernando, led me along. Later we dropped into a shallow valley with several ravines before ascending another hill of five hundred feet, again in steps, at the top of which we came to some flat ground. Finally we descended to the village of Pucuru. The journey, in all, took three hours and ten minutes of really hard walking. The track was indistinct; snakes were plentiful. [In fact one large black one slithered over my boot].

Reaching Pucuru at 14.40 hrs, we were surprised to see Jeremy Ainsworth and his girl friend[1] who had arrived at the same time. They had

1. Jeremy Ainsworth had earlier tried to follow the expedition in his own Land-Rover, but had been forced to give up. His winch was in use on the Pathfinder.

come overland on the Capeti route with their horses. Jeremy had lost his wallet and we lent him ten dollars to keep him going.

Leaving James and Tony to organise the clearing of the route from Pucuru to Paya, I returned with Fernando to the river. My own feet are riddled with 'jungle foot' and it is painful to walk. Fernando, whose feet are hardened, marches like a fury and I had great difficulty in keeping up. We became lost on two occasions, but in the end reached the river just before the last light at 18.00 hours. The Pathfinder was at Cruso Mono and ready to start out on the track we had recce'd.

Skilfully driven by their crews, the Range Rovers made a triumphal entry into Boca and, by early afternoon on 28 March, the leading car was safely aboard Ticky's raft to cross the first deep pool. Thereafter the big blue vehicle was able to speed up the process by towing the raft, like a bargee's horse, as it motored along the sandbanks. Using its snorkel, the Range Rover could wade in about two feet of water and continued motoring where the Land Rover had been forced to raft.

The next day the Range Rover reached Cruso Mono and was now only two days behind the Pathfinder. Everyone was working flat-out and in high spirits, the psychology of the Pathfinder was paying off. I was feeling elated when I scribbled in the faded waterproof notebook that night.

We reached Cruso Mono ahead of the vehicle and were able to do some useful reconnaissance on the river-bed. My great fear is that the rains will start in earnest and the river will rise. If this happens our current road will disappear! The Rover reached Cruso Mono at 14.00 hours and, while we were having tea, it started to rain. In the downpour that followed, the piraguas returned to Boca. We hear on the radio that the Pathfinder is in Pucuru, the recce section has reached Lomas, Sergeant Farrell is on the Cacarica river with the Colombian army and Richard Summerton has his base at Sautata. The picture generally looks good for once!

However I went on to express some doubts and fears:

I should like to move my Headquarters forward now, but I dare not do so until the vehicles are all safely on their way to Pucuru. The problems of maintaining our column in this jungle is enormous and I calculate there are only about one box of rations and a few gallons of petrol ahead of the requirements. The piragua re-supply system cannot go on much longer and we keep praying for the Beaver to be back in the air. Horses are going forward to Paya and we are even using porters to get stores ahead. Whatever happens, our flexible system of supply must hold out. It is necessary to use local food whenever possible and to reduce the scales of supplies to the barest minimum.

But the gallant little Pathfinder and its team continued to inspire us.

Two and a half months of unrelenting physical labour are certainly beginning to tell. There are reports coming back of further difficulties on the track to Paya. The Tirfor jack is constantly in use heaving the vehicles up the near-vertical slopes and the sappers are being bruised black-and-blue as they slip and slide on these contours. The Land-Rover is in a terrible condition, but still goes on. What an amazing vehicle it is. Its bumpers are battered and bent and the body-work dented and torn, its exhaust pipe went on the first day it was in the jungle. The brakes have failed several times, and this usually results in its nose-diving into a ravine or sliding backwards into a stream. Now its bodywork is evidence of the countless collisions with trees and rocks.

I thought things were going too well, and when we brought the second Range Rover up-river we suffered a few minor setbacks.

My piragua was towing the raft across some fast water at the exit of a rapid, when, looking back, I saw with horror the raft rear up like a stricken beast. Words would not come quickly enough, and anyway I could not really think of anything to say. I heard one of the helmsmen yelling, 'She's going lads, get away, get away, we are going over.' The tow-rope slackened as the raft and its swaying Range Rover spun out of control in the foaming water. The engines were racing and men were plummeting over the side. Water was pouring up through a two-foot gash in the hull of one pontoon. Like a whaler's longboat the piragua was dragged backwards. Only one man was still aboard the raft and that was the commander, Ticky Wright, who was struggling to regain control. Canito, instantly realizing what must be done, sliced through the tow rope with his razor-sharp machete. Amazingly enough the raft was still upright and what was more the Range Rover, still aboard. Men were struggling in the water, clearly visible by their bright red life-jackets. Downstream the raft spun, but by a miracle Ticky was winning control and, as we watched, he rammed the wreck into a shingle bank on the far side of the river.

Most of the survivors had reached the edge of the river and were clinging onto the trees, but few had the strength to climb up; they had been working for hours in the heat, and for many, who were suffering from 'jungle foot', every step was agony. Canito swung the long piragua round and we picked up some of the survivors. The vehicle was unharmed but the raft had been ripped open and was badly crippled; it would need much more work before it could continue. Quite what caused the accident is hard to tell, but it was probably a combination of several things. Firstly, the hull of one big boat was torn by a sharp stone, and secondly, a number of the crew were sitting on the upstream side. The result was that when they struck the fast water the upstream pontoon sunk down and immediately, because the raft was being towed, dipped under water.

However, by next day the indefatigable Ticky had repaired the damage and the Range Rover was on its way once more. But Phil Church who had led his engineers with such determination had collapsed. Returning from Boca next day, I found him semi-conscious in a hammock beside the river, his teeth chattered with the rigors of a high fever and he mumbled incoherently as Wayne, the gentle hobo, mopped his brow with a piece of wet parachute material. But I reached the raft party just in time to witness another accident. The Range Rover was attempting to motor through some shallow rapids between two sandbanks, and suddenly hit a deep hole in the river-bed. Immediately, water poured over the bonnet and the engine cut out. Fortunately the snorkel tube prevented any water doing down the exhaust for the time being. The men's actions were slow, as if they were mesmerized by the sheer weight of the vehicle in the foaming cataract and, luckily, with the aid of a loudhailer I was able to issue orders quickly above the roar of the river. Corporal Bob Russell the senior sapper NCO leapt into a piragua and rushed up-river to Cruso Mono for the Tirfor jack, which had been taken ahead with the other stores. While he was away, members of the team fixed ropes and got as much kit as possible out of the stricken vehicle. We evacuated a very large quantity of equipment from the car. Its presence explained why Ticky found it much more difficult to manage the raft than with the previous vehicle. It was simply over-loaded and this made me very angry indeed. The Tirfor arrived in the nick of time and the engineers worked with tremendous speed to get it fixed to a tree and pull the vehicle clear of the river. Within twenty-five minutes we had it ashore and opened up to see the extent of the damage. Water had come up to about the top of the doors and everything inside was soaked; it would certainly take some time to dry out.

I now turned my attention back to Phil Church. He needed to be taken out by helicopter and so, on the afternoon radio schedule, we asked for one. Going down to the original sandbank, we waited in the pouring rain and prepared a firework display to attract the helicopter. However, night fell fast and by the time the spotter aircraft, which was leading the helicopter, came overhead it was almost completely dark. We launched a fusillade of flares to light up the ground around us. The giant helicopter, looking like an enormous insect, came hovering in aided by its searchlights. Trees and bushes were hurled about by the fierce downdraught and waves of spray from the river lashed us. But the trees were too close to the river for this hazardous operation to be completed, and, after several attempts, they turned and flew out towards Panama saying they would return at dawn. The jungle became silent again, save for the sound of the rain and the distant thunder. However Private Wilmott found an Indian house where James, he and the sick Phil could spend the night. Sitting in the water-filled piragua, I returned upstream to the main camp.

On passing the exhausted Rover group, I found that both Ticky and Brian Blackford, their feet a mass of bleeding sores, were now sick with high fever, which I hoped was only temporary. Canito flung his boat through the swollen rapids with amazing skill as black logs, invisible in the surging torrent, thudded against our hull. Suddenly the storm returned with new violence, and above the noise I could hear Vincente, the bow lookout hoarsely screeching instructions to Canito on the motor.

The imperturbable little Panamanian boatman stood upright like a statue, his left hand clutched the gunwhale and his right held the throttle. The rain and spray drenched him, but his face wore the same contemptuous expression as it always did when he was driving his streamlined craft on this treacherous river.

'How long to Cruso Mono?' I shouted.

'Five minutes,' he replied with a shrug, his white teeth and eyes reflecting a flash of lightning. At Cruso Mono I heard news that the Pathfinder was five miles beyond Pucuru. 'Well,' I thought, 'as long as something goes right somewhere I'm happy.'

Soaked to the skin, I sat eating an avocado pear that Kay had prepared. My right hand felt rather stiff and, looking down, I saw it was puffy and infected. Earlier that day I had nicked it with a machete and, as the cut was so small, had thought no more of it. By midnight the pain was so intense I couldn't sleep. Climbing wearily from my hammock, I woke Kay whose bed was slung to the same tree.

'What's the matter?' she yawned.

Right: David
Bromhead prepares
a marker balloon

Below: Rafting on
the Bayano River

Above: Many fallen trees made our going very difficult. Ernie Durey at the wheel of the Land-Rover

Below: We cross the bridge at the beginning of the southern part of the Pan American highway

Right: Ulster, 1973

Below: An incident in Armagh. *L to r:* Captain Mike Evans RE, Major Dick Jarmen RE (my successor who was killed two months afterwards), a Fusilier sergeant, L/Cpl Sim (my driver)

The Scientific Exploration Society gives a dinner to announce the Zaire River Expedition. *L to r:* J. B-S, Livingstone's grandson, H.R.H. Prince William of Gloucester, Stanley's grandson, H.E. Mr Walter Annenberg and Richard Snailham

'Nothing,' I lied and dug around in my rucksack for the first-aid kit. By the time I found it I could hardly move my fingers, and pains were shooting up and down my right arm. Oh my God! I thought. That is all we needed – something serious to go wrong with me. I had about eighteen Tetracyclin tablets in the pack. The infection was obviously pretty virulent, and I hoped these antibiotics would be more successful than on the Blue Nile. Washing the two orange-coloured pills down with a long gulp of whisky, I sat listening to the hiss of the river and the calls of the animals. I glanced at my watch, it was 1 April and I wondered what they would be having to eat for dinner that night in Camberley, where it was Judith's birthday. The whisky had reduced the pain, but sleep was still not possible. In the cool of the night my thoughts became very clear.

James Beattie badly needed a rest and I wanted to have someone to take the burden of signals, administration and overall co-ordination off Ernie's shoulders, so I had brought Kelvin in to take command of the Pathfinder group. Most of the administration for the expedition was now being done from Colombia anyway and, with his considerable experience, Kelvin was as valuable in the field as he had been running the logistics. Furthermore, if anything happened to me Kelvin could assume command. Now that Phil was a casualty, I had to find a new leader for the Range Rover group. Temporarily, Tony Stansfeld could take over until I got Jim back from Paya, where he had gone to recce with Peter Marett. All along the line men needed replacement but I could only spare the worst cases. In fact, by about 20 April, I must lose some of my best men who had to return to military duty in Britain.

For three months I had played an endless game of snakes and ladders. At times I wondered if the dice were loaded against us, was there some supernatural force that was determined to defeat those who dared to challenge the Darien Gap? I began to wonder whether my decisions were being overruled by my own obsession: perhaps nature just did not intend mere men to conquer her. Was the self-assurance I had gained from the Blue Nile giving rise to false optimism?

Back in Panama City, where the sick and depressed were concentrated, I knew many of our fellows had written us off as lost and me as insane. Some of my officers had urged me to give up.

'You've done a good job, John, we've all worked hard, but we can't beat this, it's only common sense to give up,' said James, who had worked as hard as any.

But logic and common sense had long since ceased to play a part
in my plans. For everything the Gap threw at us we had so far found
an answer. True, we had been delayed and at times severely pun-
ished, but in the end we had always won. To suggest we had a private
god on our side would be the highest vanity, but somehow I found
my faith in our team, our spirit and our will to win gave me confidence and apparently my confidence assured the others. Now after
seventy days in this living hell our wits were honed to a fine edge and,
having learned the law of the jungle, we were turning it to our
advantage.

Two Tetracyclin tablets and a quarter of a bottle of whisky later
the swelling in my hand began to subside. By dawn I had filled in
ten pages of the grubby little notebook with my plans for reaching
the Atrato. Written with my left hand by the light of a fading torch
the notes were barely legible. but the plot was fixed in my mind.

At dawn Phil was lifted out by the rescue helicopter. Ticky and
Brian Blackford recovered quickly, and the following day Gavin
succeeded in getting the drowned Range Rover going. The race was
on again and, not even pausing to see the last car winched up the
cliff, we loaded Headquarters, plus all the reserve supplies, into two
boats and set off for Paya.

The river got shallow and at each rapid we had to get out and
push. As it grew dark the boatmen begged me to halt, but if humanly
possible I wanted to reach the last village in Panama that night, so
that I could issue instructions for the next phase.

In the pitch black we struggled in a particularly fierce set of rapids.
Kay, a weak swimmer, pushed with us without complaint and
suddenly a red flare illuminated the river, bathing the surrounding
jungle in a gentle pink light. We were at Paya. Here too were Keith
Morgan-Jones, his horses, the Pathfinder group, Jim and Peter and
a mass of astonished Cuna Indians.

'Would you like a cup of tea?' said a voice from the darkness. It
came from Keith Forrester, who with his wife lived amongst these
gentle people to learn the Cuna language, so that they could translate the Bible into the Indian tongue. I had little rest that night. We
were accommodated in the open-sided village hall and it was a
change to find a dry roof and plenty of beams from which to sling a
hammock. At around midnight I was woken by Keith Forrester who
said, 'Major, we have a problem; there is serious trouble amongst the
Indians.'

Ungluing my eyes I spied a gathering, which included the chief and several armed warriors outside the hall. Keith hurriedly explained that the people had caught a man of a rival tribe sneaking into the village, and indeed he had been peeping into the chief's hut when he was seized by sentries. The chief alleged that this man was a spy, a murderer or at least a thief and had come to plan a night attack on them. This was a new problem because formerly all questions of law and order had been dealt with by the Guardia, and I suggested that the chief should take the prisoner along to the Guardia hut, some twenty minutes' walk from the village. It was quickly explained that, in these frontier districts, the Guardia had little influence over the Indians, and that anyway, if the small party were to go down the narrow jungle trail, they would surely be ambushed by the spy's friends. The argument seemed rational enough, if one appreciated the background of these people.

I then suggested that the spy would be better tied-up for the night and the matter could be decided at dawn. But this would not satisfy the chief, who said the man must die now. Furthermore he proposed to shoot him with his ancient shotgun, the only firearm in the village. Keith Forrester placidly argued against such a drastic course and then, between us, we cooked up a possible solution. I told the chief that all my men were heavily armed and that no rival tribe would dream of attacking the village while we were there. Had he not seen the display of pyrotechnics which had greeted my arrival? Furthermore, I would guarantee his safety with my word as a British officer. The chief, who undoubtedly had never heard of a British officer before, let alone his word, eventually nodded and agreed to accept our security. The matter was to be decided at dawn, and meanwhile the prisoner would be roped to a pole in the village centre and guarded by the young men. Any attempt to escape would mean an arrow or certainly a fish-spear through his back.

As the little party strolled away, apparently with honour satisfied, I whispered to those members of the expedition who had woken up, 'Who has got a gun?' We found that the particular group including myself were only carrying two revolvers and a few Pains-Wessex ministar projectors.

In the morning I was able to persuade the chief to release the spy unharmed; however, this was not the only strange incident to occur at Paya. Quite suddenly a convention of witch doctors arrived, and took over part of the hall for purposes which intrigued our medical team no end. An earlier arrival had been a young Equadorian lady named Estrella, the daughter of a very wealthy man. Promised by her family to an elderly and influential suitor against her will, Estrella had fled north and, attempting to reach the United States, had come to the Darien Gap. At El Real she had been arrested as an illegal immigrant, and when I first saw her at the Guardia post, she looked no more than a scruffy little urchin. However, Estrella had used all her womanly wiles to escape from the clutches of the Guardia and, finding the same smugglers' trail that we had used, had reached Paya. There she was seized by the Cuna who asked the Forresters' advice on how to dispose of this unwelcome foreign woman. Ever the peacemaker, the missionaries took her into their care and, by the time David Bromhead's recce section reached the Indian village, Estrella was looking groomed and presentable.

'These are honourable Englishmen,' explained Keith Forrester to the chief. 'I think you should allow them to take the young girl to Colombia, where the proper authorities can look after her.'

Lance-Corporal Davies had not failed to notice Estrella's flashing eyes and long flowing black hair. 'Thank God I'm Welsh,' he thought.

With an impressive display of reluctance David agreed to take the girl and put her in Davies' care. Morale was high when this gallant little band set out once more.

Few appreciated the work of the recce section. Always miles ahead in the jungle, rarely seen by anyone and often no more than a faint signal on the radio, they lived a life apart. Travelling light, one horse, few rations and the minimum of equipment they marched hundreds of miles as they scouted the way. Their reports came back to me by Indian runner, or sometimes I found notes pinned to the trees. When they made a mistake everyone cursed, but when they found a route after weeks of backbreaking work no one praised them.

As far as re-supply was concerned, they were the end of the line, but David Bromhead, George Baker and Taffy Davies were the sort of soldiers who, more than any of us, learned to live at one with the jungle. We all ate some local food to conserve our precious rations, but the recce team virtually lived off the land. My faith in David, built up from the time when he probably saved my life in the Ethiopian bush and enhanced by his cool courage on the Blue Nile, was well rewarded.

'We're through to Lomas,' his voice crackled over the radio. 'It's a terrible route, but you can make it.'

David's team had completed their task and had led us at last to the end of the twilight world of the jungle, beyond which lay another obstacle—the flat, open mire of the Atrato valley. All but the final route across this swamp was now known. Now he must return to his Army helicopter unit in Britain. Sergeant-Major George Baker, his back still alive with a family of maggots living in an infested sore, would go ahead into the stinking morass with Richard Summerton.

Taffy would become a power-saw operator with Ernie's sappers who were already blasting, winching, pushing, laddering and jacking their way forward to Palo de Las Letras. From this ridge it would be generally downhill to the edge of the vast bog.

Following David's route, I used some local mules to recce forward to the frontier. They were the first we had seen and belonged to the small Guardia detachment at Paya. However these were not as sure-footed as the Blue Nile beasts, and within two hours I had been rolled on in the Tuira River and pitched head-first into a tree-stump when a vine tripped up my mount. Luckily a topee makes a good crash helmet!

Sergeant de Leon was my constant companion. His wiry frame was always immaculately uniformed, as, shaded by his bush hat, he rode his mule with the same expertise with which he had handled the long piragua in the rapids and guided me to Cruso Mono. Of all the Guardia who had helped us we probably owed most to this smart little Panamanian NCO.

On 6 April we closed the base at Paya. A Colombian mule-train awaited us at the frontier, and Keith Morgan-Jones, his job done and now four stone lighter, waved goodbye as he set off down-river in Canito's piragua. With him went Kay and Carolyne to help at Panama City, and then fly over to join us in the Atrato. Charles Keyes and Private Wilmott would take our faithful pack-ponies back down the Pucuru track to sell them to the kindest homes they could find.

The Forresters came to say goodbye with the young chief to whom I presented a splendid all-steel British hand-axe.

It was a significant moment in the expedition, the curtain was dropping on another act; teams welded together by their battle against nature were breaking up after a long time. The old cast had hardly dispersed before the new actors came on stage.

'Buenos Dias,' said the living image of Mussolini in a sombrero. Francisco, muleteer extraordinary, strode into our camp at the head of his column. His massive, muscular beasts dwarfed our ponies. 'If you are ready my mayor, *I* will load mules,' said Francisco firmly, and we stood back to admire his skill. 'The mules will march by themselves, you go ahead and I will meet you at Palo,' said our self-assured friend. Enormous trees soared skyward for over a hundred feet. An occasional ray of sunshine filtered through the canopy, but for the most part the forest floor was a gloomy green world, through which flittered electric-blue butterflies and tiny humming birds. Above us raucous macaws, big-beaked toucans and brightly coloured parrots clucked and called with ear-splitting shrieks. The air was heavy with the scent of blooms that I had not seen when moving on my feet because of the need to pick a path with care. Now from muleback I could observe brilliant flowers, beefsteak plants and thousands of tiny creatures who lived in this vast overgrown hot-house. On the way we paused to photograph the rusting red Chevrolet that reminded us that we had not beaten the Darien Gap yet.

We reached Palo at 13.50 hours and, apart from the broken-down concrete plinth that marked the frontier, the little clearing was empty. I had said we would meet the Colombians at 14.00 hours. Sergeant de Leon stood with his mule on the Panamanian side and I walked forward to the plinth to photograph our four-man headquarters with the Union Jack, which the American hobo was clutching incongruously.

It was exactly 14.00 hours when the jungle around us seemed to move and I looked up to see that we were facing the Colombian Army. A platoon of swarthy, purposeful soldiers clad in camouflage uniform, their weapons spotlessly clean, stood watching us. From their midst an officer stepped forward, and said, 'Captain Sierra of the Fourth Brigade Infantry,' clicking his heels with Prussian precision and saluting. I introduced my staff and Sergeant de Leon. With the officer was a sergeant-major who suddenly seized our Union Jack. I was certain that we had committed some unpardonable breach of international law, but he put my mind at rest saying, 'It is your right to carry your flag into Colombia, according to the Treaty of 1821.' This was true, but I was surprised that our friends were so well briefed. The sergeant-major then asked if he might be allowed to carry the Union Jack into his country as indeed the Duke of Wellington's veterans had done one hundred and fifty years before. The hobo happily handed it over and, with a final wave to Sergeant de Leon, we marched downhill into the thickening jungle of the Atrato valley.

Captain Sierra told me that Kelvin and the Pathfinders group were already a day ahead and going well. That night we reached the riverside camp of the Colombian Commander, Major Alberto Patron. Sitting by the fire, we ate a communal meal with our allies and enjoyed the first of many cups of local coffee. Alberto briefed me on the campaign that was being waged against the communist guerrillas throughout the more remote regions of Colombia.

'I think the Atrato is too unhealthy a place – even for the communists,' said the unusually fair-haired officer, 'but we must take normal military precautions; seven soldiers were killed in an ambush near Barranquillito last week.'

I agreed and we discussed joint tactics in the unlikely event of a meeting with the rebels. Well, I thought, so far the Darien Gap has thrown everything at us except bandits. I carefully checked my revolver when I cleaned it that evening!

After dark, Limbu and I decided to do a night hunt along the river-bed and, equipping ourselves with head-torches, we went out for a few hundred yards. Armed with a .22 rifle and a twelve-bore shot-gun, we waited on a ledge beside the water, but although we saw several pairs of eyes, we were unable to recognize their owners and came back empty-handed an hour later. The camp was completely silent and, but for the smell of wood smoke, it would have been difficult to detect. Even the mules were quiet. Using my flashlight we found our way in, and, just as I was entering, I felt Limbu stiffen beside me. A voice from the deep darkness said, 'Buenos noches, Mayor' (Goodnight, Major). Somehow it did not surprise me that, standing with his rifle at the ready, in the shadow, was Private Ortiz. His camouflage and concealment were perfect; in the flash of my light I saw the whites of his eyes and his immaculate teeth. I said, 'Buenos noches,' and went to bed feeling very secure.

At dawn we broke camp and marched on in pursuit of the Pathfinder, which we soon overhauled. Kelvin, Ernie and the sappers were working like demons, assisted now by the Colombian infantry.

Pausing to watch them cross the Cacarica River, we enjoyed a fantastic lunch of avocado and papaya at the little Indian family house. Meanwhile the American hobo entertained us with the stories he had heard about us from the Indians. The Choco of the Bayano valley had found him lost and starving in the jungle, and in their kindly way had given him food and shelter. His knowledge of Spanish and various Indian tongues enabled him to understand them. They said we had very powerful gods, and that our cars were made of plastic so light that we could throw them across the ravines. Apparently we were guided by a very tall and clever Indian who came from the mountains – obviously Sergeant Limbu. But what impressed them most of all was our magic box. Whenever we needed anything, they said, we would place the box in a clearing, and dance round shouting at it. Then the box would speak. Shortly afterwards our gods would send over the great bird who would drop us everything we wanted. What a splendid way for them to describe the use of radio to call for parachute re-supply!

By 8 April, we reached the Bataille River and I noticed that the jungle was getting thinner and hotter. But there always seemed to be another hill to climb and, as I staggered up an especially steep ascent, I saw Private Ortiz, who, with Sergeant Limbu, was acting as a lead scout.

'Mayor,' he said, beckoning me, 'come, we have something to show you.' Sweat was seeping out of every pore and at the hill-top a refreshing breeze fanned my face. The wind was blowing through a gap in the trees. I gasped, for through the gap I could see the great Atrato Swamp. It stretched from horizon to horizon. Swirling mist rose from the stunted trees that stood in the stinking green bog and in the far distance, barely visible, towered the dark outline of the Andes.

Without warning the jungle ended and we stepped on to the beaten earth road that led to Lomas de Rumie. I could have kissed that track, but marching down it we felt the full heat of the tropical sun and longed for a patch of shade.

That afternoon an oil company float-fitted helicopter flew me the last few kilometres to Lomas where our next base was being established. As we landed beside the Colombian naval vessel I saw someone, dressed in a superb white sailor-suit, waiting for me on the shore. The short blond hair and large circular dark glasses told me it was Rosh.

'Which poor sailor did you pinch that outfit from?' I roared.

'You are bloody rude, I'll have you know it cost me a bomb in the Kings Road,' she answered back. Rosh, as I should have expected, had everything well under control and had become, whether she liked it or not, 'the Queen of the River'. The hot-blooded latin sailors had been unable to believe their eyes when the expedition's liaison officer and radio operator had turned out to be an attractive young English girl. The captain moved into the engine-room and gave her his cabin, and the crew saw to it that her every wish was fulfilled with the utmost expediency, which was as well because the expedition had many wishes. Meanwhile the sailors lived in hope, awaiting the day when the English would arrive, with, it was reliably reported, dozens more young ladies like Rosh. I was a sad disappointment.

Back in the jungle, dramas continued. At Paya Junior Sapper Duffy had been evacuated by helicopter with a dangerously enlarged appendix. On reaching Palo, a Range Rover broke another differential, and, when unpacking the replacement, they discovered a venomous-looking black snake coiled in the box. The latter turned out to be a rubber version popped in by some joker at the Rover factory! However, the vehicles were still advancing, and I turned my mind to the final battle, writing that night in my log:

The gun boat, *Teniente Hernando Gutierrez*, was named after a hero of the 1934 War between Colombia and Peru. She was not an especially beautiful vessel, but her twin .50 inch machine guns mounted in their barbette on the upper deck looked business-like. Her square grey-painted structure gave her the appearance of an early iron-clad. While the all-ranks wardroom on the open poop deck gave her a more friendly look. In reality *El Buque*, as we called her, was a combined peace-keeper and hospital-ship for the Atrato. Lieutenant Lara, her young captain, was accompanied by a crew of some twelve enthusiastic sailors who seemed ever cheerful and clearly most interested in their unusual support task. With twin screws and a flat bottom, she is going to be of the greatest possible use to us as a floating headquarters for the assault on the swamp. She is also equipped with a flimsy tin ship's boat driven by a forty horse-power out-board. It was such a boat that had been involved in the tragic accident at Turbo and, although the gunboat's crew still mourned their lost friends, they were one hundred per cent behind us. Major Carlos Duque, a friendly marine officer, was also on board and acting as another liaison officer to us.

Having had a rapid discussion with Richard Summerton on his recce results, I saw that there were only two routes open to us, the Tumarado or the Tumaradocito. They are both creeks leading across the great bog.

The oil company's helicopter pilot had promised me a quick flight into the swamp and this I gladly accepted. We flew first to the Tumarado Creek and, as Richard had stated, I found it clogged with thick water-weed for much of its length. The area was completely uninhabited. Mile upon mile of boundless, melancholy marsh, with the occasional lake breaking up the surface, stretched in front of us.

To permit me to examine what appeared to be a relatively firm spot, the pilot obligingly landed. As the floats touched down I felt the ground subside beneath us and, on stepping out, I found it was like standing on a giant blancmange. The only thing there to welcome me was a small alligator that scuttled off into a pool of peaty brown water. Stunted grass grew through the top of the morass and with my stick I found it very easy to penetrate the surface. Obviously, this will not carry the weight of the Range Rover.

Meanwhile, at Lomas de Rumie the logistic build-up for the swamp crossing had begun. The Beaver flew in low over the village and in an effort to drop a load of petrol on the minute area of solid ground, slightly over-shot, and put the forty gallon drum, plus its parachute, through the roof of the largest house. It crashed through only ten feet from an open fire, but did not burst. The house was full of Colombian soldiers and civilians. No one was touched and every-one thought it terribly funny. I reckoned there must be a guardian angel on our strength! Other stores including Ticky's raft were air-landed at a ranch down-river and brought up by the inflatable boats. Carolyne Oxton came to take over the administration, and the reserve personnel, who had been restored to good health by Suzie's nursing in Panama, arrived to replace some of the exhausted men who would come in with the vehicles.

As the flaming orange orb sank behind the mountains, I sat on the hill-top and described what I saw and my thoughts for the final move in this campaign.

On my return to the gunboat, I had lengthy discussions with Richard and we plan to go to the Tumaradocito tomorrow. At 16.00 hours my colleagues in headquarters came in, and we established the new HQ in a murdered engineer's hut on the hill, which is in fact the Lomas de Rumie. It appears that our final headquarters is on a peak of Darien, looking out, not across the vast Pacific, but across the great Atrato Swamp.

Turning to look towards the Andes, one first of all sees three low hills in the centre of the swamp. These represent to me an outer-bastion of the Andes and a narrow point in the obstacle. I believe, from what I have seen from the air, and now know from Richard's reconnaissance, that I must make for these hills. The distance is some twenty-six kilometres, but somehow we have got to find a way through the liquid morass before we can set foot on what may only be relatively dry. The route I shall look at tomorrow seems the most promising, for this was the way that Brendan O'Brien went last year. However Richard tells me that it is completely blocked with at least fourteen major log jams. Most of the logs are hard-wood which will defy even our fine power-saws. As a result I have issued a warning order to our base that I may require large quantities of dyna-mite at short notice. The swamp, apart from the few hills, is completely flat and from it, in the mornings and evenings, rises a strange grey mist which hangs about for several hours. The sunset tonight was quite fantastic and one of the most beautiful I have seen in Darien.

My first aim is to establish a good transit camp here at Lomas so that, as the exhausted teams come in, they can be fed and re-supplied before being pushed on into the swamp. I plan to use the gunboat but to maintain my command post at Lomas. The situation is ideal and, for once, I could brief people by standing on a peak and pointing out objects on the horizon over twenty kilometres away.

The next day we moved off to examine the Tumaradocito creek by piragua. The boatman was not up to the standard of Canito and my log tells of a trying day:

The log jams were certainly difficult. They began after a few kilometres, and in many places they completely blocked the river. At these points sometimes we could lift the piragua onto one of the obstructions and then, using the outboard engine to drive it, hop over the top. Eventually we reached the house of a man named Passilidas, where we arranged to hire some labourers to start clearing away the logs.

I noticed several strange lizards that appeared to have a form of wing tissue on their backs, but they were moving so fast that it was difficult to identify them. This creek is, in fact, purely a drain. The firm ground only extends for a few feet on either side of it; beyond is the swamp again. On investigation, I found it to be quite impassable for a vehicle. It is just liquid mud. Probing with a twelve-foot bamboo, I could feel no resistance. However, Richard assures me that, as we go further into the bog, the banks around the creek get wider and eventually form a crust above the liquid, and this extends right the way over to where the Pan-American highway is now entering the swamp at Barranquillito.

Time did not permit us to go as far as I should have liked, and eventually we turned back and made our way slowly through the log jams. We had just cleared one especially difficult jam when without warning our piragua shot sideways and capsized. We were all pitched into the water. There was nowhere really to swim because the banks were pure mud and most of us clung on to the boat which, fortunately, being of wood did not sink. The reason for our plight was plain to see. The boatman had started the engine at full power at right angles to the piragua. It took little effort for us to right it and to collect our belongings. Meanwhile one of the Colombian soldiers and the shame-faced boatman duck-dived repeatedly for a lost shot-gun. Eventually, to our surprise, they found it deep in the mud at the bottom of the creek. Everyone was soaked to the skin and several cameras were damaged. Realising that mine was probably finished I went on taking pictures in the hope that something might come out, which it did. Eventually, we were all abroad again and continued our journey, cold, wet and smelly.

That night my mind was made up. The best route was, as Brendan had predicted, the Tumaradocito Creek, and then gingerly over the crust. I believed this would bear the weight of the cars, but when the rains came it would flood. However, the rains were still holding off and the Pathfinder was on its way in. My log recorded their arrival:

This afternoon the weather was unusually clear and visibility was still good, but towards the late afternoon ominous black clouds began to appear from the South, and obviously the rains are on the way. At 18.00 hours we heard the distant rattle and roar of the Pathfinder and, within minutes, it had rolled in festooned with its crew who were in tremendous heart. What a fantastic achievement! They were nearly drunk with joy and arrived in the nick of time, for as they dismounted there was a flicker of lightning right overhead and the rains started. For some two hours we were subjected to the heaviest deluge I have ever experienced. Visibility was cut to a few yards and, as night was falling, the flashes of lightning lit up the gunboat on the river and the swamp around us in an eerie yellow light. Standing in the headquarters building one could actually feel a mild electric shock in the feet when the lightning struck the ground. It amazed me that it took so long to pass and, indeed, appeared to circle around us for a very long time. We were right in the centre of the storm and it seemed to enjoy playing upon our lonely hill. At the foot of the slope we could hear the mules kicking and jumping in the shelter, not used to this sort of thing either. The radio, of course, was unusable and for safety we removed the aerial. After the brief respite, the storm returned and, as I write, the building around me is positively shaking with the violence of the elements.

At dawn we sent a recce party back up the road. Alas, they found it was washed away in many places and could see no sign of the Range Rover. In fact it was still struggling through the hills, painfully slowly, urged on by Jim Masters who was determined that, having come so far, they would get through if it killed them. Meanwhile, another struggle was going on above the high Andes where the Beaver, laden with dynamite and detonators for the log-blasting, was being tossed about like a feather in the storms. Having no long-range radio with which to contact our aircraft, we could only hope and pray, when it did not appear at dusk.

It was 14 April when Ticky ferried the battered green Pathfinder forward to the Tumaradocito. Kelvin had returned to Panama and Ernie was alone with his engineers. 'Hello, hello,' he cried, as we approached the first log jam, 'JBS has found a new obstacle for us.' Following the raft in a fleet of rubber boats, the sappers swarmed into the attack with machetes, power-saws, explosive and bare hands. As they worked, the filthy bedraggled soldiers sang, swore and joked. Clouds of birds flew up in alarm as the power-saws ripped at the hardwood and explosions thundered over the swamp.

Darien will not break these men, I thought as I returned to Lomas where the mail awaited me.

I noted one item of interest in my log:

An important-looking package arrived from the British Ministry of Defence, and on opening it I discovered it was a letter from Mr. Geoffrey Johnson-Smith. Another letter was also enclosed from Mr. Tam Dalyell, MP, who had heard about our encounters with the peccary. He expressed the hope to the Secretary of State, that the expedition would not massacre these beasts, but might bring some home for the zoos in Britain. The mind boggles at the thought of trying to catch an angry peccary in company with 299 of his chums, hell-bent on destruction in the jungle, late at night. Nevertheless, I suppose all things are possible.

Jim reported he was still making slow progress, and Ernie called for more explosive. The weather forecast was ominous; the big rains would start any day.

Returning from a re-supply sortie to Ernie on 17 April, I saw a crowd on the shore at Lomas. In the middle of the people were the two blue cars. The men, hollow-eyed and exhausted, gazed out across the mire.

'How on earth are we going to cross this?' said Bob Russell.

'The Pathfinder's almost through, and you'll follow in a couple of days,' I assured him.

But we still had problems. The raft crew had been working round the clock for weeks, the hull of their craft was in urgent need of repair and every moment the rains got nearer. It would be a desperate struggle to get the Pathfinder and one Range Rover to Barranquillito anyway. I doubted if we could get the third vehicle across before the rains and thus, to the disappointment of its crew, I decided that one Range Rover would avoid the swamp, going to Turbo on the gunboat's stern.

On 20 April the raft bearing the Range Rover reached the half-hidden entrance to the Tumaradocito. From the bridge of *El Buque* I saw a vast island of waterweed blocked the creek. Mixed with the weed were logs and branches that must have floated downstream from Ernie's demolitions. So, the Gap still had another trick up its sleeve.

We tried using grapnels to pull the weed out, but as fast as we made a hole it closed up again. Thankfully, we still had a good stock of explosive on board, and within an hour had fashioned some long necklaces of dynamite. Jim watched me ruefully. I knew what he was thinking. 'What a time for John to start playing with bombs.' But an hour later, as the column of spray that had been hurled upwards for several hundred feet settled, we were all delighted to see that the necklaces had done the job and a clear channel led through. Two days later my HQ said farewell to the gunboat and followed the Range Rover up the muddy waterway. On the way we met Ticky who was coming back with his boats almost out of commission. The raft had done a magnificent job and great credit was due to Ticky, as well as our friends who together had produced this superb item of equipment. Without this the Gap would never have been conquered. Ticky was very weary, but with the rain running down his drawn face, he still managed to raise a smile; however, I knew that we were right to only bring one Range Rover across. I doubt whether the crew or the raft could have done another trip.

It rained almost continuously as we sailed upstream. We saw several animals including a rather unusual giant otter. The creek was quiet, the roar of the demolitions had gone and, in spite of the rain, I was able to sit back and enjoy the scenery, knowing that the vehicles were now safely on the crust. At first the Tumaradocito was no more than a narrow creek bounded by a rich green, vaguely defined shore line. Although our ears were plagued by the clattering roar of the motor, there was an impression of stillness, for there was little wind and the only noise that of the rain on the water. We were in a different world, a world that was almost dead until you saw the movement of some large snake or a fascinating bird. On every side and from every clump of trees, fern or luxuriant growth there rose birds as we approached. Brilliant kingfishers dodged in and out of the tree stumps and wild turkeys watched from the high branches as herons, looking almost reptilian with their long necks and close plumage, rose gracefully from the reeds. White egrets poised on logs against a perfectly green back-drop and dignified storks surveyed us from the water. Perching ducks flopped into the stream from fallen branches and long vines dangled like bell-ropes from the living hard-woods. Spanish moss fell like grey cotton-wool from every tree.

I was brought back to life by a jarring crash which meant we had hit a submerged log. When the engine stopped I could hear the croak of the frogs and the harsh cry of the birds.

By early afternoon we had reached the track that led through the swamp forest. The way led around grotesque plants and tall trees which arched over us like a cathedral roof. Deep shafts and sink-holes punctured the slippery surface and I imagined that it was up these that the water would rise when the rains came, turning the whole place into a vast lake.

For the moment the terrain could be likened to a huge sponge that was rapidly filling with water.

In the darkening jungle the Range Rover was slipping and sliding its way, inch by inch over the muddy surface. Stripped to the waist, their bodies a mass of sores, bites and cuts, their trousers coated in greasy mud, the engineers and the car crew toiled on in the rain. A few miles ahead the jungle ended as suddenly as it had begun. Here, reaching out into the morass, there stretched a low grass-covered embankment. It was this embankment that would one day carry the Pan-American Highway. Now, beside the massive concrete pipes of an unfinished culvert, there sat a crumpled green Land-Rover surrounded by a bunch of very weary but proud men; men who were so tired that it was hard to believe that next morning they would plunge back into the steaming bog to help their rivals. Yet that is what they did. Anticipating that the last vehicle would not make it until the following day, I went on to make arrangements with the authorities for the arrival of the expedition. Eventually, in a tropical downpour, I returned to the school at Barranquillito at 01.30 hours, where, to my joy, I found the Range Rover, and all about lay exhausted men asleep, fully dressed, where they had dropped. A note pinned to the radio set told me that following my instructions, Jim had sent the message, 'Mission Accomplished' at 21.00 hours when they got in. The Gap was crossed.

As usual, the Range Rover had experienced more difficulty on the journey than the Land-Rover. Rain had been falling in torrents some of the day and hazardous ravines had plagued it to the very end. Many times it sank down in the mud and had to be painfully jacked out again. With the help from Ernie and his men, however, they had got through. In the final twenty yards of jungle the winch had broken for the last time. Below the causeway the car had stopped again and the last few yards to the road were only made with the aid of the Tirfor jack. As darkness descended over the swamp the Range Rover eventually caught up with its rival, the Pathfinder. More than once we had thought they would never make it. Now they had proved that it could be done with the help of some hard-working sappers and good drivers. The next day we entered Barranquillito officially. The log records:

Monday, 24 April 1972
The ninety-ninth day since we started.

Before crossing the bridge we held a joint service with our Colombian friends and stood in silence for a few moments in memory of the five who had been drowned. We then sang the national anthems of Britain and Colombia. Some of the expedition members from base house in Panama had come by Beaver to see the finish, bringing with them members of the press. At precisely 11.00 hours we marched forward, led by the Colombian detachment under Alberto Patron and Carlos Duque. Following us came all three vehicles flying the flags of Britain, Colombia and Panama. Smaller flags of Jersey and Wales were also to be seen. The procession advanced with the Colombians singing their marching songs and the sappers singing 'Hurrah for the CRE.' We halted at the bridge to hear the formal speech of welcome from the Inspector-General of the province, who also announced that there will be a public holiday in the surrounding towns and that we were to be Freemen of Chigorodo. Behind him stood a crowd of onlookers, a column of school-children in their Sunday best with their national flag. Just as the inspector cut the tape across the bridge, the Beaver throttled back and roared over the heads of the crowd. The timing was immaculate. The tape fell and our column crossed over. Sergeant Major Baker gave the order to halt and then 'Fall out'. With a tremendous yell, the team charged into a bar where already the tops were off the beer bottles.

Eventually we all packed up at Barranquillito and like the captain leaving the ship, I departed from the once more deserted village street, with my headquarters. The drive to Chigorodo was along a bumpy but straight track, the surface of which was covered in a layer of fine white dust. We passed through plantations and vegetable gardens and orchards of the fruit-canning companies. As we swung into Chigorodo the scene changed, and it appeared the town was in the middle of a fiesta. The bars were open, doing a roaring trade, the streets were decked with flags, whooping horsemen rode up and down joyously and it took me several moments to realise that the cause of this merriment was us. In almost every bar there was a member of the expedition, his tattered clothes showing him up against the smarter dress of the citizens. The fact that no one spoke much Spanish did not matter, for today Britains and Colombians are all friends. The men were being plied with drinks, kissed by the numerous bar-girls and encouraged to ride bucking broncos or tell exaggerated stories of their feats in the dreaded gap.

The party lasted until the early hours, when suddenly the clouds opened and rain such as we had never seen drenched the revellers to the skin and flooded the warehouse in which the exhausted and inebriated lay side by side. The rains had finally come.

The long bus journey to Medillin next day was not enjoyed by those with aching heads. Climbing the road up the Andes in one of the Range Rovers I dozed and thought. There had been many narrow escapes. David Bromhead had been bitten on the boot by a deadly six-foot bushmaster. Feeling the reptile strike him, he had drawn his revolver and shot its head off with a speed that would have done credit to one of the better gun-fighters of the Wild West. On another occasion, only the timely arrival of the United States helicopter at Paya had saved young George Duffy's life.

Near the frontier Limbu had a lucky escape from serious snake bite when he was struck at by a huge bushmaster which reared up behind him. It struck twice but each time, through good fortune, Limbu was taking a pace forward for his next swing at the vegetation, and the snake missed him. Behind Limbu was Ruby, a Colombian cutter who spoke no English and no Gurkhali. Limbu spoke no Spanish, and therefore Ruby's timely warning went unheeded. However, he raced up and pinned the reptile down with a forked branch. Even so he could not manage to hold it. But Limbu saw the danger and had spun round to despatch his attacker.

Although the British Trans-Americas expedition could not be called the most hazardous of operations, there was always danger round the corner. And on the last day Ticky and a sapper had almost lost their lives when returning to Turbo with the Colombian gunboat. They were working on the raft which was tied alongside the ship, which in turn was moving at approximately five knots. Suddenly, something must have hit the front of one of the inflatable boats, for without warning the bow of the raft doubled up and water swept over it. Both men were hurled into the river and sucked under. They found themselves bumping along the rusty, flat hull and suddenly being spun with enormous force by the screw. Fortunately the gunboat had lost one propeller the previous week, which increased their chances of survival. Nevertheless, they were extremely fortunate to be hurled out into the wake, having lost all their clothing and watches. With only superficial bruises and cuts they were hauled aboard and congratulated on their lucky escape.

In Medillin we were received with warm hospitality, and found a message of congratulation awaiting us from Her Majesty the Queen. More parties, a triumphal motorcade and a ceremony at Simon Bolivar's statue followed in Bogotá. Checked and serviced, the Range Rovers drove on.

Complete success for the expedition came later, on 9 June 1972, when Jeremy Groves sent the signal 'Mission Accomplished' from the Cape Horn area. The Range Rovers had driven through every type of terrain. The frozen wastes of Alaska had almost stopped the undertaking when one car slid two hundred yards on the ice-bound

Alcan Highway to smash into a huge lorry blocking the way. The Rocky Mountains had presented some challenging drives on roads from which vertical drops of thousands of feet descended into rushing, boulder-strewn rivers.

In Mexico they met desert conditions and in Guatemala the Pan-American Highway became a rutted track. They beat the jungles and swamps of Darien, and then climbed up into the high Andes.

In May 1972 they sped on through South America, crossing more mountains and once again meeting desert in Chile. Here they covered 2,375 miles in four days, and one day made eight hundred miles cruising at ninety miles per hour on a straight desert road. In the Gap they had only averaged three miles in a day!

As they neared their goal, they hit snow and ice once more. Many mountain passes were blocked and it took five long days to break through this last obstacle belt. On one occasion they had to cross a lake on a very Heath Robinson local raft to avoid the blocked passes. One can imagine the feeling of achievement as the drivers gazed at Cape Horn and switched off their engines after seven months and seventeen thousand miles.

The project had been the most ambitious expedition[1] ever undertaken by the British army and, many times during the journey, we found it hard to believe that we could win, but still we pressed on. Indeed, it had been an incredible adventure, accomplished by determination, flexibility, excellent equipment and good practical engineering, coupled with a generous help of all the sponsors and governments concerned. Already our track had become known by the Indians as the Carretera Inglese – the Englishman's Road, and they are using sections of it to travel to market or visit distant relatives. Later we learned the Pan-American Highway had been given the hundred and fifty million dollars it needed and will follow our path. One day I should like to return and motor through in comfort, but I sincerely hope that the road-builders will spare a thought for the animals, the people and the flora of this strange land, whose environment may now be changed for ever.

1. The official book of the expedition is Russell Braddon's *The Hundred Days of Darien* (Collins, 1974).

12

THE REASON WHY

Till a voice, as bad as Conscience, rang interminable changes
  On one everlasting Whisper day and night repeated – so:
'Something hidden. Go and find it. Go and look behind the Ranges –
  'Something lost behind the Ranges. Lost and waiting for you. Go!'

The Explorer – Rudyard Kipling

IT seemed strange to be returning to England in the early summer.
For some inexplicable reason I have always fancied it is winter when
one comes home from a long journey. There was the usual round of
dinners, press conferences, radio and television appearances which
had to be shared out amongst the team. Lectures had to be given,
the film edited, articles written and work started on my personal
burden – the Expedition Report.

For several weeks after our return from Darien we were wined,
dined and questioned. The girls, looking glamorous again, refuted
suggestions of jungle love affairs and the sappers shyly answered
flattering enquiries with studied understatements. Ernie, his waist-
line refilling rapidly to more comfortable proportions, made our
audiences howl with laughter. Colonel Julian Du Parc Braham and
his committee radiated their happiness over the success that had
rewarded their confidence in us. Our modest overdraft was quickly
reduced, thanks to the income from lectures, philatelic sales and the
book rights.

Meanwhile the sponsors heralded our return with well-deserved
advertising and exhibitions of equipment.

But in the midst of the euphoria there were more sober moments.
The Gap had cut us to size, not always a pleasant process. Self-
confidence and self-respect had been taken away in some cases, but
in others it had been enhanced. Some had bugs inside them that
would take months of treatment to cure, while others, feeling perhaps

that in the heat of the campaign they had acted selfishly or under strain had lost faith, would brood quietly or in contrast, continue to argue bitterly in an effort to find sympathy and justification for their actions. I recognized such occurrences as a perfectly usual result of an arduous, large-scale expedition. Happily, those who felt this way were few in number and the majority could be proud of their performance and walk tall.

'To what do you attribute the expedition's success?' was the question I was asked again and again. Of course there were many factors. Our equipment had been good. True, there were troubles with the Range Rovers, but in the end the great cars had demonstrated their power and strength and had triumphed. No praise was too high for the Pathfinder Land-Rover. The Avon raft, the Mexe ladders and the Husquvarna power-saws had enabled the sappers to perform miracles of field engineering.

The sponsors and the various governments had backed us to the hilt. Without the magnificent support of the Army Air Corps Beaver, the Panamanian, Colombian and American aircraft, re-supply would have been impossible. Brendan's recce and the careful planning that followed had all contributed, but in the end there is one factor that must not go wrong, and that is the team.

Although I believe in all honesty that about one person in ten did not quite reach the expected standard, the other nine more than made up the deficiency. In any expedition I may organize I feel that any individual failure must ultimately be my responsibility. I select the majority of members, prepare them, brief them and lead them. If anyone does not come up to the mark, there is a good chance that I have failed somewhere along the line.

Individuals do matter and everyone has a vital part to play. There were no passengers in Darien. Without the girls' mental toughness and strength of character, Kelvin's meticulous logistics, Jim's undauntable sappers and Ernie's Anglo-Saxon dogged determination and humour, I doubt if we could have done it. In the jungle, it was David's tireless recce that found the way, Keith's painstaking care of his horses that kept them moving, and Ticky's expert rafting that got us across the rivers and swamps. While, throughout the game, there were the relatively silent, uncomplaining players who, by their loyalty, hard work and skill, kept the wheels turning: Kay, Peter, Sergeant Limbu and over the horizon, Jennie Kent in Panama and Jeremy Groves in Bogotá. All these, plus many others and our allies too, I must have driven nearly mad, yet they asked nothing for themselves, only that the team should succeed.

Of course we had all had our selfish inclinations, our moments of false pride and had all been totally unreasonable to each other, but somehow most of us had managed to subjugate our whims and pull together when it really mattered, and this was how I think we won. But now it was done, I must return to a spell of conventional soldiering.

'Good morning, sir,' snapped the wiry Scot. 'Sergeant-Major Donald reporting.' Standing in front of me was the erect figure of my new squadron sergeant-major. Had I not already heard that he was a very high-grade soldier, I should now have guessed that here was a man with fire in his belly. The greying hair and weather-beaten features made him look rather older than he was, but his twinkling eyes were those of a man young in heart and spirit.

'Do sit down,' I said. 'How do you like the idea of joining 48th Field Squadron?'

'Very much,' he replied sharply, the bristle of his short moustache twitching.

'Any reason in particular?' I asked.

'Weell – they say that you're a wee bit of a mad bugger and so am I, so I think we'll get on together,' he said slowly with a broad grin. I decided I liked Sergeant-Major Donald.

We both enjoyed being with the squadron. For my part it was a pleasant change from a desk job in the War Office. Instead of dealing with a foot-thick pile of paper each day, there were the more human conflicts.

'You've been absent for nineteen days, eight hours and three minutes,' I roared at a diminutive sapper one morning. 'What have you to say for yourself?'

'I'm sorry, sir,' he stuttered. 'The train was late.'

In the months that followed, we exercised, and it was a bitter February morning when we came ashore at Belfast Docks. As the sapper squadron to the Third Infantry Brigade we were to provide engineer support to the British troops, covering some two thousand square miles of the Ulster border counties. One of our major tasks was searching for terrorist arms, explosives and equipment and, for this purpose, we had formed a special search troop. It was a difficult, hazardous and unpleasant task. Houses were often booby-trapped and a 'tip off' on the robot telephone system could be a lure to get us into a trap. I needed my best leader for this troop, and without hesitation, appointed the sergeant-major as its commander.

The squadron worked around the clock for four long months, building defences, hunting for mines, clearing obstacles, manning boats, patrolling the streets and searching, searching, searching. From time to time we got shot at, usually by a sniper, unseen behind a darkened window or a leafy hedge. Mines exploded beneath vehicles, and on one occasion it was only a short stop for tea that saved me from being blown up by a three-hundred-pound bomb, placed in a culvert. Tragically it got a Ferret armoured car a few minutes ahead of us, killing a young officer.

In Ulster I met the most friendly, hospitable people in the world, but I also met the most bigoted and the unreasonable. I saw hatred that I would have hardly believed possible in the United Kingdom, and I saw love and compassion beyond compare. I came away as perplexed as the day I arrived, but sadly I left a good friend behind.

Donald's Goblins, as we knew the search troop, had quickly gained an enviable reputation for their dogged determination and skill. For fourteen weeks the rugged Scot encouraged and led his men from one success to another. In the face of danger Ian Donald set the highest example of courage, initiative and leadership and his happy manner, devotion to duty and tireless efforts were an inspiration to all. It gave me a tremendous thrill to watch this team at work. One could not help admiring the cool, matter-of-fact way they searched, cheering themselves up with a continuous good-humoured string of obscenities, knowing all the time that they were a prime target for the bomber and sniper.

On 24 May 1973 they had been engaged on a variety of searches since well before dawn and it was a bright, sunny afternoon in South Armagh, when they found the first collection of bombs and booby-traps in a post office. Leaving an expert to deal with these, the Goblins moved on to examine a house that was thought to contain another bomb. The sergeant-major arrived by helicopter to find that the infantry had already cleared the council estate of civilians and children. The house, a semi-detached dwelling, surrounded by a small low-walled garden, stood at the end of the street. The border was a hundred yards away. It looked innocent, but Donald had been at this game long enough to trust nothing. Rightly, he decided to blow a hole in the rear wall of the building. Doors and windows are likely sites for booby traps. Thus he deployed his men to minimize the risk and began a methodical search of the garden.

'No one is to enter the house until I am satisfied that it is safe.'

So saying, he moved forward as a single risk to clear a safe lane across the lawn. A hundred yards away women in curlers, grubby children and sullen men watched in silence. On the hills around, red-bereted paratroopers scanned the hedgerows for any sign of a terrorist, and over the border the Irish Garda watched too. To the Goblins it was just another job. There were always these tense minutes when someone must go forward alone and it was usually Ian Donald who did so. Two of the team were circling the house, their cautious movements watched by other sappers from behind the village store. On the lawn the sergeant-major inched his way probing for the concealed menace and feeling for trip-wires. Only fifteen yards from the back door, he paused and looked up.

At that moment the house disintegrated into a mass of flying slates, bricks and splintered timber. The distant roar of the explosion was heard in the sand-bagged police station at Crossmaglen where Lance-Corporal Szade, one of the search team commanders, was waiting with his men. Long before the first radio message came through, they all felt a dreadful foreboding.

At Castle Dillon the rising trout were sending concentric ripples over the mirror surface of the lake. At my desk as I finished off some paper work, the operations room intercom crackled – 'OC, sir – there's been an explosion near Crossmaglen – we've got Corporal Szade on the phone.' The hair on the back of my neck rose a little. I knew Szade would only use a telephone if it was a real emergency. The line was bad. The NCO had no definite information, but he could not raise his commander on the radio.

In minutes I was aboard the helicopter, hurtling over the lush green countryside. The village of Cullaville appeared in the distance and, as we got nearer, I could see the damage. The little estate was littered in debris. A burst water-pipe was sending up a fine spray from the pile of rubble that had been the end house.

Donald was lying in the garden, partly covered by wreckage; he had died instantly. In the road outside, a sergeant in the Parachute Regiment, who had chanced to walk down the street, had been killed by a piece of flying timber, but thanks to the care with which their leader had positioned them, the remainder of the search team had survived.

We decided to wait until nightfall before getting him out; just in case there was a second device, possibly rigged to be fired by remote control. Thus it was 11 p.m. when, crouching behind the garden wall, we carefully pulled aside the wreckage with a length of rope. Then two of us carried the limp body out of the ruins to the waiting

Saracen armoured vehicle. I collected his sheath knife and holster
for his sons and then wrapped him in a blanket, before giving him a
final salute. I knew that the army had lost an outstanding soldier,
Margaret Donald had lost a fine husband and I had lost a friend
I was not likely to forget.

In June 1973 we handed over to 11th Field Squadron – its commander, my old friend, Major Dick Jarman, waved us farewell.

'Look after yourself, Dick,' I shouted. Three weeks later he too
was killed by a bomb.

Four days after Dick's death I stood on the banks of one of the
mightiest rivers in the world. The Zaire (formerly the Congo) looked
as formidable an enemy as any I had met before.

It had all started in 1970 when Richard Snailham, aware of the
forthcoming centenary of H. M. Stanley's Anglo-American Trans-
African Expedition of 1874, had drawn SES's attention to the need
for scientific exploration in what was then called the Republic du
Congo. Now renamed Zaire, it is one of the largest nations of
Africa, but in spite of its development, it still holds back some secrets
from man. Our research had shown that, although the country was
mapped, it had still not been wholly explored on foot, nor had its
natural resources been fully charted. Many indigenous diseases still
caused misery. Communications could be improved and, symbolic-
ally, the Zaire River itself still presents a challenge, since as far as we
could discover, it has never been navigated over its entire length.

Flowing from its source near the Zambian border, it runs for over
2,700 miles to the Atlantic, crossing the Equator twice and dis-
charging a volume of fresh water second only to the Amazon. I am
told that the outflow is visible on the surface of the Atlantic for three
hundred miles. Unlike the Blue Nile, its flow is unusually even, for
there is always heavy rain over some of its feeders. Although steamers
cover great distances of the waterway there are approximately five
hundred miles of long and dangerous rapids, which are considered
unnavigable.

Diego Cao, sea captain of Portugal, was the first European to discover the Zaire, in 1482. In 1485, he returned and penetrated about
one hundred miles upstream, where the first rapids tumble hundreds
of feet from the great basin beyond. The first British expedition, in
1816, was led by Captain J. H. Tuckey, RN. Fifty-seven strong, and
well-equipped, it ended in disaster; within three months, eighteen,
including Tuckey, were dead. But the expedition penetrated one
hundred and seventy-two miles inland, passing the first set of rapids.

In 1874, Henry Morton Stanley left on his second great voyage, crossing Africa from east to west in nine hundred and ninety-nine days. Three hundred and fifty native bearers set out with him; only one hundred and fifteen reached Boma at the mouth of the Zaire River.

They met extraordinary fates: smallpox, dysentery, 'fever' – 69
'Battle and murder' – 58
Starvation – 8
Drowning – 14
'Smoking wild hemp' – 1
'lost in jungle' – 1
'caught by crocodile' – 1
Missing – 13

In addition, Stanley's three white colleagues died, two of fever, one drowned in the rapids. Stanley began his descent of the Zaire River six hundred miles below its source. The remaining 2,118 miles took eleven months, during which he was attacked on thirty occasions. Under constant threat of ambush, forced to portage his heavy un-suitable boats round long rapids, it is understandable that Stanley could accomplish relatively little scientific work; survival was achievement enough.

Freddie Rodger pointed out the need for a thorough study of river blindness, along the river, while biologists, botanists and zoologists indicated the value of an opportunity to work in the region. So we planned to launch an expedition with the aim of navigating the river, carrying out important scientific research *en route*. I believed that the earliest date we could carry out the project was late in 1974 and so we made our preparations.

HRH Prince William of Gloucester had announced the expedi-tion on 3 November 1971, at a dinner given by the Society to com-memorate the centenary of the uttering of the famous words, 'Dr. Livingstone, I presume.' The event was held in the Grocers' Hall in the City of London and was attended by over a hundred explorers and their friends. Amongst the guests were the grandsons of Living-stone and Stanley, the US Ambassador, Mr. Walter Annenberg and his wife, representatives of the governments of the Congo and Tan-zania and members of the US Explorers Club. Thanks to Dennis Miller and the staff of the publicity department of *The Daily Tele-graph*, the organization was superb. Richard Stanley kindly allowed a great many items of his grandfather's equipment to be put on display and other items were brought down from the Livingstone Memorial Museum in Scotland.

The next month Richard Snailham and Martin Romilly flew to Africa to carry out a full-scale reconnaissance, while the rest of us moved off to fight another battle – in Darien. Now, eighteen months later, it was my turn to see the river down which I had been asked to lead one of the largest expeditions ever to visit tropical Africa. Our plans were already well advanced. General Caldwell had accepted the unenviable job of Chairman of the Expedition Committee. Kay and her daughter, Jill, organized our London office. A slim and attractive blonde nurse named Pamela Baker became my PA in the absence of Rosh, who had married Jeremy Groves. Once more the wheels began to turn and we all felt – here we go again.

One of my first tasks was to select the group leaders. Very often I have been asked what I looked for when picking such people. I know that on an arduous expedition men can be tired, hungry, cold and wet, or they might be hot, thirsty and covered in sores. There will be times when they have no idea what is happening or where they are going. This is when the strength and flaws in a person's character will show. So I have always looked for leaders whom I believed would go on leading under the worst conditions they might face.

Such men need to possess unusual ability and understanding to knit together the soldiers, scientists and other civilians into a team and the team must have confidence in the leader. Thus I feel that, although he should not ignore setbacks, he must remember that if he is seen to despair, the morale of his group will deteriorate rapidly. Therefore I hope that expedition officers will display cheerful, reasoned optimism and by their enduring courage press on when lesser men might falter.

'But how can you tell from an interview if a man has courage?' I was once asked. My answer was that firstly I try to discover if a person has fear – for one who does not can have no courage. He simply does not need it. Such people do exist and they can be frightening company, often leading their comrades to take unnecessary risks.

Next, I try to find out if the candidate has will-power, because in very many cases I believe courage is simply resolute will-power. But as well as sheer physical courage, there is moral courage – the sort that will lead a man to make an unpopular decision or stake all on his own judgment. Strangely, men who appear to possess unbounded physical courage do not always display the moral variety. On the other hand, I have never known a person who had moral courage to be found wanting in the face of physical danger. The Duke of Wellington's advice to leaders to be 'cool in crisis and decisive in action' still holds good today.

Being a leader is a lonely business, and too often one's own thoughts are of little comfort when there is no-one to tell you that things may not be as bad as they seem. On an expedition I occasionally find myself listening to two internal voices. Perhaps they represent two sides of my personality. One voice is complaining and moaning, urging me to rest, to turn back or take the easy way out. Fortunately, the other is more forceful, determined and able to suggest alternatives when plans fail. This voice tells me to cheer up and keep going. At times of crisis I have witnessed a confrontation between the two personalities in my dreams. Sometimes the image is so vivid that different courses of action advocated by the voices are played out as if on a television screen. I have even found it possible to replay the scene, sometimes on a different night. At one time I thought I must be going round the bend, until I met a very normal sort of chap who had exactly the same sort of experiences under stress.

The ordinary members of the team must also be selected carefully. Basically, I think one is looking for somebody who is cheerful, compatible, unselfish and tolerant. Both mental and physical toughness are important, but a person who tends to be over-competitive can be a very disruptive element.

Loyalty to the leadership and to the aim of the expedition is very necessary, but under the stress and strain of expedition life there is always the person who will grumble and knock the system. This is inevitable; however, if one person is constantly complaining there may well be something wrong with him. Indeed, he may need to criticize in an effort to satisfy his own ego and restore his own self-confidence. Whatever the reason, anyone who disintegrates rather than integrates the group under stress is a bad influence and should be removed at the earliest opportunity.

Unfortunately, expeditions attract prima donnas. Although a confounded nuisance on a prolonged venture, they are fairly easy to spot. Their vanity and self-interest will usually give them away. On the rare occasion when I have met such characters, I have found that they are often bad mixers or will usurp the leadership and can become quite irrational. In extreme cases they become rather exhibitionistic and complain bitterly of persecution if they do not get their own way.

Masochists sometimes join expeditions hoping for the opportunity to prove themselves under the ordeal. Being an idle person who believes that any bloody fool can be uncomfortable, I also regard such people as a potential danger to a team.

I have found that political and religious extremists, or for that matter anyone with strong views, can cause friction. But I have absolutely no doubt that faith can help one to overcome difficulties. My own view of religion is that it is best described as a bank account, into which one must pay regularly so that in times of need you can draw on it. But you cannot arrogantly demand to cash a cheque when you need a miracle – it is very much up to the bank manager to decide on the timing and amount of his support. Although one hopes that by maintaining a credit balance he might be better disposed to assist.

Of course not all explorers believe in a god, and many of my friends claim to be atheists or agnostics. Whether someone has or has not a religion only really concerns their selection for an expedition in that it is quite useful to know if you have to bury them! Even so, whenever possible I try to hold a simple service on Sundays. Apart from being appreciated by some members, I feel it has moral value and helps us to retain a sense of time. Congregations are usually poor at the start of an expedition, but increase in proportion to the tension. There are few atheists before a battle!

I have tended to talk about men, but the same remarks apply to women. For many years I was very much against taking girls with us. I felt that, human nature being what it is, they would be an unwelcome distraction and could not really pull their full weight. However, I soon discovered that there were certain advantages to having women members. In Darien there were five girls in the team and they showed themselves to be mentally as tough or even tougher than the men. I found that their inbuilt capacity for survival more than made up for their limited physical strength.

As far as sexual distraction is concerned, it is a question of selecting your girls carefully. They know all men are interested and explorers tend to be a particularly virile lot, but in the end it is the girl who calls the tune and if you have the right sort of women, they will keep even the most ardent suitor at bay. On one expedition a delightful continental lady scientist accompanied us. She had a charming personality and was an attractive woman, especially when wearing a rather under-sized bikini. A few days after the start of the venture, I realized that at least three of our members were vying with each other for her favours, which, in fairness, I must say she kept to herself. Even so, at the end of the first week, I had to rebuke two of my colleagues for quarrelling, and that evening I asked her as discreetly as possible if she wouldn't mind wearing a one-piece costume. Giving me a delicious smile, she said in her husky voice, 'Well, John, which piece would you like me to wear?'

Nevertheless, if you get good women, they are worth their weight in gold. They bear the brunt of the planning and secretarial work, they can be excellent fund-raisers, and on the expedition they even provide a useful listener for worried men to pour out their troubles to. But one of their great assets is that they add tone. Men are often inspired by the women's good example and are far less likely to be petty when girls are around.

The difficulty facing the leader is to select the people with the right characteristics. I do not claim to be an expert, but I do have a method which seems to work pretty well. However, while I still hope to lead some more expeditions, I cannot afford to reveal my system!

A major problem that faces most explorers today is money. Very often the battle for funds is far tougher than the expedition itself. Few are sufficiently well off to be free from this worry, although those of us paid by Her Majesty are in a better position than the professional expeditioner, who must not only pay the costs of the project, but earn a living as well. Of course, the British, who are usually short of everything, should be able to cope with such problems better than most! The real trouble is that until you have successfully completed the venture, there is nothing to sell and anyone investing in you is taking a risk. So if you want to sell your story or film in advance you must be something of a salesman. Many of the least-explored regions are almost unknown to the general public, and therefore it is terribly important that you present your case in the best possible light.

I believe there is a distinct danger that if you are desperate for money, you will take foolhardy risks to satisfy your sponsors' wishes, although it is my experience that newspapers and television companies are very reasonable and would not dream of asking anyone to hazard life simply to satisfy the readers or audience. But it is important to avoid becoming so committed to sponsors that the initiative passes out of your hands. Alas it usually happens that when an expedition organizer is required to become a PR executive and a fund-raiser, it is the very time when he needs to devote all his energies to actually planning the enterprise. To neglect this planning may prove fatal, so it should be a question of balance and, where possible, getting other members to help with the PR and appeals.

A few misguided individuals fancy there is a fortune to be made out of exploring. How wrong they are! But this is one of the dangers of commercial sponsorship, that it may lead people to explore for the wrong reasons. Even so, that does not mean to say that an explorer should not recoup some of his expenditure by lecturing or writing. Yet it never ceases to amaze me how many people will begrudge a few pounds for a good lecture. On more than one occasion I have given up my only free evening in a week to motor over a hundred miles to talk to folk, who will just give you a cup of tea before rushing off to their dinners, without pausing to consider how hungry the speaker might be! While some organizations even express indignation and surprise when asked to pay one's travel expenses!

But fortunately not everyone believes it is the explorer's duty to be at the beck and call of the nation and, indeed, many are very appreciative. One of the most moving experiences I have known was to lecture to a group of blind people, many of whom had never seen and could not really imagine what anything I had described looked like. However, their gratitude and interest were overwhelming.

I suppose we all get asked the same questions. What's left to explore? Why do you do it?

It sometimes surprises people to learn that there are still very many regions to be fully explored, for although there are few places man has not trodden or overflown, there are numerous areas where scientific investigation has yet to be carried out. As the world's population expands, food and energy grow scarcer. Coal, gas and oil fields are still being discovered, as are stocks of nuclear fuel. But, whereas years ago it was largely the profit motive that prompted the search, today it is a desperate need to maintain our standards of living and the quality of life. Apart from this, there are important aspects of medical research, the possibilities of new drugs being discovered, and the endless battle against disease. We still have much to learn of nature and of life, both above and below the sea. Only in very recent history have we been able to penetrate the watery depths effectively, and I believe that in the next century our attention will turn more and more to the ocean floor.

The exploration of space is beyond the means of all but a select few, nevertheless it is as fascinating to me as any terrestrial endeavours. However, on earth we still have opportunities for discovery and exploration in Asia, Africa and South America. New Guinea and the Pacific area also offer interesting possibilities and who knows what lies in Mongolia and China?

There are legends and myths to be investigated by the score, including our own hardy annual, the Loch Ness Monster, the Yeti and the great sea serpent. Was there an Atlantis? Is Stella's sea cow really extinct or do small colonies still feed on the coast of Russia? What happened to Colonel Fawcett? Was there a canal connecting the Pacific to the Atlantic a thousand years ago? How many lost cities are covered by the Amazon jungle?

I feel that long after we have gone from this earth our descendants will still be trying to solve many of these mysteries, but while we are here they provide tantalizing objectives for the adventurous and the curious. As far as I am concerned, it is curiosity that drives me on. I have no particular desire to conquer a peak or an ocean or to be the first man to complete some particular feat. Although I must confess that even if the challenge is not of primary importance, I still derive satisfaction in striving 'to seek, to find' without yielding. But it is the quest for the unknown that is paramount. Therefore, I believe that I am justified in using every possible human and technical aid to achieve the aim and solve the problem.

I know it has been said that with the huge amount of equipment, manpower and technical expertise, it is hardly surprising that we have got through where others have failed. In reply I will argue that I am not in the exploring game to find out something about myself or to compete with others, therefore I do not feel compelled to obey any self-imposed rules for physical challenges.

My headgear has occasionally led people to brand me as an ultra-patriotic adventurer. (The topee happens to be the most practical tropical hat I have ever worn and apart from being almost indestructible, it is very comfortable.) I am proud of my country, but I scorn those who will enjoy their heritage without attempting to contribute something more to mankind. Today we live in an international society, and I hope that we can play an important part in the future development of the world. Even so, I felt a pang of pride when I overheard a chance remark as we landed at Shafartak on 24 September 1968. A powerfully built American lady tourist turned to her husband and said, 'Elmer, these guys must be crazy.'

'Hush, dear,' replied her husband, 'they're British.'

Exactly five years after the day we had put our boats on the Blue Nile, Jim Masters and I sat beside another great river, the Colorado. It was August 1973 and, in company with our colleague, Ron Smith, we were testing different types of craft in preparation for the forthcoming expedition to Zaire. Probably the world's leading expert on river navigation, Ron had showed us his equipment and techniques. Now, tired and relaxed, we squatted on the damp sand, watching the sparks from the log fire swirl upward into the night sky. A guitar twanged gently, the river hissed by and the call of a night bird echoed through the canyon.

'Do you think we should have Harry in the crew?' I asked Jim.

'He's not a strong swimmer,' muttered Jim.

'Bad swimmers make good boatmen,' said Ron, drawing hard on his cigar.

That's a very profound remark, I thought, and probably sums up a lot of what makes us tick. But is it the challenge or curiosity or simply, as the late Sir Francis Chichester once said, 'that it intensifies life'?

Probably every man has his own reason. For me, it is what is on top of the mountain, or beneath the waves, or hidden by the jungle that really matters. I find, that in the words of Kipling, I must always go and look behind the Ranges – where the trails run out.

CHRONOLOGY

1936 Born
1955–1957 Sandhurst
1957 Commissioned into Royal Engineers
1958 World tour in forty-two days
   Joined 33rd Field Squadron RE in Cyprus
1959 Aphrodite expeditions started at Paphos, Cyprus
   Began to visit Libyan Desert
1960–1961 Married
   Aphrodite expeditions and desert exploration continues
1962 Instructor at Junior Leaders Regiment, RE, Dover
1963 Instructor and adventure training officer at Royal Military Academy, Sandhurst. Sandhurst SE Libya Expedition
1964 Emma born
   Sandhurst Ethiopian Expedition, 1964
1966 Sandhurst Ethiopian Expedition, 1966
1967 Adjutant, 3 Division Engineers, Tidworth
   Victoria born
1968 Staff College Course at Shrivenham
   The Great Abbai Expedition
1969 Staff College, Camberley
   Scientific Exploration Society founded
   The Dahlak Quest Expedition
   Joined Sealed Knot
   Wrote *Weapons and Tactics* (Penguin)
   Revisit Cyprus
1970 Working at Ministry of Defence in Whitehall
   Sealed Knot battles
1971 Ministry of Defence
   Planning British Trans-Americas Expedition
   Sealed Knot battles
   Rear Party officer for British Roraima Expedition
   British Trans-Americas Expedition
1972 British Trans-Americas Expedition
   Squadron commander, 48th Field Squadron RE, Ripon

1973 With squadron in Ulster
 Recce for Zaire River Expedition
 Visit USA for boat trials on Colorado
 Revisit Panama
1974 With squadron in Oman
 The Zaire River Expedition

INDEX

INDEX

34/17